Green Politics and Global Trade

American Governance and Public Policy

A SERIES EDITED BY

Barry Rabe and John Tierney

This series examines a broad range of public policy issues and their relationship to all levels of government in the United States. The editors welcome serious scholarly studies and seek to publish books that appeal to both academic and professional audiences. The series showcases studies that illuminate the successes, as well as the problems, of policy formulation and implementation.

Green Politics and Global Trade

NAFTA and the Future of Environmental Politics

John J. Audley

GEORGETOWN UNIVERSITY PRESS / WASHINGTON, D.C.

Georgetown University Press, Washington, D.C.
© 1997 by Georgetown University Press.   All rights reserved.
Printed in the United States of America

10 9 8 7 6 5 4 3 2 1   1997

THIS VOLUME IS PRINTED ON ACID-FREE ⊗ OFFSET BOOK PAPER

Library of Congress Cataloging-in-Publication Data

Audley, John J.
    Green politics and global trade : NAFTA and the future of
environmental politics / John Joseph Audley.
        p.   cm. — (American governance and public policy)
    Includes bibliographical references and index.
    1. International trade—Environmental aspects. 2. Commercial
policy—Environmental aspects. 3. Environmental policy—Economic
aspects. 4. Green movement. 5. Free trade—Environmental aspects—
North America. 6. United States—Commercial policy.
    7. Environmental policy—Economic aspects—United States.
    8. Canada. Treaties, etc. 1992 Oct. 7. I. Title. II. Series.
    HF1379.A92   1997
    382'.917—dc21   97-7907
    ISBN 0-87840-650-6
    ISBN 0-87840-651-4 (pbk. : alk. paper)

To Andrea

Your strength, love and friendship
are the greatest gifts I could ever receive

Contents

Tables

Preface

... the sovereignty of man lieth hid in knowledge ...
now we govern nature in opinions, but we are thrall
unto her in necessity: but if we would be led by her
in invention, we should command her by action.

Francis Bacon, *In Praise of Human Knowledge*

The disease of reason is that reason was born from
man's urge to dominate nature ... in the first man's
calculating contemplation of the world as prey.

Max Horkeimer, *The Eclipse of Reason*

Of all the challenges facing contemporary societies in the effort to
achieve a sustainable global economy, perhaps none is more complex
than reconciling international trade with environmental goals. Global
trade affects each of the most pressing environmental problems—global
warming, deforestation, the loss of biodiversity—in complex and often
misunderstood ways, a fact that compelled governments to begin to
address this issue only in the last few years. This is a study of one of
these attempts and about the nature of the political institutions created
as a result.

Two powerful ideas lie at the heart of this research project. Market-
based economies and their close first cousin, the principles of "free
trade," advocate constantly expanding economies to meet human
needs, while ecologically centered "sustainable development" asks humans to balance their needs with those of other species living together
in complex ecosystems. The struggle to reconcile these two paradigms
for human behavior were captured as part of the political debate surrounding the North American Free Trade Agreement (NAFTA).

Serendipity is the best explanation for the source of my interest in
this research project. In 1988 I worked on the Mexico-U.S. border in
the business environment commonly known as the *maquiladora* community. For two years I traveled the border, working with large

multinational companies and their Mexican laborers to design more efficient packaging systems. What I found there both fascinated and puzzled me. Some of the largest companies in the world had located assembly operations just south of the U.S. border to take full advantage of highly skilled, low-cost workers in Mexico, yet remain close to their principal consumer market. Here some of the poorest people in America worked ten hours a day, six days a week, living with social and environmental problems few people would ever believe exist so close to their own comfortable homes: raw sewage floating down streams dividing the two countries, filling the air with a stench I've never before (or since) experienced. Homes were made of little more than cardboard boxes and discarded pallets. Community members drew their water from discarded industrial drums that often were marked with labels indicating hazardous materials were once stored there.

At the same time I also saw opportunities for personal advancement where once there were none, and individual spirit to take advantage of that opportunity. While laborers worked for virtually nothing, the jobs represented a chance for a better life for themselves and their families. They were devoted to their jobs and worked hard to take full advantage of the chance to work for a company that paid a higher wage than they could find elsewhere and that provided them with transportation to work, hot meals, and health insurance. In short, I saw one of the many ironies that make up the border culture often referred to as *la frontera*.

I returned to college in 1989 to begin working on my Ph.D. At the University of Arizona, I was fortunate enough to work with Professor Helen Ingram at the Udall Center for the Study of Public Policy. One of our first projects involved a water quality study in "Ambos Nogales," the twin sister border cities of Nogales, Sonora, Mexico, and Nogales, Arizona, USA. Professor Ingram's insights into how communities work to make and implement policies were instrumental in guiding me toward the kind of research project that ultimately became my dissertation.

My experience on the border helped me understand the relationship between economic policy, social and environmental conditions, and the quality of human life. I was able to pursue that interest after transferring to the University of Maryland, College Park. Due entirely to dialing the wrong campus phone number, I had the good fortune of meeting Georgia Sorenson, director of the Academy of Leadership at Maryland. I can only thank Dr. Sorenson for listening to her instincts when she provided me with the necessary financial resources and moral support to get involved in national politics. In January 1991 I went to work for Senator Dennis DeConcini (D-AZ) as a Policy Fellow, to work on issues related to "Fast Track" reauthorization scheduled for May of that same year. Fast Track is a term that refers to special privileges granted the President to negotiate trade agreements between the United States and other countries. Due entirely to my ignorance of the members of the environmental community, I naively called each organization to ask for their input to help explain why they were so concerned about trade liberalization with Mexico. Four months later I began representing the Sierra Club in trade policy negotiations.

From April 1991 through July 1993, I worked as program director for the Sierra Club. In this capacity I was privileged to testify before Congress on trade-related matters, work with administrative officials from the executive branch responsible for trade policy negotiations, and work with representatives from pro- and anti-NAFTA industry, government, and community groups. I participated in many formal discussions focused on the trade and environment debate, including meetings in England, France, Mexico, and Canada. Each of these opportunities to work with both pro- and antitrade elites helped to shape my view of the politics and policies surrounding the emerging area of trade and the environment.

It was during this period that I came to know the people who eventually became the heart of my research project. I owe an incredible debt of gratitude to Mike McCloskey, chairman of the Sierra Club, and Larry Williams, the Sierra Club's director for international programs. The Club and its staff became my home and family for that entire period. During the early stages of the debate, Lori Wallach of Public Citizen and her vast network of activists were largely responsible for helping me secure the financial support I needed to remain involved in the debate. Stewart Hudson and Rodrigo Prudencio from the National Wildlife Federation (NWF), Alex Hittle from Friends of the Earth (FoE), Cameron Duncan of Greenpeace, and Justin Ward of the Natural Resources Defense Council (NRDC) became my professional colleagues and sometimes sparring partners. Working with these folks eventually introduced me to my partner, Andrea Durbin, an event that made all the hard work and endless hours more than worth the effort. Others offered their advice and support in numerous ways: Daniel Magraw, Bryan Samuel, David van Hoogstraten, Jan McAlpine, Dan Brinza, and Carmen Suro-Bredie to name just a few working for the United States government; Rod Leonard of the Community Nutrition Institute (CNI) and Mark Ritchie of the Institute for Agriculture and Trade Policy (IATP) believed in my ability to remain a committed activist despite my scholarly intentions. As much as anything else, this book is about you and your efforts to resolve the important conflicts.

While dialogues and meetings with business and government officials played an important part in the political process surrounding NAFTA, the majority of my energies were spent working with other representatives from U.S. environmental organizations focused on trade policy. In most instances the environmental community functions largely as a loose coalition of interest groups centered on similar policy interests and goals. Common positions were adopted by organizations after lengthy discussions regarding the content of policy and the strategies designed to see them implemented. As a large, grassroots organization, the Sierra Club focused its attention on developing policy positions in response to its activist members, who then focused their political attention on their elected officials. In the process of adopting these positions, a great deal of energy was devoted to reconciling the broad differences of opinions among U.S. environmental groups focused on NAFTA.

This degree of participation in NAFTA negotiations acted as a double-edged sword when it came time to start my formal research. My years directly involved in discussions surrounding NAFTA, the General Agreements on Tariffs and Trade (GATT), and policy discussions at the Organization for Economic Cooperation and Development (OECD) unconsciously inform my approach to this analysis. Few people enjoyed the kind of access to meetings, private documents, and the events that surrounded NAFTA. But as I began the task of sorting through information, developing theories, and writing this manuscript, the dilemma I faced was one of separation. How could I, a former representative from an organization that spent considerable energy trying to defeat NAFTA, distance myself from my own experience to write an objective analysis?

The first ally I found in my effort was separation. Knowing I wanted to write this, I purposefully left the Sierra Club before the political battle over NAFTA began in earnest. When the policy process moves from development stage and enters the voting stage, issues become very black or white, and professional colleagues become either allies or enemies. Avoiding the pitched battles that often characterize the end of a policy event helped me put my experiences into perspective more quickly than had I remained part of the lobbying effort to defeat the Agreement.

My second ally was time. I could not begin to interview participants until after NAFTA was completed. January 1994 was six months after I returned to teaching, and it gave me time to soften the "bias blinders" created by my own participation. I did not begin to write the first draft of this manuscript until the summer of 1994, one year after I left the Sierra Club.

Finally, I made every effort to validate my own experiences by interviewing other elites who took part in negotiations but had a different perspective. The extensive interviews I conducted helped to verify or refute my own impressions taken from the detailed notes I kept. In this regard, numerous conversations with Charlie Arden-Clarke of the World Wide Fund for Nature, David Schorr of the World Wildlife Fund (WWF), Robert Housman of the Center for International Environmental Law (CIEL), and William Snape of Defenders of Wildlife were of immense value. Of particular help at this stage was the access I enjoyed to the Washington, D.C. publication *Inside U.S. Trade*. No other source of information on the politics and process of trade policy negotiations is more complete. Regrettably, many of the documents I had obtained during meetings could not be used for reasons of confidentiality. In the complex world of U.S. politics, loss of one's reputation for trustworthiness exacts a very high price, so verifying this information through interviews with others was a very important part of the interview process. I also have my dissertation committee to thank for keeping me on a scholarly track. Of all the committee members, Mac Deslter was most familiar with the politics of U.S. trade policy. He kept me intellectually honest when it came to viewing the contributions of environmentalists. Ric Uslaner and Ken Conca read everything I wrote, even when it was not "ready" to be read, and offered helpful comments that kept me focused on the real issues. Peter Brown was my moral compass; he urged me to never forget why I cared about these issues as I struggled under the yoke of scholarly analysis. Finally, my chair, Karol Soltan, believed in me and in my ability to complete this project, with the kind of confidence and friendship all too often missing from the Ph.D. ordeal.

In the end, I believe my participation in trade policy negotiations was a positive experience. I developed a more precise appreciation for the importance of formal and informal relationships among policy elites. College alumni, association members, even neighborhood friendships opened the doors for participation to influence one another during negotiations. My experience as a participant in negotiations taught me that, generally speaking, all the people involved truly cared about doing the right thing. Whether they believed trade meant higher environmental standards of living, or lower standards and more degradation, they all strove to do the best they could. Self-interest, while obviously a factor in some instances, was not what drove people to work fourteen-hour days, six days a week, three years in a row. These folks all cared about the issues, cared to see the United States act responsibly, and cared about the quality of the environment.

As a colleague read this manuscript he reminded me that the entire process of negotiation is a political event, and avoiding the last stage of negotiations did not shield me from those politics. The reader will have to determine the degree to which I was able to extricate myself from my own experiences and offer an honest rendition of the events as I saw them. I hope I was successful; however, as we are all products of our own experiences, I do not apologize for the perspectives I bring to this analysis, nor for any bias the reader may detect. We all have our biases; in this instance, mine may be more apparent than others.

Finally, I want to take a moment to thank the people at Georgetown University Press. For me writing this book was a very humbling experience, as I've learned how much time, patience, and effort is required by others to realize a good end product. I want to thank John Samples for believing in this book, Patricia Rayner for her patience and skill editing the manuscript, and Gail Grella for her professional assistance in marketing the final product. To them go any credit for a quality finished product.

Green Politics and Global Trade

1

Regimes, Institutions, and Public Policy

... the debate over trade and the environment has
become a political mine field that reaches into virtually
every country, industry, and ecosystem. As much as
any other issue, it is this that will test the ability of
governments to meet the demands of a world in which
"instability" is no longer just a political condition but
a biological one.

HILLARY FRENCH, *Costly Tradeoffs:
Reconciling Trade and the Environment*

In November 1993 the U.S. Congress approved the North American
Free Trade Agreement (NAFTA). Its passage concluded two and one-
half years of policy negotiations between Mexico, Canada, and the
United States designed to increase trade by expanding market access
and reducing investment barriers. The results of negotiations were
profound. NAFTA combined the economies of the three countries to
create a tariff-free, $6.5 trillion market of 360 million consumers. The
new rules for investment and market access enabled North American
business to "rationalize" their investment and production throughout
the region, creating tremendous synergy among the three economies
to enhance international competitiveness (Hufbauer and Schott, 92).
U.S. exports to Mexico were predicted to expand by 16.7 percent by
1995, while Mexico would gain unprecedented access to the largest
market in the world. Canada and Mexico would begin to forge an
economic relationship that had not yet been realized. In short, the
negotiation of adoption of NAFTA promised to reshape the economic
face of North America.

Liberalizing trade is not unusual for the latter part of the twentieth
century: the United States had already negotiated bilateral trade agreements with Israel and Canada during the same decade; members of
the European Union were working through the initial stages of their

new political and economic relationships; and the world was struggling to complete the Uruguay Round of the General Agreements on Tariffs and Trade (GATT). But among these efforts designed to liberalize trade, NAFTA is unique because of the role played by environmental issues and their representative interest groups throughout negotiations. From the start of preliminary trade talks between Mexico and the United States in 1988, local and national environmental organizations expressed concern that a trade agreement with no regard for the environment would be disastrous for the long-term ecologically sustainable goals. Their concern, combined with their influence in U.S. politics, made environmental interests central to NAFTA's future.

It took almost two years and two presidential administrations to overcome the political hurdles facing NAFTA's passage. When it was completed, the environmental provisions in the NAFTA Package were without a doubt unprecedented. NAFTA admonished trading partners to adhere to the principles of sustainable development and to avoid attracting businesses through loosely enforced environmental regulations, developed new language that recognized the complicated relationship between trade rules and environmental goals, and created new mechanisms designed to address these complications. Yet the environmental community was bitterly divided over the merits of the Agreement. Divided into two clearly defined camps—one grassroots, the other national—environmental groups allied themselves with traditional participants in trade policy debate and fought each other to win the day in Congress. What pressures were responsible for including environmental issues in NAFTA, and what caused the environmental community to break apart over the outcome?

One year later Congress passed legislation implementing the Uruguay Round of GATT. Despite new rules for trade policy negotiations, formalized access to trade policy elites, and a virtually united environmental community, environmental groups were unable to negotiate enough improvements in the Uruguay Round to merit their support for its passage. Minor changes to portions of the agreement, including the creation of a committee on Trade and the Environment as part of the newly created World Trade Organization (WTO), did not satisfy U.S. environmental groups' demands for more environmentally sensitive trade. In an effort to appease them, the Clinton administration proposed procedural changes in U.S. trade policy, linking environmental issues to all future negotiations. However, the administration just as quickly removed such a proposal, after angry pro-GATT Republicans and business representatives threatened to withdraw their support (Marcich, 95). Despite nearly unanimous objections by the environmental community, the Uruguay Round passed easily in November 1994.

For environmental organizations the period following NAFTA and GATT's passage has been marked by a steady downward movement toward institutionalized obscurity. Formal appointments as advisors to trade negotiations, conferences between government officials and interest groups, and newly created institutions mandated to study the complex relationship between trade liberalization and environmental protection mark the institutionalization of the environmental community participation in trade policy, but continued progress toward balancing trade and environmental objectives in other trade policy forums has not been successful (Gingrich et al., 94a, 94b). At the same time the international dialogue between trade and environmental advocates has continued, creating new opportunities for environmental principles to influence trade negotiations. Unfortunately, few environmental organizations express much confidence in their ability to effectively move the trade agenda toward environmental issues. Five years after the linkages between trade and the environment were forged in NAFTA, environmental groups no longer possess the political leverage to continue progress toward establishing a balance between the desire for constantly expanding trade and constraints on human activity suggested by environmentalists. Why didn't the unprecedented inclusion of environmental interests in NAFTA endure?

The answer to these questions can be found by analyzing the political forces responsible for the formalized linkages between trade and the environment established in NAFTA. NAFTA's environmental provisions, and the role played by U.S. environmental organizations, are the product of the institutional relationship between these organizations and the political actors involved in NAFTA's negotiations. This relationship empowered environmental organizations with heretofore unknown political leverage and granted them access to members of the political regime responsible for making and implementing U.S. trade policy. When I analyze both the relationship between these actors and environmentalists, and the source and use of environmental leverage during negotiations, I conclude three things. First, *historical circumstances and political sequence of events created a unique opportunity for environmental groups to modify the political agenda for trade policy negotiations to include environmental issues.* Two previously independent regimes—trade and environment—intersected under the aegis of political demands for expanded trade. Due to the unique circumstances surrounding NAFTA negotiations, this intersection empowered environmental groups to play a critical role in the formation of governing coalitions to pass NAFTA.

Second, *the source of political leverage used by environmental organizations during negotiations was their ability to threaten NAFTA negotiations.* Environmental groups pushed their concerns onto the negotiating agenda by credibly threatening to defeat any agreement that did not include concern for the environment. This *preemptive leverage,* the ability to block political efforts to negotiated expanded trade relations in North America, forced trade advocates to incorporate environmental demands as part of the "Fast Track" negotiating reauthorization. Sustaining preemptive leverage after Fast Track reauthorization and converting it into substantive policy recommendations were difficult; the solution environmental groups came up with happened unconsciously. Some environmental organizations worked in coalition with other anti-NAFTA interest groups to sustain the threat to defeat NAFTA. They sustained the threat of preemption and kept negotiators sensitive to environmental demands made during negotiations. Other groups used their access to negotiations to develop policy alternatives that recognized environmental concerns but did not threaten the overall policy goal of expanded economic activity. These groups used *cooperation* with protrade members of the regime to compel officials from both the Bush and Clinton administrations to concede to some of the demands in exchange for their support. Positioned as the moderate environmental organizations willing to compromise with trade advocates, these groups actually *controlled the conflicts* among environmental groups by defining the terms of the compromise and neutralizing environmental opposition to NAFTA with their support.

The third point is more speculative. Despite the changes to the scope and rules characterizing the trade regime generated by environmental communitys' version of the "good cop/bad cop" roles in negotiations, *environmental concerns over trade policy lacked sufficient leverage or opportunity to substantively alter the norms and principles of trade policy.* Gains in procedural rules and formal roles that institutionalized participation and increased informal access enabled environmental interests to find a niche in trade policy but not substantially alter it. In the final analysis, environmental issues were not pivotal to the voting decisions of members of Congress; consistently resisted by traditional trade policy elites, unwanted by both Mexico and Canada, environmental groups were forced to accept substantially less than they had originally hoped to achieve or risk losing any improvements in trade policy. Two political realities—elite demand for constantly expanding economies and the domination of the powerful symbol of "free trade"—would not be replaced by environmental norms that suggested limits to the scale of human activity.

The broader questions raised by studying the intersection of trade and environmental policy in NAFTA stem from two areas of inquiry. One area has to do with the role institutional factors play in determining public policy. This study suggests that the degree to which existing political institutions adapt to new social demands is governed by the ability (or willingness) of political regimes, organized within the institution's sphere of influence, to modify normative principles that guide their behavior. Identifying the degree to which an institution's structure, rules, and norms respond when faced with incorporating a new actor will help predict future behavior of the political actors invested in the regime. Will newly incorporated actors bring with them the political leverage they enjoyed while operating outside the regime's monopoly of players, or do they find sources of leverage among the informal relationships with other actors? Will these relations produce equitable outcomes?

The second broad question involves how the interest group community generates and uses power. Is power always situational, or do some actors consistently enjoy the power to shape policy outcomes more than others? When power is shared among a community of interest groups, what factors determine how they use this power individually? This study suggests that the individual characteristics of each group—constituency base, access to other regime elites, organizational values and philosophies—help to differentiate the behavior of one interest group from another.

To support my claims regarding environmental interests in trade, I analyze the interaction between political actors involved in the creation and implementation of trade policy. In particular, I focus on the efforts of national environmental organizations to reform trade policy. Three questions guide this analysis. How and why were environmental issues included in NAFTA negotiations? Scholars and some business and political leaders acknowledged a relationship between trade rules and environmental protection going back more than twenty-five years, so why was NAFTA the first political opportunity for these two issues to become part of a single policy initiative? Second, why did environmental groups differ in terms of the participation and perception of NAFTA's environmental provisions? An often misunderstood "community" of environmental organizations brought dramatically different philosophies and strategies to trade policy. Finally, what is the nature of the changes to the regime responsible for U.S. trade policy? Analyzing how political compromises between environmental groups and traditional trade policy elites resulted in NAFTA's environmental provisions will explain why procedural rather than normative changes characterize the intersection.

POLICY MONOPOLIES, POLITICAL ACTORS, AND TRADE POLICY REFORM

For more than forty years, a small group of congressional representatives, the executive office, and interest groups controlled U.S. trade policy. Through a combination of limited access to decision makers, formal rules, and informal norms these political actors shaped the rules and rewards associated with U.S. trade. The regime they created was designed to hinge the U.S. economy to the rapidly expanding global market and to keep access to trade policy making and implementation limited. Although not as old as trade policy, crafting and implementing environmental policy created its own regime, characterized by unique goals, rules, and access to political power. For two decades these regimes had little in common; independent policy domains produced outcomes directed at serving the interests of their seemingly autonomous goals. Policy tools were used that initially had little impact on one another.

Beginning in the late 1970s, a series of events forced these two worlds to collide, compelling elites from both communities to tackle some very difficult issues. Efforts to liberalize the global economy and facilitate trade among nations was hampered by national policies directed at protecting and preserving the environment. Environmental policy efforts to stem the constant growth in human consumption met head on with efforts to meet that insatiable demand. Should trade policy recognize ecological limits on human behavior? How can you reconcile unilateral action to protect the environment with a desire to promote multilateralism? Should trade agreements allow governments to restrict market access to products not produced in an environmentally safe manner? What are the implications for trade and for the environment when different national environmental standards create competitive advantages for companies where conforming to environmental laws is less costly?

To analyze how NAFTA responded to the intersection of trade and environmental regimes requires an examination of the political process responsible for crafting the "environmental provisions" found in the Agreement. By this I mean directing analytical attention to the political process itself, how relationships between political actors engaged in the process of forging environmental linkages in trade policy develop the capacity to effect changes within the existing norms, rules, and decision-making procedures of trade policy.

Institutions, Regimes, and Public Policy

Incorporating environmental issues in trade policy is one example of how political institutions make and implement collective choices. It is also an example of how political regimes operating within the sphere of one or more institution influence the changes in policies considered or choices made. Representative organizations from a host of institutions—the U.S., Mexican, and Canadian governments, interest groups, and academic experts—played important roles in the political regime responsible for creating NAFTA and its environmental provisions. Within the intersection of these institutions, the political regime responsible for U.S. trade policy made choices among alternatives targeted at incorporating environmental issues. To help explain how this occurred, one must begin by clarifying the meaning of the terms used to describe these actors and their interaction.

Institutions play important roles in everyday life. According to political scientist, Jack Knight, ". . . institutions are prevalent wherever individuals attempt to live and work together. From the simplest to the most complex, we produce them while conducting all aspects of our social life." (Knight, 92: 1). Examples of institutions abound; religious organizations, such as the Catholic Church, structure relations between the sexes, set standards for behavior within a community, and transmit important social knowledge from generation to generation. Interest groups, such as the Sierra Club, educate citizens about the importance of environmental protection and organize political pressure directed at influencing elected officials. Private companies, such as the Honda Motor Company, organize workers' efforts to produce products for sale on the international market. Political institutions, such as the U.S. Congress, make and implement collective choices in a democratic society. Each organization, described briefly here, is an example of the broader institutional categories of religion, interest groups, private business, and governments. What differentiates one institution from the next are its characteristics, namely, the differences in *organizational structure, formal rules,* and *norms* or *principles* (Jackson, 91: 10; March and Olsen, 89).

Institutional structure determines the scope and range of an organization's activities (March and Olsen, 89; Jackson, 91; Knight, 92). For example, political institutions make and implement decisions regarding (among others) public law or the expenditure of public revenues. Private organizations make similar decisions about private behavior. Their individual structures can and do overlap, creating situations where individual behavior has conscious and unconscious implications for the behavior of other institutions and on society overall (Schelling, 78).

Formal rules determine how decisions will be made and shape interactions between actors with vested interests in maintaining existing institutional structures. Rules affect both the behavior of actors and the outcome of their interaction. The formal hierarchy of private institutions usually locate decision-making authority with greater responsibility for the long-term welfare of an organization than line or staff employees. In contrast, democratic political institutions are characterized as having dispersed decision-making authority, usually structured by constitutional mandates. As with the structure, the overlapping nature of institutional interaction often means that formal rules have consequences for other organizations and for society. For example, when the U.S. government attempted to modify its rules regarding gays in the military, the decision rippled through religious and political organizations around the country.

Norms or principles guide behavior by acting as a "moral compass" when actors consider "appropriate" behavior (Jackson, 91; Knight, 92; Baumgartner and Jones, 93). They also help to constrain the realm of possible alternatives by helping to shape individual expectations around an agenda consistent with current normative beliefs (Baumgartner and Jones, 93). Governments may be democratic, authoritarian, or some combination of both. Businesses and other private organizations may be benevolent or hostile and aggressive, competitive or collaborative, profit-oriented or nonprofit. The differences in environmental "norms" are often cited as a source of conflict between nation-states as governments attempt to negotiate international environmental agreements. These differences shape the priorities of governments, for instance, population control or growth policies, pollution prevention or economic development (Caldwell, 90; Mazur, et al., 95).

While the norms held by different institutions may differ, they all share two characteristics. First, every institution has a strong survival instinct (Wilson, 73). Regardless of what the circumstances are, when faced with a crisis that threatens the continuation of the organization, people will usually make decisions that help ensure its survival. This characteristic has important consequences, especially when trying to explain the differences in behavior among the national environmental organizations selected for study. Second, at this time in history, the principal motivations for organizing are economic (Lindblom, 77; Hechter, 87). Society is organized largely around the need to make and distribute wealth, and this underlying theme has important consequences for the range of possible alternatives considered by political decision makers.

Institutional analysis is widely used as a tool for research in sociology (Powell and DiMaggio, 89; Knight, 92), history (Robertson, 93), political science (Keohane, 96; Williamson, 75; March and Olsen, 89; Shepsle, 79; Ostrom, 90), and economics (Shepsle, 79; Shepsle and Weingast, 87). Such application has made it more of an "emerging intellectual persuasion, as opposed to a fixed blueprint or a clearly defined school" among social scientists who believe that the institutional variables just identified are important in explaining the outcome of collective action (Occhipinti, 94: 1). To help focus the ability of institutional analysis to analyze the role norms, rules, and procedures play in developing policy,

I turn to a discussion of the political regimes that link the various organizations involved in public policy and empower them to make and implement public choices.

The concept of regimes is as widely used in political science as the concept of institutions. For clarity, I will use one of the most widely accepted definitions of regimes—"a set of implicit or explicit principles, norms, rules, and decision-making procedures around which actors' expectations converge in a given (policy) area." (Krasner, 83: 2)—to discuss the similarities and differences implied by these two terms. Both concepts emphasize stable, long-term relationships between actors engaged in efforts to influence policy. Principles and norms constrain participant beliefs and expectations about their own behavior and that of others. Rules encompass both the decision-making rules necessary to make and carry out social choices and the informal rules necessary to facilitate human interaction. Both also emphasize the importance of organizing disparate interests to compel actors to cooperate to achieve a socially desirable outcome. But there are also a number of differences between the concept of regimes and that of institutions. In application institutional analysis seems to place greater emphasis on the historical sequence of events as a variable to explain behavior (Jackson, 91: 13; Robertson, 93). While institutional analysis is associated with both national and international issues, regime theory is most often associated with international relations, and is usually applied to analyze the relationships between nation-states, supranational organizations such as the United Nations, or important private actors such as multinational corporations (Krasner, 83). In this sense both theories tend to focus analysis on organizations as decision makers, not the people actively representing those organizations.

To understand the relationship between political process and national policy outcome, the focus of attention must be on those people actively engaged in the process of making policy. While institutional analysis identifies the larger factors influencing individual behavior, it also tends to focus on the institution as its principal actor. While regime analysis tends to follow in this direction, it is more flexible in that it can also make the individual the analytical unit. In an important study of local politics, Clarence Stone uses the term *urban regime* to refer to informal arrangements between private and public actors that empower formal political decision makers to make and implement collective decisions (Stone, 89; Chapter 1 and Part III). Stone's analysis focuses on the role informal relationships play as a means of overcoming institutional rigidity that often constrains actors operating within a particular political institution. He shares the international regime theory belief that regimes are best characterized by long-term arrangements between participants and that interaction between actors results in the constant "restructuring" of the rules and procedures that characterize a particular regime. But because he is focused on local politics, he is able to center his analysis on the formation of the loosely networked governing coalitions necessary to make and implement public choices. For Stone, regimes adapt to changing political demand but remain largely intact unless some dramatic shift in normative beliefs or principles fundamentally challenges the nature of a regime's structure (Stone, 89; Part III).

This discussion of regimes and institutions offers the hypothesis that institutional understanding of the nature of public policy requires an analysis of both the macro variables that set the stage for a policy debate and the micro variables involving the individuals who make the decisions that produce policy. Institutions provide overarching norms, rules, and procedures for interaction among the individual actors. More than one institution may exert influence over behavior; in fact, overlapping institutions is more the rule than the exception. Political regimes—loose coalitions of individual actors who represent themselves or their organization—form to organize the interests of a small group of actors and respond to demands placed upon the institution. Some call these groups *policy monopolies*, small but highly influential groups of actors who rely upon shared beliefs and formal rules to limit access to the process of policy making (Baumgartner and Jones, 93). The degree to which existing regimes respond to changing social demands is a function of the ability of new actors to reshape the rules, norms, and procedures of institutions responsible for structuring their behavior. For example, until NAFTA negotiations began, the regime responsible for crafting trade policy in the United States was comprised of members of the executive office, Congress, and political elites from the business, labor, and agricultural communities. These actors constituted a policy monopoly where a limited number of actors share common values and interests regarding the maintenance of existing trade policy. Interaction between the actors was both formal and informal; actors relied upon procedural rules and informal norms to facilitate interaction and limit access. These rules were established by the larger political institution represented by Congress, the administration, and the international trade community.

Political Actors, Private Resources

Institutional analysis of policy outcomes creates a template for understanding how formal rules, decision-making procedures, and normative values influence members of political regimes as they respond to changing social circumstances. And while this is an important means of understanding policy outcomes, it does not explain how individual actors influence one another to reach a policy compromise. A fuller understanding of the nature of policy outcome requires knowing who the relevant actors are, the nature of their relationships, and their capacity to influence one another as they consider which alternative to choose. What I am referring to here is the political power necessary to make and implement social choices.

Contemporary liberal discourse usually refers to political power in terms of the "cost of compliance," where social control is the objective and the ability to maintain control is a measure of the degree of power necessary (Stone, 88). In this sense power is often divided into the ability of one party to dominate another (Dahl, 61) or the ability to control the political agenda and keep certain issues outside the social agenda (Bacharach and Baratz, 70), or the ability to keep those dominated unaware of the power exerted upon them through hegemonic control (Gaventa, 80; Edelman, 77; Piven, 77). While these views of political power provide useful insight into an important aspect of political science, they each tend to regard power as an independent variable. However, in many political circumstances power is circumstantial, created and used within the context of certain events or interaction, or political regime. In this sense power and its use is best understood within the institutional framework of the policy domain.

Jack Knight examines the use of political power in an institutional framework. Knight argues that powerful actors use their private resources to control conflicts between political elites as they compete for private rewards; "Institutional evolution is not best explained as a Pareto-superior response to collective goals or benefits, but, rather, as a by-product of conflicts (between actors) over distributional gains" (Knight, 92: 19) [parentheses added]. More powerful actors use their political resources and access to political decision makers to shape a policy alternative that maximizes personal interest and at the same time limits competition from alternatives that distribute benefits more broadly. Weaker actors are compelled to accept the compromises shaped by the more influential participants because such acceptance offers some measure of political reward for their participation. For Knight the characteristics of the policy compromise, namely the distribution of private rewards associated with new legislation, act as a proxy for measuring the distribution of power among participating elites.

Other scholars argue that to focus solely on power as a cost of compliance issue oversimplifies power because it fails to recognize the importance cooperation plays between actors to empower elected officials to make and implement social choices (Stone, 89; Ostrom, 90; Coleman, 90). Policy decisions occur when actors, bound together by common interest, can agree upon a course of action. The issue is not who has more power—rarely is there ever a situation where actors have relatively equal power—but how actors use their resources to establish an adequate level of cooperation. "... the issue is how to bring about enough cooperation among disparate community elements to get things done—and to do so in the absence of an overarching command structure or a unifying system of thought" (Stone, 89: 227). For example Stone's study of Atlanta's post–World War II development shows that cooperation between community elites led not only to the renovation of downtown Atlanta in response to changing social and economic demands, but it also promoted "civic cooperation" among competing community members (Stone, 89).

From these two seemingly incommensurate positions on the use of power in shaping policy, a number of important areas in common stand out. First, we know that (in democratic societies) *power is fragmented*. Rarely does any one individual or organization possess enough political power to control all aspects of the political process. But power is not broadly fragmented; instead it is usually enjoyed by a political elite or political monopoly surrounding particular policy issue areas (Dahl, 61). To empower formal political institutions to make and implement social choices requires some means of organizing that power support for a particular alternative. Second, *power is situational*. In many instances power is a function of institutional structure or formal political office or a consequence of a series of events that position actors to have power over others. Situational power may also be the product of epiphenomenal forces, such as the power inherent in the rhetoric surrounding "free trade" or "environmentalism." These factors suggest that power is constantly changing, providing a single group or political actor with specific leverage at one point in time denied them in another. Finally, we know that *power is used throughout the political process*, from the way the agenda is shaped to the selection of possible alternatives to the actual vote.

Preemptive Leverage

Challenges to existing structures, rules, and norms often serve to modify public perception of existing policy issues (Baumgartner and Jones, 93). New information brought about by technological or scientific innovation or shifts in social values create opportunities for actors to use their private resources to try and redefine the political agenda surrounding a particular policy (Baumgartner and Jones, 93; Gaventa, 80). John Kingdon refers to this as the intersection of "political streams" and "policy streams," an analogy which suggests that a unique opportunity for change has occurred (Kingdon, 84). The intersection is often initiated by exogenous social events or by a formal rule that enables actors to focus their private resources on efforts designed to influence the agenda setting and outcome of policy making (Ripley, 85). But once these streams intersect, how do political actors use their resources to influence policy?

In an important reexamination of Floyd Hunter's analysis of community power, Clarence Stone suggests one explanation for changes in the public agenda can be explained by identifying the ability of some actors to *preempt* or block the policy process (Stone, 88). Political actors otherwise not part of the elite network are able to gain political concessions from policy elites in exchange for their willingness not to block formal efforts to respond to social demands. Otherwise insignificant political actors can exert tremendous leverage on the political agenda when they hold strategically important positions in the policy process. Chapter 2 will explore the use of preemptive leverage during Fast Track reauthorization to explain how an otherwise uninvolved interest group community could so dramatically affect the nature of U.S. trade policy negotiation.

Accommodating and Adversarial Leverage

Once a policy issue agenda has been altered to respond to new political pressures, the task facing policy elites is how to reforge the political regime to ensure its long-term survival and an adequate level of private reward for participating. Actors use their political resources—constituency pressure, money, organizational status, membership, and access to other elites—to influence the components of the policy alternative under consideration. Returning to the discussion of power presented earlier, the second two uses of power will explore the degree to which environmental groups relied upon *adversarial* or *accommodating* leverage. Chapters 3 and 4 will compare how environmental groups used their leverage during both the NAFTA negotiations and the voting period to determine whether adversarial or accommodating leverage offers the best explanation for the inclusion of the environmental provisions in NAFTA.

The analysis of events surrounding NAFTA negotiations and the source and use of political leverage enjoyed by national environmental organizations will show that historical circumstances combined with procedural rules created the opportunity for environmental groups to preempt negotiations if their issues were not included as part of the negotiating agenda for trade. Once established as participants in negotiations, both adversarial and accommodating leverage were essential to gain concessions from negotiators. What the analysis will also show is that the coalition of "accommodating" environmental organizations used their access to trade advocates and their support for the overall principles of "free trade" to control conflicts within the environmental community and neutralize any opposition to NAFTA's passage offered by their more adversarial environmental counterparts.

METHOD OF ANALYSIS

The research task outlined above can be broken into three specific tasks. I will begin by presenting the nexus of the trade and environment regimes. This presentation serves two analytical objectives. An historical analysis places the nexus of trade and environmental political regimes within the context of events leading up to NAFTA negotiations. It also presents the powerful normative principles of *free trade* and the not-so-well-established principles of *sustainable development*. These two normative principles underlie the entire trade and environment debate. The predominance of free trade and the institutions of trade over sustainable development and the institutions of environmental protection help to explain the nature of NAFTA's environmental provisions. Chapter 2 will be devoted to developing this history of the trade and environment debate.

The second analytical task centers on analyzing the role played by key national environmental organizations involved in negotiations. Although hundreds of nongovernmental groups tried to influence NAFTA's outcomes, only eleven groups were selected because of their long-term participation in negotiations and the degree of political leverage they enjoyed. Analysis of their participation in trade policy negotiations is divided into three stages: Chapter 3 focuses on the Fast Track period beginning with preliminary trade discussions between Mexico and the United States in 1989 and ending with the Fast Track vote in May 1991. Fast Track set the agenda for negotiations between Mexico, Canada, and the United States and perhaps represents the most important stage in negotiations. Chapter 4 analyzes the role played by these environmental groups during the negotiations themselves. This period (May 1991 through September 1993) is highlighted by the transfer of administrative power from George Bush and the Republican party to Bill Clinton and the Democrats in January 1993. Chapter 5 focuses on the voting stage, beginning with President Clinton's 17 September 1993, White House speech marking the formal signing of NAFTA's Supplemental Agreements and ending with the congressional passage in November 1993. All three chapters pay particular attention to the nature of the formal and informal relationships between environmental organizations and other political actors engaged in trade policy reform.

The final section of this book is devoted to presenting the institutional reform of trade policy resulting from the inclusion of environmental interests in NAFTA. While it is still premature to measure NAFTA's environmental effects, a review of the changes in scope, rules, and normative principles responsible for U.S. trade policy in the aftermath of the NAFTA debate is possible. NAFTA's environmental provisions are briefly discussed, but greater attention is devoted to describing the changes in participation by environmental organizations and the implementation of NAFTA's environmental provisions. In the years following NAFTA, a great deal of formal dialogue has taken place among trade policy experts, but the degree to which it has resulted in continued reconciliation between trade and environmental goals will be challenged. I conclude the book with a discussion of the implications of the way in which environmental issues were institutionalized into trade regimes through NAFTA, with particular focus on the 1997 negotiations involving the three NAFTA countries and Chile.

Data Sources

Most analyses of NAFTA's environmental provisions focus on the environmental benefits or costs associated with liberalized trade. While numerous studies attempt to model NAFTA's environmental effects (Magraw, 95; Costanza et al., 95; Charnovitz, 92), there is very little analysis of the role played by environmental organizations in the formation of trade policy.[1] To piece together the complex details of this story requires a research methodology that relies upon content analysis of the original documents, congressional records, and media coverage.

Congressional Documents

Congressional attention to the possible relationship between environmental issues and trade policy focused principally on the period of the NAFTA discussions (January 1991 through November 1993). The more than one hundred congressional hearings, countless reports to Congress by various research agencies, and correspondence between members create a tremendous wealth of information that documents formal interaction between representatives of the environmental community and elected officials. Particular attention is given to congressional hearings specifically addressing environmental issues, although all of the hearings were examined for information content pertaining to issues related to trade and the environment. A full list of hearings can be found in Appendix D.

Private Documents

Environmental organizations documented the dialogue between themselves and other members of the trade policy community with consensus statements that spelled out political demands, consensus positions, and detailed political strategies. These documents were obtained either as a product of my own participation[2] or, in the months following NAFTA, during contacts with environmental representatives and administrative officials.

Information on membership, organizational philosophy, source of finances, and personnel commitment to trade policy was obtained through direct contact with each organization's headquarters. This information was then used to draw distinctions among the national environmental organizations who participated in the NAFTA negotiations. In most instances, this information was available in annual reports, and, where possible, information was obtained for the years 1988–1993. Data detailing the level of foundation support awarded each organization by U.S.-based foundations was obtained directly from the foundations themselves and verified with information provided by each environmental organization. Only foundation support directly identified as "trade and environment" resources was counted in this study. See Appendix A and particularly Appendix A: Explanatory Information.

Personal Interviews

The paper trails created by congressional and private documents provide important information regarding the nature of relations between elites and the progress toward consensus, but the documents themselves can leave gaps in information that can only be obtained through direct questions with the political actors involved. Interviews with more than forty political elites involved in the development of trade policy between 1991 and 1993 were conducted in the winter of 1994, three months following successful conclusion of NAFTA. Interviewees can be divided into four different groups. First, attention was directed toward representatives from each environmental organization that participated in negotiations. The second group consisted of staff and political appointees in the Departments of State and the Interior, the Environmental Protection Agency, the Office of United States Trade Representative (USTR), and from key committees and offices in the U.S. Congress. The third group consisted of key actors from the business, labor, and agriculture community in order to balance the perspective on environmental issues with others in the negotiations. Finally, I interviewed staff from leading House and Senate officials involved in NAFTA. Details pertaining to the personal interviews can be found in Appendix A.

A second wave of interviews took place one year later. I interviewed the same representative from each of the national environmental organizations, two USTR representatives, one labor and one industry representative, and two trade and environment policy experts. With the exception of one of the USTR officials, each person interviewed was also part of the first wave of interviews. The goal of these interviews was to assess the status of the trade and environment debate one year after NAFTA's implementation. Finally, during revisions to the last section of this book, a third wave of interviews was conducted with remaining active participants from the environmental community, along with several representatives from the USTR. These interviews were designed to update the section with the most recent activities of the trade and environment debate, and to gather information describing the most recent trends toward continued reconciliation of these two policy domains.

Media Coverage

NAFTA was an important media event; according to NEXIS research service, more than twenty thousand articles covering NAFTA were published between January 1991 and November 1993. From this tremendous volume of coverage, four daily newspapers—*The New York Times, The Washington Post, The Chicago Tribune,* and *The Los Angeles Times*—and three business papers—*The Wall Street Journal, The London Financial Times,* and *The Journal of Commerce*—were selected to provide detailed information regarding the sequence of events which outline the three years of negotiations. In addition to these daily publications, one Washington, D.C.-based newsletter, *Inside U.S. Trade,* was of tremendous help in filling gaps in the timeline of events, obtaining copies of significant documents, and providing its own perspective on the relationship between environment and trade matters in NAFTA.

Analyzing the response of the political actors to challenges by environmental organizations to the trade regime provides a unique opportunity to observe a number of important characteristics that help explain policy outcomes. Modifications to the scope, rules, and principles of the U.S. trade regime suggest how far the members of this policy regime had to go to incorporate environmental demands yet remain intact enough to ensure the continuation of their monopoly. Had their response resulted in a fundamentally different regime, it would have signaled that environmental organizations had organized and used tremendous political leverage to dramatically reshape the direction of trade policy. But these organizations did not enjoy such power; however, the outcome of negotiations shows the source of the power they used to become involved in trade negotiations and how they used that power to force compromises with trade advocates that recognized some of their concerns. Finally, environmental interests in NAFTA show how environmental organizations used power within their own community to shape a common set of demands and to overcome their internal differences to remain involved in negotiations.

ENDNOTES

1. See Esty, 94 for an important exception.
2. Refer to the Preface for a discussion of my own participation as an advocate for the Sierra Club and as an advisor to numerous environmental organizations.

2

The Complex Relationship between Trade and the Environment

Of all the challenges facing contemporary societies, perhaps none is more complex than reconciling international trade with environmental goals. The challenge begins with the fact that global commerce and efforts to protect the environment are central to everyday life. Trade between countries has risen elevenfold since 1950, exceeding $6 trillion in 1990. Twenty-five percent of this trade involves natural resources—petroleum, timber, fish, minerals—the "building blocks" of a consumer society. Over an even shorter period of time, environmental protection has become central to both domestic and international policy. Concern for environmental protection runs deep; eight in ten U.S. citizens consider themselves environmentalists. In less than three decades, environmental issues have found their way into almost every agenda in the national and international arenas, from population to nuclear disarmament to urban development and issues of social justice (Merchant, 87; Mazur, 95). The total annual budget for both public and private investments in environmental protection in the United States is currently estimated at between $120 billion and $140 billion (Cascio, 96).

While both trade and environmental policy are central to today's policies, all indicators suggest they will become even more central within the next twenty-five years. Global population is skyrocketing, surpassing five billion in 1995. Each new citizen is born into a world increasingly oriented toward market-based economies; and as nations around the world try to meet their demands for consumer goods and jobs, the scale of activity must expand. Trade between countries will undoubtedly play a central role in national efforts to provide each of these citizens with the goods and services offered by modern, technologically driven societies. The requirements of expanded trade mean an increase in the significance of trade policy and the concomitant pressure upon policy makers to take steps to protect the environment. Trade liberalization is a part of the equation that explains deforestation in Indonesia and Latin America; worldwide fish stocks have been seriously depleted, exacerbated by trade (French, 93). Trade liberalization and its relationship with the environment compel us to face the fact that the earth has limits to what it can withstand and still provide a hospitable place for humans to live.

The political institutions charged with reconciling these policy domains are themselves constrained by their own institutional characteristics. National governments struggle to retain sovereignty over domestic and international matters at a time when global trade agreements rewrite the rules of national governance. While elected officials struggle to create attractive business environments, they must also respond to increasing public demand for environmental protection. In the end both actions have implications for national sovereignty; collective solutions to both protect the global environment and encourage trade and investment are not easy for political institutions designed to respond to national, not global, political pressures.

Over the past ten years the political struggle to reconcile the relationship between trade and the environment has produced strong and often bipolar public views toward each issue. Both "free trade" and "environmental protection" have been lionized and demonized as the solutions to, or the root causes of, our most pressing global, environmental, human health, and democratic problems.[1] How did we come to think of these two vital areas of public policy in such extreme terms?

Understanding the political relationship between trade and the environment begins with analyzing the history of each policy domain. Policy history provides the reader with a number of important elements. First, it acts as a narrative of the sequence of events behind the creation of each political regime. While subject to a researcher's own bias, careful presentation of a policy's history sets the stage on which current policy takes place (Ripley, 85). Special attention must be given to the key political actors who took part in the historical development of these two formerly independent political regimes. Understanding policy history also helps to explain how each issue has become an important symbolic lightning rod in contemporary discourse. Once these institutional factors are identified, the intersection of trade and the environment can be characterized to locate the current debate in terms of its contemporary substance and participants.

THE PUSH FOR FREE TRADE IN THE POST–WORLD WAR II ERA

International commerce has existed since men learned how to transport goods across distance to exchange for items not available at home. While ostensibly meant to enrich one's personal fortune, trade has also been intertwined with political goals. Early trade policies extended political power through commerce, empowering countries like Great

Britain to claim that the "sun never sets on the Union Jack." Besides securing geopolitical power, mercantile systems like those in Spain and Britain were also important sources of national revenue; import duties helped to transfer the financial resources from periphery to core nations while enabling national politicians to exchange tariff protection for private rewards at home (Miller, 95).

The intellectual argument favoring trade liberalization grew out of dissatisfaction with this mercantile trading system. Local citizens objected to the high prices they paid for products offered by domestic producers who enjoyed the benefits of higher prices and the protection from competition secured through import duties (McCord, 70). During the 1840s economists Adam Smith and David Ricardo argued against this system, postulating that "freer trade"—trade less constrained by customs duties—promotes competition which encourages specialization. Specialization, in turn, results in expanded output, ultimately maximizing the individual welfare by offering more goods and services to consumers (Winham, 92; Bhagwati, 88). Modern economists rely upon these basic tenets to develop econometric models that extend these theories to argue trade under *any* circumstance is beneficial. According to noted economist, Paul Samuelson, "International trade is mutually profitable even when one of the countries can produce every commodity more cheaply (in terms of labor or all resources) than the other country." (Samuelson, 87: 669). Any domestic policy that either directly or indirectly blocks trade imposes costs on consumers in the form of higher prices, fewer alternatives, and poorer quality products (Krugman, 87).

Beyond the economic arguments in favor of free trade lies the basic belief in individual liberty. The symbolism of free trade implies the guarantee of two "freedoms." First, it suggests a "cost-less" solution to expanding human scale. Economic growth and free trade are now intertwined in the development of contemporary economic policies because trade encourages growth, and growth is regarded as the solution to expanding demand. Proponents of free trade argue that the solution to wealth disparities is not to redistribute but to expand. If more people have greater access to global markets, then economies grow and there is more wealth for all to share (Lang and Hines, 93; Daly and Cobb, 89). The second symbolic argument in favor of "free trade" involves freeing individual entrepreneurs from an intrusive government. "Freedom from" government restrictions that may hinder the manner in which individuals use their own resources to make money becomes an important component of efforts to democratize governments by protecting individual liberties from government intrusion (Held, 87).

While the intellectual argument in support of free trade developed during the nineteenth century, the political momentum to promote global free trade did not begin until the 1930s. Following the end of World War I, national governments expanded the use of restrictive trade barriers to restart national economies and promote industrial development (ul-Haq et al., 95; Schattschneider, 35). The slump in national economies brought on (in part) by protective tariffs sparked the Great Depression of the 1920s and 1930s. The term "protectionism" gained popularity as a pejorative term used to describe policies designed to benefit a small group of business interests by imposing higher costs on society overall (Schattschneider, 35; Winham, 92; Bhagwati, 88).

International demand for wartime goods caused by the start of World War II enabled governments to refocus popular attention away from the political debate between free and protectionist trade policy. Business leaders who had benefited from liberal trade policies adopted during the war began to work with politicians to develop a policy framework based upon their belief that freer trade was essential for modern industries to take full advantage of economies of scale and promote economic stability for their home countries (Kock, 69). According to a report written for Congress by business leaders representing the United States' largest companies:

> The United States has a major interest in the expansion of world commerce. We are a powerful industrial nation. We need vast quantities of goods and services of many kinds. We have a large margin of efficient, productive capacity which can be put to work making things for international trade. We can exchange these things with the people of other countries who, themselves, make other things available for trade. . . . A restrictive course by America toward foreign trade is contrary to American interest. (Committee for Economic Development, 1945)

It was, however, long before Allied forces were confident of their victory in World War II that political and economic leaders from the West began to anticipate and plan the nature of economic arrangements necessary to expand the world economy at the end of the war. Fearing a collapse in world trade similar to that which followed the end of World War I, Western leaders envisioned the creation of global institutions that would stabilize currency evaluations, provide a ready flow of capital for investment, and develop rules to govern national policies and prevent a return to protective policies (Kock, 69; Dam, 70). The three "pillars" of the 1942 Bretton Woods Conference—the International Monetary Fund (IMF), the International Bank for Reconstruction and Development (World Bank), and the General Agreements on Tariffs and Trade (GATT)—grew out of these visions to meet these global needs. All three institutions play vital roles in the promotion of trade liberalization, but GATT is particularly important because of the unique role it plays building the institutions responsible for trade.

GATT's Central Role in Trade Liberalization

GATT was created in 1946 to establish a multilateral framework for trade liberalization. It is embodied by a formal Secretariat and small staff located in Geneva, Switzerland. While its formal structure remains small, its influence lies in the ability to foster norms that facilitate cooperative trade arrangements. GATT scholar Gilbert Winham identifies the first fundamental normative principles as *external and internal nondiscrimination* (Winham, 92: 46). *Most Favored Nation* (GATT Article I) prevents Parties to GATT from treating an imported product (for example, French wine) any differently than they treat the same product from another country (Australian wine). *National treatment* (GATT Article III) requires Parties to treat imports no less favorably than they treat domestically produced goods and services (California wine).

The second normative principle is designed to eliminate tariff restrictions. *Tariff reduction* (GATT Article II) is considered to be GATT's most fundamental principle because Parties agree to eliminate formal restrictions to market access. For the first two decades, quantitative trade restrictions were the focus on GATT deliberations. But over the past twenty years, a particular version of tariff barriers began to plague trade liberalization efforts. *Non-Tariff Barriers* (NTBs), policies through which countries indirectly restrict access to domestic markets, have proliferated. For example, a regulatory requirement calling for particular metal edges on skis (which only domestic ski manufacturers use) because the special quality of a country's snow "requires" a particular kind of metal would be considered an NTB in violation of GATT principles for trade liberalization.

The two principles just described refer to the methodology and values adopted by GATT to reduce trade restrictions. But GATT also embodies a number of procedural norms based upon the premise that changes to national policy must occur voluntarily. *Reciprocity* between Parties exists when one country reduces tariffs in exchange for an equal amount of reduction by a trading partner (Article XVIII). *Commercial consideration* occurs when Parties agree to support the values of the free market and eschew government intervention in trade. Indirectly addressed in Articles XVI and XVII, commercial consideration embodies a faith in market mechanisms and unrestricted trade to improve individual welfare. Each of these steps, including policies that restrict trade based upon GATT-recognized trade restrictions, must occur in a *transparent* manner, where the intentions of the policy are understood by all Parties affected by the restrictions.

GATT relies on a relatively informal, closed, rule-making procedure to implement its principles in national policy. The GATT Secretariat engages nations in a cooperative process to negotiate mutually beneficial rules to govern trade and bind Contracting Parties to rules which restrict partisan behavior on domestic issues (Low, 93). Until the adoption of the Uruguay Round of GATT in 1995, creating the World Trade Organization (WTO), the process normally involved negotiating "Rounds"—voluntary negotiations involving interested "Parties" to GATT. Successive GATT Rounds focused international attention first on reducing direct tariff barriers, such as import quotas, then focused on NTB, such as specific product requirements that effectively prohibited sale of foreign goods.

GATT also acts as an arbitrator between Parties. Disputing countries discuss their different interpretations of GATT's trade discipline in an effort to reconcile differences and avoid formal action. If reconciliation does not occur, aggrieved Parties initiate a dispute process where a panel of trade experts judge the merits of the case. The proceedings are private, involving only the disputing Parties and their representatives; information and subsequent decisions can be withheld from public comment or review (Winham, 92; Dam, 70). The reason for this relatively secret proceeding is because dispute proceedings are not intended to find fault but to resolve differences of opinion that block trade. The greater the privacy, the greater the chance Parties can resolve their differences of opinion and begin to trade.

With the successful completion of the Uruguay Round negotiations in 1995, the GATT was transformed into the WTO. The Marakkesh Declaration expanded the WTO powers by creating a fully operating institution capable of self-adjustment. Revisions to multilateral trade rules and procedures no longer require long negotiating Rounds that characterized early negotiations. The WTO itself is capable of implementing its own changes in trade rules and procedures. The WTO has also expanded its scope of influence over specific sectors of trade, expanding its influence over agriculture, antidumping, services, investment, and intellectual property. A new dispute mechanism gives the WTO much greater authority to enforce its guidelines and to use trade sanctions against member nations who do not abide by decisions rendered by its dispute settlement process (Charnovitz 94a, 94b).

GATT norms, rules, and scope act as the foundation for efforts to liberalize trading rules. Voluntary, cooperative, and informal, its underlying principle is a belief in the principles of free trade and of the importance of informal arrangements between Parties to avoid constituency pressure that often compels government officials to respond by using protective legislation.

U.S. Trade Policy Regime and Fast Track
Negotiating Authority

The political and economic role of the United States give the U.S. trade policy important weight in efforts to liberalize trade. Unlike the negotiators representing most other countries, U.S. negotiators must convince Congress, during congressional ratification, to accept the outcome of their negotiations without modifying the terms. Congressional consideration of a completed trade agreement may result in modifications to the agreement that disrupt the compromises struck by negotiators. To avoid this outcome, Congress developed Fast Track, a process described by trade scholar I. M. Destler as a "pressure-diverting policy management system" in which Congress cedes trade negotiating authority to the president in exchange for political protection from the short-term, negative effects of liberalized trade policy (Destler, 92).

Article I, Section 8 of the United States Constitution grants Congress authority over U.S. commerce, including direct responsibility over the content of bilateral and multilateral trade agreements. Direct responsibility over policies that often impose serious hardships on voters whose jobs are affected by trade made it difficult for members supportive of more liberal trade policies to avoid using tariffs and quotas on foreign imports to protect local industry from international competition (Pastor, 80). In his seminal work on the politics of tariffs, E. E. Schattschneider argued that the ability of these "pressure groups" to convince Congress to use tariffs and duties to protect their own interests precipitated the 1929 Stock Market Crash and the advent of the Great Depression (Schattschneider, 35). To divert this pressure and to facilitate trade liberalization, Congress began the slow process of removing itself from direct authority over the content of trade policy.

The first important step taken by Congress was the 1934 Reciprocal Trade Agreement Act. The 1934 Trade Act made two important changes to trade policy negotiations. First, tariff reductions were negotiated on an item-by-item basis; although more cumbersome, the specific item procedure eliminated some of the political pressures against liberalizing trade by reducing the tendency to package issues together for congressional consideration. The second major step was to change the negotiations from treaties (which require a super majority vote in the Senate) to executive agreements. At the formal request of the president, Congress granted authority to negotiate bilateral executive agreements; it retained the right to rescind any agreement (with six months' notice) and could withdraw the negotiating authority if it chose.

Between 1945 and 1988 the United States relied upon this new format for trade policy negotiations to forge relations with the emerging GATT. The office of the president negotiated multilateral tariff reductions under the framework of GATT, or through bilateral negotiations with other trading partners. Under the guidance of the House Ways and Means and Senate Finance Committees, the president prepared and submitted *enabling legislation*, legislation designed to make U.S. laws consistent with the new trade rules (Hudec, 86; Low, 93). With a bill (not a treaty), the president needs only a simple majority vote to pass the enabling legislation and formalize the negotiations into U.S. law.

Under this complex arrangement, the United States continued its lead toward reduced tariffs and increased trade. Successive trade acts between 1945 and 1984 continued the downward trend in both tariff and nontariff trade restrictions (Destler, 92; Low, 93). Congress was

TABLE 2.1 Components of Trade Regime

Executive	Interest Groups	Congress
Office of the United States Trade Representative	**Business Associations** —U.S. Chamber of Commerce —Business Roundtable —United States Council for International Business	**House Ways and Means** —Subcommittee on Trade
Interagency Advisory Process —Departments of State, Interior, Labor, Commerce, Agriculture		**Senate Finance Committee** —Subcommittee on Trade
Private Advisory Committees —Advisory Committee for Trade Policy Negotiations —Seventeen Issue-Negotiating Committees	**Labor Unions** —AFL-CIO–American Federation of Labor-CIO —UAW–United Auto Workers —USW–United Steel Workers —ACTWU–Amalgamated Clothing & Textile Workers Union	
	Agriculture —NFU–National Farmers Union —NFFC–National Family Farmers Coalition	

still sensitive to the short-term repercussions of tariff reductions and retained the power to modify the terms of the enabling legislation using amendment procedures and legislative "mark-ups" of the proposed bills. The process often produced changes to the delicate balance achieved by negotiators and made negotiators from trading countries suspicious of the "firmness" of positions negotiated by the United States. To help strengthen the hand of U.S. negotiators and further distance congressional members from constituent pressure to protect their industries, the 1974 Trade Act removed these obstacles by creating a set of procedural rules commonly referred to as "Fast Track."

Fast Track represents the last step to disentangle Congress from the politics of protective tariffs. Fast Track involves a set of self-imposed procedural limits to congressional members' ability to alter the terms of an agreement. First, it prohibits amendments to the enabling legislation. Second, it limits the period for consideration; once the enabling legislation is submitted for consideration, Congress is compelled to take action on the subsequent implementing legislation within sixty days. In exchange for these new privileges, the president is now required to notify Congress of the administration's intention to enter into a formal agreement within ninety days of initiation. Congress can withdraw Fast Track procedures if it votes against the president's request within ninety days of the request (Destler, 80).[2]

Downward Trends in the Growth of Trade Foster Fears of Protectionism

The trend toward trade liberalization initiated following World War II continued on its path of tariff reduction until the 1970s, when global inflation and increases in petroleum prices slowed the growth rate of the international economy (Low, 93; Bhagwati, 88). Governments responded with two forms of trade legislation. Laws such as sections 201 and 203 of the United States Trade Act of 1974 and Section 301 of the 1988 Trade Law Act allowed domestic industries to receive temporary protection (in the form of direct trade barriers) from imports, and compelled the U.S. government to take unilateral steps in defense of "unfair" trade practices (Lawrence and Litan, 86: 3). The second form of protection arising from the 1970s was the proliferation of NTBs. According to the GATT Secretariat, voluntary restrictions on trade and other NTBs were identified sixty-three times between 1978 and 1982 (Bhagwati, 88). The 1974 Tokyo Round of GATT negotiations was principally dedicated to the elimination of NTBs in an attempt to halt this movement toward trade protectionism; however, it wasn't until the completion of the Uruguay Round in 1994 that a more comprehensive limit on the use of NTBs was agreed to by Parties to GATT.

Through a combination of regional and multilateral trade expansion, global trade has become an important part of domestic economic policies of both industrial and developing countries. The trade policy regime created by formal and informal rules of trade propelled trade between nations to more than $6 trillion each year, an elevenfold increase since 1950. Trade between nations grew two and one-half times faster than the growth of total output; as a percentage of annual Gross Domestic Product (GDP), U.S. imports rose from 4.7 percent in 1960 to 9.7 percent in 1990, while exports grew from 5.2 percent to 11.4 percent (French, 93). This level of growth occurred not just in the developed world; over the past ten years, the most impressive rate of growth has occurred in developing countries. Real GDP in developing countries nearly tripled from 1955 to 1990, approaching $3,000 (Bailey, 94). Pacific Rim countries are often cited as examples of the benefits of liberalized trade; according to the World Bank, Korea exported $170 million in finished goods in 1990 (World Bank, 92).

Expanding trade has become an important source for new jobs; economists estimate that for every $1 billion in exports, fifteen thousand new jobs are created. Exported goods are credited with one-tenth of all employment in the United States, now the fastest growing sector of the American economy. With the collapse of the former Soviet Union and the embrace of market economies worldwide, trade proponents stand on the verge of unprecedented growth. Citizens from Russia, China, and India want to enjoy the material benefits of a modern, high-technology, trade-oriented global society.

Broad acceptance of the principles of free trade now dominates both political and economic thinking in almost every industrialized nation in the world. Protectionism is used in the pejorative sense and advocated only by those who seek narrow personal gains at the expense of others. Faith in free trade is so powerful that, according to economist Paul Krugman, "If there were an Economist's Creed it would surely contain the affirmation, 'I believe in the Principle of Comparative Advantage,' and 'I believe in free trade'" (Krugman, 87: 131).

THE GREEN MOVEMENT AND THE INSTITUTIONS OF ENVIRONMENTAL PROTECTION

American attitudes toward the environment are rooted in our relationship to Europe. To the first settlers, the New World was both an unused land abundant in natural resources and a wilderness threatening the survival of a new people (Shabecoff, 93; Cronon, 83). Founded upon their belief in the human domination of nature and their belief in private enterprise, colonists forged a relationship with their environment based upon resource extraction for their personal use and private reward (Shabecoff, 93; Cronon 83). Resource management for maximum human use, not preservation of the environment, became the hallmark of early American environmentalism.

According to environmental historian Philip Shabecoff, the first challenge to the concept of maximum use was born in the minds of early environmental philosophers who embraced transcendentalism and rejected the trappings of an increasingly material society (Shabecoff, 93; chapter 3). Henry David Thoreau argued that nature was "valuable" even when it was not considered beautiful or useful to humans. From Thoreau's perspective, human activity was the real culprit causing environmental "damage," a thought reflected in the writings a contemporary of Thoreau's, George Perkins Marsh; "But man is everywhere a disturbing agent. Wherever he plants his foot, the harmonies of nature are turned to discord" (as quoted in Shabecoff, 93; page 56). The seeds of environmental concern sewn by transcendental thinkers produced two important trends marking the first generation of environmental policy and politics. Affluent urbanites developed an active concern for protecting and preserving nature. John Muir, early spokesperson for the cause of wild nature, formed the Sierra Club in 1892, followed shortly by the National Audubon Society and the National Wildlife Federation. These early environmentalists lobbied congress for legislation to establish wildlife preservations throughout the United States, giving birth to the national park system.

The theme arguing humanity's destructive capacity sounded by early environmental philosophers was not reflected in the early environmental policies crafted by Congress. "For most of the nineteenth century, the ebullient young country was still not ready to take a sober look at the environmental consequences of its long binge of expansion and development" (Shabecoff, 89; page 59). The second important theme growing out of the challenge to eighteenth century environmentalism was the development of the conservation management philosophy. Largely associated with Gifford Pinchot, it argues that natural resources must be conserved to ensure maximum use for now *and* for future generations. Pinchot believed that all the nations resources were linked together in an effort to expand the nation's growing economy. Exploitation and misuse threatened long-term prosperity, so government policy was required to guarantee the benefits of such a bountiful country for all of the people. Conservation management became the hallmark of early environmental legislation in the United States (Shabecoff, 89).

While Muir's ecocentrism never seriously challenged the prevailing anthropocentric view, the political era of the 1960s represented the first important challenge to U.S. attitudes to environmental management. For the first time works such as Rachel Carson's *Silent Spring*, Paul Ehrlich's *The Population Bomb*, or Barry Commoner's *The Closing Circle* used science to awaken society to the effects of human activity on the environment. Danger to human health caused by pesticides, excessive population, overconsumption of the world's resources, and habitat loss challenged the prevailing view that technology, economic growth, and environmental management made society better off (Naess 72; Merchant, 87).

The modern environmental movement that grew out of this awakening was comprised of an army of young people schooled in the political activism of the 1960s. Borrowing a page from the civil rights movement, these new environmentalists developed a combative political style to express their demands for greater environmental protection. Newer environmental organizations such as Friends of the Earth (FoE), Greenpeace, and the Natural Resources Defense Council (NRDC) mobilized older organizations to join them to stage the 1970 Earth Day celebration. They challenged the older environmental groups to help them pressure Congress for laws to protect the environment. In a span of fifteen years, their work produced an unprecedented patchwork of regulatory policies that now comprise the foundation of U.S. environmental policy (Shabecoff, 93; Rosenbaum, 91). The Clean Air Act (1970) and the Clean Water Act (1972), the National Environmental Policy Act (1969), the Endangered Species Act (1973), the Toxic Substance Control Act (1976), and the Resource Conservation and Recovery Act (1976) are considered landmark pieces of environmental legislation and are often used by other countries as models for their own environmental laws.[3]

Besides formal legislation designed to protect the environment, numerous changes to Congress and the executive branch reflect the institutionalization of environmental issues into local, state, and federal political systems. The Environmental Protection Agency (EPA) and the President's Council of Environmental Quality (CEQ), plus new congressional committees like the Senate Environment and Public Works Committee and the House Energy and Commerce Committee, became chiefly responsible for U.S. environmental legislation. Important legislative leaders such as former Senators Edmund Muskie and George McGovern, and Congressman Henry Waxman used their offices to lobby in support of environment policies. National environmental groups relocated their offices to Washington, D.C., to take part in the daily routine of politics and policy making. State governments developed their own environmental agencies and adopted laws to implement federal guidelines for water, soil, and air quality, doggedly pursued by an exploding number of environmental groups involved in state government (Davis and Lester, 89). In just fifteen years environmental issues and their representatives became formal participants in the U.S. political process.

Development of International Environmental Regimes

The U.S. environmental movement was indicative of a growing international awareness of the importance of protecting the environment. Improvements in scientific understanding of the environment increased public awareness of the global implications of environmental protection and the implications of population increase, consumption patterns, ecosystem disruption, and desertification. Political events like the first Earth Day in 1970 and the 1972 United Nations Conference on the Human Environment (the Stockholm Conference) transformed international public support for environmental protection into political pressure to protect the global environment.

The Stockholm Conference was a watershed event in the effort to internationalize and legitimize the environmental movement, both in terms of its formal output and in terms of its informal impact on environmentalism. First, the Conference redefined international environmental issues by focusing on meeting the needs of all humans, controlling pollutants worldwide, managing natural resource use, increasing education and respect for the cultural aspects of environmental issues, and creating international organizations to help realize these goals (Haas et al., 93). Of particular importance were the twenty-six principles embodied in the Declaration of the Stockholm Conference. Among these principles, two stand out as particularly important. The Declaration reserves the right of states to exploit their resources, provided they do not damage the environment beyond their border. Preserving this right was of critical importance to representatives from developing countries who were concerned that the more developed countries would pressure them to preserve their resources in a manner that would prohibit them from evolving through the early resource-maximization stage already experienced by industrialized countries (Agusto de Castro, 95). The second fundamental principle of the Declaration is that of cooperation. Nations were called upon to work together to develop international laws on liability and compensation for environmental damage and to avoid imposing the values inherent in domestic laws onto countries that do not share the same set of environmental priorities (Soroos, 94; Caldwell, 90). Differences in environmental priorities and concerns over national sovereignty established a tension between developed and developing countries as they struggled to create an international regime for environmental protection.

The Conference was also important because it created one of the key United Nations agencies charged with environmental protection. The United Nations Environmental Program (UNEP) collects and disseminates information about the environment through its Earthwatch Program (Soroos, 94). UNEP also acts as the focal point for the negotiation of multilateral environmental agreements (MEAs); between 1973 and 1990, UNEP-sponsored negotiations resulted in the adoption of a number of important MEAs that gave shape to the modern international environmental regime (Caldwell, 90); the 1973 Convention on International Trade in Endangered Species (CITES); the 1979 Convention on the Prevention of Marine Pollution by Dumping of Wastes and Other Matter; the 1987 Montreal Protocol on Substances That Deplete the Ozone Layer; and the 1989 Convention on Control of Transboundary Movements of Hazardous Waste and Their Disposal.

Evidence of the institutionalization of international environmental issues can be found by examining the responses of other international institutions to the environment. UNEP began to coordinate environmental issues involving other, older U.N. agencies, including the United Nations Educational, Scientific, and Cultural Organization (UNESCO), the World Health Organization (WHO), and the Food and Agriculture Organization (FAO). Other international and regional organizations such as the Organization for Economic Cooperation and Development (OECD) and the North Atlantic Treaty Organization (NATO) formalized a role for environmental issues in their deliberations (Soroos, 94; Caldwell, 90). The role for international Non-Governmental Organizations (NGOs) grew, along with the institutionalization of environmental issues, into these new policy forums as organizations such as the World Wide Fund for Nature, the International Union for the Conservation of Nature (IUCN), Greenpeace, and Friends of the Earth became regular participants in providing scientific and professional advice to government officials and advocating for human and environmental issues in international dialogues (Caldwell, 90).

Sustainable Development Offers an Alternative Paradigm to Economic Growth

National and international efforts to establish a regime for environmental protection resulted in the development of an alternative vision of human's relationship with their environment to that prescribed by growth-oriented trade policy. Its intellectual roots can be found in the principles of *sustainable development*, "a process of change in which the exploitation of resources, the direction of investment, the orientation of technological development, and institutional change are all in harmony and enhance both current and future potential to meet human needs and aspirations" (World Commission on Environment and Development, 87: 46). Few people have developed the implications of sustainable development better than economist Herman Daly.

In *Toward a Steady-State Economy*, Daly and his associates argue that the scale of human behavior should be based on biological laws that depict the world as a closed system of renewable and nonrenewable resources (Daly, 73). To avoid ecological destruction, human scale should never exceed the *carrying capacity* of the earth's ecosystem to act as both a "source" for natural resources and a "sink" for waste disposal (Daly, 91). Instead of advocating continuously expanding levels of economic activity, Daly argues for a more community-based economic structure, able to operate within the carrying capacity of local ecosystems yet provide adequate opportunities for individuals to provide for themselves and their families.

While sustainable development has never drawn the same level of attraction to its principles as the growth model and principles of free trade, it does serve as an alternative paradigm for organizing social and political institutions, one seemingly more harmonious with the limits to human activity imposed by nature. And while its interpretation currently lacks consensus a single definition, it remains a uniting principle linking environmental organizations around the central idea of balancing the demands made by human society with those requested by the natural one.

THE INTERSECTION OF TRADE RULES AND ENVIRONMENTAL PROTECTION

The differences in institutional structure, rules, and norms and in the political actors that characterize the trade and environment regimes set the stage for one of the most important intersections of policy domains. While their differences suggest a good deal of conflict, their similarities suggest a pattern for their intersection based upon the cooperative principles of the international components of both institutions. The emphasis on cooperation, in turn, creates tensions over national sovereignty that help to characterize the NAFTA debate.

Any comparison between these two regimes must begin with their differences in basic normative principle. Trade liberalization is grounded in the belief that economic growth promises the greatest opportunity for expanding social welfare. Technology provides answers to thorny questions about resource use and waste disposal. Market forces signal the optimal use of these technologies by relying on competition to ensure constantly expanding, economically efficient production. Sustainable development, on the other hand, implies limits on the scale of human activity. Unfettered use of technology and overreliance on market forces to determine prices for goods whose value is not amenable to such evaluations promotes ecologically irresponsible behavior.

When the principles of sustainable development and economic growth are applied to trade policy, they produce dramatically different results. For trade advocates free trade expands the level of domestic economic activity, thereby alleviating poverty and providing citizens and their governments with greater resources to spend on protecting the environment. Noted economist Jagdish Bhagwati argues, "Growth enables governments to tax and to raise resources for a variety of objectives, including the abatement of pollution and the general protection of the environment. Without such revenues, little can be achieved, no matter how pure one's motives may be" (Bhagwati, 93: 42). As economies mature, less polluting industries can take the place of older technology industries, thereby reducing the damage to the environment resulting from increased economic activity. The sustainable paradigm does not offer such straightforward visions of the future; based upon limiting human activity, its solutions suggest a more difficult path of redistributing wealth, developing national economies, and expanding the role played by government in economic activity (Lang and Hines, 93). While their vision of the future is not as well articulated, their attacks on the growth paradigm are. Solutions like constantly expanding human scale fail the test of sustainability. For example, despite the fact that the world's economy continues to grow, more and more people live under circumstances that result in deaths by malnutrition and human diseases caused by inadequate sewage and impure water (World Bank, 92). Daly argues that this occurs because growth models say nothing about the distribution of wealth, only the creation of wealth (Daly, 92). Free trade's focus on expanding the scale of economic activity fails to properly internalize the cost of resource use and degradation, the social costs of lost jobs and economic disruptions, and the limits on activity dictated by the environment (Daly, 92; Ferguson et al., 95). According to Daly, searching for solutions to poverty and environmental problems in trade policy is like a fairy tale; ". . . like Alice in *Through the Looking Glass*, the faster we run the farther behind we fall" (Daly, 93: 57).

Very little intersection exists between the political actors involved in both the trade and environmental regimes. With the exception of U.N. agencies that have internalized some element of environmental concern in their mandates (such as the OECD, the World Bank, and United Nations Conference on Trade and Development [UNCTAD]) trade and environmental actors have very little formal or informal knowledge of one another. In the United States, what little knowledge they have is not usually positive; business advocates remain concerned about the implications of environmental regulatory policies on competitiveness, while environmental groups have been largely suspicious of the influence on Congress that business groups enjoy (Jackson, 91; Esty, 94a).

Another difference between the kinds of actors involved in the different regimes is the degree of consensus around a predominant normative principle. Trade advocates enjoy remarkable consensus over the goals and principles of free trade; with the exception of organized labor, the vast majority of actors involved in the trade regime embrace the growth paradigm.[4] This fact facilitates the informal decision-making structure that characterizes trade policy development. Political actors comprising the environmental community are more diverse. Table 2.2 locates eleven national environmental organizations on a continuum whose ends are defined by the extreme opinions toward trade policy. Differences in organizational mandate, personnel, and source of revenue suggest that some environmental organizations are more amenable to trade norms, rules, and decision-making procedures. For example, members of the board of directors from organizations such as the World Wildlife Fund, the National Wildlife Federation, and the Environmental Defense Fund have much greater access to economic elites supportive of trade policy. Board members from the Sierra Club, Friends of the Earth, and Public Citizen have much different backgrounds, with few ties to the business community.[5]

Despite these fundamental differences in principles, both trade and environment regimes do share a number of similar characteristics. Both rely upon cooperation and consensus between parties to any

---

TABLE 2.2   Spectrum of National Environmental Organizations

More Opposed to Growth Model			*More Supportive of Growth Model*

Greenpeace
Public Citizen
Friends of the
    Earth (FoE)
	Sierra Club	Defenders of
		    Wildlife
		    (Defenders)
		National Audubon
		    Society (NAS)
		Natural Resources
		    Defense Council
		    (NRDC)
			The Nature
			    Conservancy
			    (TNC)
			Environmental
			    Defense Fund
			    (EDF)
			National Wildlife
			    Federation
			    (NWF)
			World Wildlife
			    Fund (WWF)

More Adversarial		More Accommodating	

agreement. While this normative principle fosters a more collaborative approach to trade and environmental policy making, it also suggests some serious obstacles. Cooperation at the international level tends to slow down the process of policy making, especially when the issues under consideration have negative implications for domestic policy. Two examples underscore this problem. The agricultural sections of the 1994 Uruguay Round of GATT still allow for special tariff protection for European agriculture (Low, 93). Negotiations were unable to overcome pressure exerted by French farmers fearful of the implications of the removal of farm subsidies on their way of life. Another example grows out of the United Nations Conference on the Environment and Development (UNCED). National politics made the adoption of the forestry protocol and the biodiversity convention difficult; without the United States as a signatory, both conventions fail to enjoy recognition as international law (Sooros, 94). Cooperation between nations as the principle adoption rule and enforcement tool complicates implementing international environmental agreements largely because of the ease with which nations can free-ride on the environmental efforts of others (Hufbauer and Schott, 93).

The two examples just given point to additional problems related to the scope of both regimes. GATT's limited scope extends beyond products; due to its voluntary nature, GATT has no influence on non-Parties to the Agreement. The combination of limited product scope and jurisdiction has the result that only 7 percent of world production is subject to GATT trade rules.[6] Setting agendas for environmental protection has proven incredibly difficult, as issues confronting developing nations were often at odds with those advocated by environmentalists from industrialized countries (Agusto de Castro, 95; Caldwell, 90). The inability to establish a common agenda severely limits the scope and effectiveness of the institutions charged with protecting the environment.

Rules and scope of the trade and environment regimes within the U.S. contest have important implications for the nature of the intersection between trade and environmental policies. By the 1980s the economic costs of the regulatory approach to environmental protection were subject to criticism; economic studies suggested that the costs associated with implementing certain environmental regulations were often greater than the benefits associated with the goals of the policy (Pearce and Turner, 90). Noncompliance with, and poor enforcement of, clean air and water regulations became commonplace, and routine inspection and reporting requirements were considered unnecessary burdens on state and local governments and businesses (Freeman, 94). The complexity of environmental problems also proved a challenge to the regulatory approach. Regulations proved effective tools with "first generation" environmental problems such as sewage treatment and certain air contaminants, but more complex environmental problems involving the increasing use of chemicals, food safety, and hazardous material use and disposal prompted a good deal of strategic behavior by industries seeking ways around the costs of complying with the performance controls set by these federal regulations (Cascio et al., 96).

The broad scope of environmental protection also produced a backlash among citizens who felt their individual liberties were infringed upon by certain regulatory laws. In particular, implementation of the Endangered Species Act and the management and use of public lands angered citizens who mobilized into political pressure groups such as the Wise Use Movement and the Sagebrush Rebellion (Switzer, 94).

Dissatisfaction with the regulatory approach to environmental protection is characterized by environmental scholar Robert Paehlke as "neo-conservatism and contemporary political realities," a phrase characterized by strong criticism of many government solutions to environmental problems, renewed faith in the private sector to stimulate the economy to generate the attitude and economic resources necessary to protect the environment, and a restoration of traditional moral and religious values which view the earth as the property of humans to exploit:

> While environmentalists once made considerable gains as special interest groups and via many negative single-issue organizations, this approach has been less effective in the 1980's. With hostile regimes in power, most recent contests have been defensive and many campaigns have been lost. It has been nearly a decade since environmentalists gained ground by political means (Paehlke, 89; 244).

The U.S. trade regime faces its own constraints. The constitutional ability of the U.S. Congress to modify trade negotiations virtually requires the U.S. government to obtain Fast Track authorization from Congress prior to the start of any negotiations. Despite this level of political protection, national politics still has considerable influence over the outcome of trade policy negotiations. Popular dissatisfaction over the merits of trade liberalization challenges any administration considering new trade policy, especially if NTBs and other tools of domestic policy are limited through voluntary adoption of the agreement.

The predominant role played by the United States in determining the outcome of trade policy negotiations is changing due to shifts in geopolitical relations (Low, 93; Destler, 92). Japanese economic expansion and the creation of the European Common Market reshuffled the balance of political and economic power, eliminating the ability of the

United States to act as hegemon in international economic relations.[7] Rising energy prices resulting from heightened environmental concerns and the 1973 oil embargo slowed the rate of global economic growth. In the United States, the combination of economic slowdown and domestic political pressures to reduce access of foreign-produced goods to U.S. markets lead President Ronald Reagan to employ fiscal policies that invigorated the U.S. economy but also expanded the U.S. public debt to its largest in history. Deficit spending drove interest rates up in the United States, attracting foreign investors whose investments sustained continued high levels of U.S. product consumption. On the international environmental scene, the weakened U.S. position makes it more difficult to dominate setting the agenda for international environmental protection. The results of UNCED revealed how difficult it now is for the industrialized world, and the United States in particular, to dominate the international environmental agenda.

Besides institutional characteristics, another theme common to both regimes relates to issues of national sovereignty. Respect for national sovereignty creates complex problems that block efforts to establish comprehensive international trade and environment regimes. The agreements themselves place constraints on issues of both internal and external sovereignty. For example, more than one-quarter of world trade involves commodities, usually natural resources thought of as "primary products" such as fish, timber, and copper. If tropical timber harvesting practices in Malaysia and Indonesia leave the local environment destroyed, is it the responsibility of other nations to try to restrict that practice? Copper mines in New Guinea and Indonesia dump 130,000 tons of metal tailings into local rivers annually, killing wildlife and destroying water sources for villages downstream. Nearly 100 percent of these minerals are exported for consumption elsewhere, but the principles of the international environmental policy regime ask other nations to respect this right. At the same time these developing countries argue that the industrialized world enjoyed a long period of resource exploitation before they developed an internal desire to protect the environment.

Characteristics of the Trade and Environment Nexus

The combination of shifting political power and inadequate institutional scope of the GATT and of international environmental institutions have had the perverse consequence of actually promoting greater bilateral and regional arrangements. Regional agreements like the European Common Market and the U.S.-Canada Free Trade Agreement (CFTA) coordinate trade between neighboring countries. Similar regional arrangements proliferate in the environmental community; since the initiation of UNEP there has been a proliferation of regional and bilateral environmental agreements, far outnumbering the complicated and difficult-to-enforce, large-scale agreements like Law of the Sea of the Montreal Protocol (Haas et al., 93).

Another characteristic of the trade and environment nexus has to do with the outline of the conflict itself and involves the **competitive implications** of national and international environmental policy. Business leaders from multinational firms worried that competition with manufacturers operating in countries where they are not required to internalize similar environmental costs may enjoy price advantages created by policy. On the other hand, developing countries argued that trade policies that require imports to meet domestic environmental standards effectively restrict access to larger markets (Snape, 95; Pearson, 93; McAlpine and Le Donne, 93; Office of Technology and Assessment, 93). The rise in NTBs reported by GATT sparked concern that environmental policy would become a new form of nontariff protection. Under the guise of environmental policies, foreign products might be prohibited from access to markets where domestic products were more expensive (Snape, 95; Stokes, 92). Policy standards such as auto emissions or agricultural regulations controlling pesticide residue were already criticized by trading countries who believed these policies were actually crafted to restrict market access for foreign products under the guise of insuring food safety or promoting cleaner air.[8] Fear that "green protectionism" would take the place of more traditional NTBs became a popular concern voiced by trade advocates.

Environmental groups responded that, in the name of trade liberalization, competitive pressures would put downward pressures on efforts to set higher environmental standards. They relied upon their ability to pressure national governments to set standards and to impose those standards on trading partners as part of their effort to set international standards for environmental protection. Absent an effective international enforcement mechanism, environmental groups from industrialized countries relied upon **unilateral action** taken by national governments. Trading partners, especially countries whose geopolitical power made it difficult to alter the course of international affairs unilaterally, objected to the use of unilateral trade sanctions to achieve domestic environmental objectives. Under most circumstances unilateral action was a violation of existing GATT jurisprudence (Bhagwati and Patrick, 90; Durbin, 95).

Concerns over asymmetries in national environmental standards and unilateral action taken by industrialized countries to protect the environment and establish the international agenda for environmental protection were key issues underlying the intersection of the trade and environment nexus. From 1982 to 1991 nine disputes between environmental policies and trade rules were addressed by international dispute resolution bodies.[9] These trade disputes validated trade advocates' concerns that environmental regulations were another form of NTB, meriting attention by GATT negotiators as part of the agenda for the Uruguay Round.

What these characteristics point to is the fact that the intersection between trade and environmental policies is framed by the norms, scope, rules, and participants that make up the trade regime. The implications of this outcome cannot be overemphasized. Environmental issues would need to frame themselves in the language of trade, guided by the rules and norms inherent in trade policy legislation. Options for implementing environmental policy, such as a higher degree of public participation in decision making, would be constrained by the trade regime's tendency toward informal, relatively secret interactions among elites. Not being a part of this particular monopoly, environmental organizations needed some kind of fundamental challenge to the successful continuation of the existing policy monopoly. Their opportunity would not come at the international level, but within the context of the three-nation negotiations surrounding the North American Free Trade Agreement.

ENDNOTES

1. See Lang and Hines, 93; Bhagwati, 93; Daly, 93; Krugman, ed., 88. To review literature on environmental protection, see Merchant, 87.

2. In particular, sections 201 and 301 of the 1974 Trade Act give Congress greater authority over the president by directing the executive to take unilateral actions against trading partners. See Destler, 92; Bhagwati and Patrick, eds., 90.

3. For a complete listing of important environmental legislation, see Sale, 93.

4. Until the 1970s U.S. labor participants in trade policy were also supportive of trade liberalization. See Bauer, Pool, and Dexter, 1972.

5. For details on the makeup of the various environmental organizations, refer to Appendix A.

6. Prior to completion of the Uruguay Round, agricultural commodities, tropical products, textiles, services, capital and labor flows, and intellectual property resources were not subject to GATT trade rules.

7. For a discussion of the importance of a hegemon in international trade institutions, see Kindleberger, 86.

8. The European Community annually publishes a list of U.S. regulations they argue are inconsistent with GATT trade rules. Among the regulations targeted are Corporate Average Fuel Economy (CAFE) standards, the Marine Mammal Protection Act, and product content laws in California.

9. For information on these disputes, see United States Congress, 92a.

3

Fast Track

In May 1991 the U.S. Congress voted to reauthorize Fast Track negotiating authority, enabling the Bush administration to begin formal NAFTA negotiations with representatives from Canada and Mexico. As part of the conditions for reauthorization set forth by Congress, President Bush committed to address environmental issues on a "parallel track" to negotiations. For the first time in U.S. trade history, environmental issues were linked to trade policy negotiations.

The linkages forged between NAFTA negotiations and environmental concerns would not have happened without the active participation in the Fast Track reauthorization of numerous national environmental organizations. Resisted by most trade advocates, they used the circumstances surrounding Fast Track and their access to Congress to convince the Bush administration to modify their negotiating agenda to include environmental issues. The political leverage they used to become formal participants in negotiations came from their ability to threaten Fast Track reauthorization and the willingness of some groups to cooperate with trade elites and accept the parallel track for environmental issues. Members of the environmental community played "good cop/bad cop" with members of the trade regime to secure a spot on the negotiating agenda and as members of the trade policy monopoly.

This chapter analyzes the institutional factors responsible for creating the political environment that empowered environmental groups with this kind of preemptive leverage. It also explains how environmental organizations used that leverage and how members of the trade regime sought compromises with more moderate environmental groups, enabling them to agree to some of their terms without diverting themselves from the larger agenda of expanding economic activity through trade liberalization.

The parallel track offered by President Bush and accepted by Congress resulted in three important things. First, it deflected any direct conflicts between trade negotiations and progress on environmental issues. This was particularly important regarding environmental remediation of the Mexico-U.S. border; fears that linkages between these

longstanding environmental and social concerns to successful negotiations could stall any agreement. Deflecting environmental issues to
the parallel track also enabled negotiators to avoid addressing the
fundamental questions raised by the trade and environment debate.
The second effect of the parallel track was to formalize access to negotiations for some environmental organizations. Participation in formal
negotiations created important avenues for influence and policy sug-
gestions. Finally, the provisions of the parallel track split the environmental community. The split among environmentalists over Fast
Track became one of the defining characteristics of their participation
in negotiations; it may also have become an important component for
maintaining their leverage throughout negotiations.

INSTITUTIONAL FACTORS SHAPE ACCESS TO TRADE POLICY NEGOTIATIONS

A variety of institutional factors set the stage for national environmental
organizations to pressure Congress to include environmental issues as
part of the conditions for Fast Track reauthorization. These factors will
be explained here.

GATT Resists Linkages between Trade and the Environment

The first venue for discussion of any linkages between trade and the
environment was the completion of the Uruguay Round of GATT.
Negotiating a trade agreement with Mexico was not a high-priority
trade issue for the United States in 1990. In 1986 at Punta del Este,
Uruguay, the eighth Round of GATT negotiations began with three
objectives uppermost in the minds of negotiators. Negotiators were
committed to resolving longstanding trade obstacles in areas such as
NTBs and special treatment for agriculture and textile products. They
were also interested in expanding GATT's influence over new areas
of trade such as services, investment, and intellectual property which
had never been influenced by GATT discipline (Schott, 90). The last goal
was largely symbolic; the changing geopolitical nature of international
relations and the relatively small portion of global trade covered by
GATT discipline discussed in Chapter 2 weakened confidence in
GATT's ability to provide an overall structure and scope for trade
liberalization (Schott, 90). Contracting Parties were committed to reas-
serting confidence in GATT, as reflected in the statement made by the
leaders of the world's largest economies during their 1990 G-7 Economic Summit meeting:

The successful outcome of the Uruguay Round has the highest priority on the international economic agenda. Consequently, we stress our determination to take the difficult political decisions necessary to achieve far-reaching, substantial results in all areas of the Uruguay Round (Low, 93: 1).

With such an ambitious agenda and timetable, leaders from GATT-member nations were not interested in the exhortations of a small group of environmental organizations concerned about the implications of GATT policy on food safety and product standards. In particular, Switzerland-based World Wide Fund for Nature and Greenpeace International were among NGOs working with European farmers concerned over the loss of farm subsidies as a result of GATT negotiations (Arden-Clarke, 91b; Hines, 94). However, outside the context of their coalition with influential farm lobbyists, European governments were not responsive to environmental concerns related to trade negotiations.

Representatives from environmental organizations were not able to convince GATT officials of the importance of expanding the negotiating agenda. Linkages between French farmers seeking the continuation of subsidies did not provide them adequate political leverage to convince trade proponents to expand negotiations to include the environment. Besides limited access to formal meetings of GATT officials, they did not have access to negotiators through informal channels to press the case. Leaders from influential GATT countries were also not supportive of expanding the negotiating agenda, preferring instead to complete the task already mandated in 1986. With no real history or competence on environmental issues, GATT advocates found no reason to respond to pressure from environmental organizations.

The failed efforts in Europe shifted the focus of environmental efforts to influence trade policy toward a small group of U.S. NGOs trying to alter the U.S. government's agenda for negotiations. In 1988 the U.S. Department of Agriculture drafted product standard language for Uruguay Round negotiations designed to harmonize product standards toward international norms normally established by international bodies such as the United Nations *Codex Alimentarius* (Fisher, 94; Leonard, 94).[1] These efforts alarmed NGOs, such as the Community Nutrition Institute (CNI) and the Institute for Agriculture and Trade Policy (IATP), which were concerned that government policy toward food safety would weaken domestic political pressure for higher food safety standards by subjecting any domestic standard to international norms (Meade, 92). By the end of 1990 the concerns over trade policy held by smaller environmental groups attracted the attention of Friends of the Earth (FoE) and the National Wildlife Federation (NWF). Relying on political pressure generated by these national organizations, a coalition of NGOs attempted to modify the U.S. agenda for negotiations to include concern for the environment (Blackwelder, 94; Hudson, 94).

The change in institutional venue increased access to negotiators, but this access did not prove to be enough of a change to win concession from the U.S. government. As with European governments, the Bush administration relied upon the same institutional characteristics of the GATT trade regime to resist efforts to link environmental concerns to the completion of GATT talks. The administration argued that the Uruguay Round's mandate did not include environmental issues and that progress toward the completion of negotiations was already threatened by other, more conventional, trade issues like subsidies. Their resistance to broadening the agenda was bolstered by the unwillingness of the other GATT countries to consider environmental issues within GATT.

Fast Track Rules Create Opening for Environmentalists

To gain access to trade policy negotiations, environmentalists needed more than just formal access to the U.S. and international trade regimes. The closed, largely informal nature of GATT negotiations, combined with its limited scope and normative history excluding environment, did not provide any new opportunities to alter the agenda. The structure and scope for negotiations could be modified; intellectual property rights issues were not part of the original Punta del Este mandate but were added in mid-1988 at the behest of the U.S. government. And while intellectual property issues were of great concern to many of the existing members of the U.S. and international trade regimes, the U.S. negotiators could resist the pressure directed at them by national groups because they could rely upon the institutional rigidity of their trade monopoly colleagues.

There was, however, a procedural issue in the United States which gave environmentalists the footing they needed to pressure U.S. negotiators. Fast Track authorization was about to expire on the Uruguay Round, forcing the president to request reauthorization no later than March 1991. Reauthorization gave (from multilateral GATT negotiations to include trilateral NAFTA negotiations), environmentalists the opportunity to press their case for linkage.

There were two principal motivations behind expanding the scope of U.S. trade policy negotiations to include discussions with Canada and Mexico. The first motivation came from Mexico. Mexican President Carlos Salinas de Gortari believed that securing a trade agreement with the United States would reinforce the Salinas administration's policy steps designed to reorganize Mexico's economy and create a market-driven, investor-friendly environment that would produce jobs for Mexican workers and help him to overcome internal opposition to strengthened economic ties with the United States (Hufbauer and Schott, 92; Weintraub, 91; Pastor and Casteneda, 89). In turn, bilateral negotiations with Mexico offered the U.S. government the opportunity to address two important components of their North American political-economic agenda. Negotiations could expand trade with Mexico's growing consumer market. Improved legal protection for intellectual property rights and expanded investment opportunity in an increasingly important economic market for U.S. manufacturers would help allay investors' concerns about doing business in Mexico. Second, formal trade arrangements could help "lock-in" the democratic and economic reforms made by Salinas, making it more difficult for future administrations to return Mexico to a government-controlled economy (Hufbauer and Schott, 92; Morici, 90).[2]

The second motivation was political. Poor progress in GATT negotiations, particularly in the areas of domestic subsidies and in the establishment of property rights, threatened to end negotiations (Stokes, 90). Congressional leaders began to voice their opposition to extending Fast Track authority beyond the June 1991 deadline unless tangible progress was made. The threat of congressional removal of Fast Track was of great concern to administration officials who believed Fast Track authority was essential to sustain negotiations. Fearing stalled GATT talks might kill the political momentum to liberalize trade, the Bush administration elected to increase the likelihood of sustaining GATT negotiations by linking Fast Track reauthorization to trade talks with Mexico.

The idea of trade liberalization with Mexico created two camps among members of the U.S. trade regime. Support for trade liberalization came principally from most multinational businesses and from most leaders in Congress. Mexico and the United States had been engaged in preliminary discussions devoted to trade liberalization since 1989. These negotiations had already resulted in some important changes to the nature of U.S.-Mexico trade. In 1989 U.S. exports to Mexico rose to $25 billion, a 21 percent jump in trade activity in one year. Mexico's exports to the United States reached $27.2 billion, up 15.5 percent since 1988. Business associations such as the U.S. Chamber of Commerce, Business Roundtable, and the regional business group, Border Trade Alliance (BTA), encouraged President Bush to respond positively to Mexico's request for negotiations (Senate Committee on Finance, 91a; House Committee on Ways and Means, 91a). Early congressional support came from representatives from Southwest delegations. Congressman Jim Kolbe (R-AZ), a longtime supporter of expanded economic relations with Mexico, stated, "We should seize the opportunity presented to . . . link the markets of Mexico and the U.S. . . . we should not hesitate or waffle on this issue" (House Committee on Ways and Means, 91a). Despite party differences, Democratic leaders, such as Senate Finance Committee Chairman Senator Lloyd Bentsen (D-TX) and House Ways and Means Committee Chairman Congressman Dan Rostenkowski (D-IL), were also supportive. Support from these two men was critical; as Chairmen of the Senate Finance and House Ways and Means Committees, they had jurisdiction over Fast Track reauthorization.

Support for trade liberalization with Mexico was bolstered by academic analysis that argued NAFTA would improve U.S. economic performance. Economic experts concluded that trade liberalization with Mexico would expand the domestic economies of all three NAFTA parties through access to larger markets for goods and services (Almon, 91; KPMG, 91; USITC, 91). But while these reports argued that a trade agreement would expand aggregate economic performance, they cautioned that trade would neither reduce nor expand overall employment in the United States. Instead, liberalized trade would shift jobs from sectors negatively impacted by competition with Mexican producers to those which would benefit from increased access to Mexican markets.[3]

The second group of trade regime actors opposed negotiations with Mexico as strongly as their counterparts supported it. As early as June 1990, the AFL-CIO, United Auto Workers (UAW), and the Amalgamated Clothing and Textile Workers Union (ACTWU) announced their opposition to expanding trade with Mexico. According to AFL-CIO international economist, Mark Anderson, "The AFL-CIO views the prospect of such an agreement with considerable alarm. . . . A free trade agreement will only encourage greater capital outflows from the U.S., bring about an increase in imports from Mexico and further harm the U.S. industrial base" (House Committee on Ways and Means, 91a). The AFL-CIO opposed Fast Track reauthorization as part of their strategy to postpone or perhaps end trade discussions with Mexico. Sector-specific industries such as the citrus, sugar, and vegetable industries in agriculture and automobile parts, glass, and steel in manufacturing also opposed trade liberalization, but it was labor's opposition to Fast Track reauthorization that attracted most public and political attention.

Labor opposition to expanded trade with Mexico was supported by some members of Congress, particularly by House Democrats from "rust-belt" states already economically hurt by firms relocating their assembly plants to Mexico under the *maquiladora* program. Congressman Jim Kolter (D-PA) stated, "If this administration continues its policy of free trade negotiations with Mexico, unfortunately, I can see a situation where the majority of American manufacturers will move the bulk of their operations to Mexico to take advantage of this cheap labor at the expense of the American work force" (House Committee on Ways and Means, 91a). Opponents to negotiations established the "Fair Trade Caucus" to publicize their concerns and redefine opponents to Fast Track as "fair traders," not "protectionists" (Fair Trade Caucus, April 1991).

Labor and rank and file congressional opposition to Fast Track was bolstered by public concerns over potential U.S. job losses resulting from expanded trade with Mexico. Historically, public opinion on trade liberalization has been mixed, with a general tendency to support trade liberalization mixed with fear it may cause personal pain through job losses in the United States. (Audley and Uslaner, 96; Destler, 92). Economic uncertainties associated with the 1980s had weakened public opinion toward the potential benefits of trade liberalization, as more and more Americans believed that trade liberalization actually had a negative effect on the quality of life in the United States (Audley and Uslaner, 96).

Armed with a high level of public concern over the implications of expanded trade with Mexico, trade opponents were prepared to stop negotiations by blocking Fast Track reauthorization. The showdown between them would occur in Congress. Proponents were better positioned to push the agenda for Fast Track reauthorization for some key reasons. First, political discussions surrounding NAFTA took place within the normative language of economic growth and "free trade"; as was made evident by the efforts of the Fair Trade Campaign to redefine the agenda, opponents to negotiations were forced to respond to the agenda for trade liberalization by borrowing from this language. The editorial boards of every major newspaper in the country supported negotiations and attacked opponents to trade liberalization as "protectionists." Support for reauthorization from the chairmen of both committees responsible for trade policy aided trade proponents in their effort to cast a favorable light on trade liberalization with Mexico. Elite Democratic support for negotiations would make it difficult for rank and file Democrats to develop an effective political strategy against Fast Track. Finally, trade supporters enjoyed academic support for their policy position, while opponents lacked "credentialed" academic or scholarly support for their position.[4]

Opponents benefited from public concern over the implications of trade liberalization and from broad support for their position among traditional Democrats in the House. They were also able to exploit the social circumstances of U.S. business relocation to Mexico under the *maquiladora* program. Therefore, despite elite support from the Bush administration and from leaders in Congress, antitrade Democrats generated a good deal of political opposition to Fast Track reauthorization. Constituent pressure focusing on job loss was effective with members whose districts are well represented by labor unions (Audley and Uslaner, 96). In particular, House Majority Leader Richard Gephardt (D-MO) was an early critic of the conditions for negotiations because they failed to take into consideration the implications for U.S. workers (Gephardt, 29 March 1991). Finally, partisan politics was also an important factor generating opposition to Fast Track. President Bush was facing elections in November 1992, and the Democratic Party was not happy about the prospect of aiding a Republican president, and possibly extending Republican control of the White House to sixteen years.[5]

The combination of institutional factors—historical circumstances, procedural rules, and presidential politics—created a situation ripe for an interest group not formally part of the trade regime to gain access by acting as a pivotal player in establishing a compromise that enabled pro-trade elites to pursue their agenda for trade liberalization. Environmental organizations exploited this opportunity to formalize their participation in negotiations by unconsciously utilizing the strong differences of opinion over the merits of trade. The outcome set the stage not only for NAFTA negotiations but for the role environmental groups would play until NAFTA was passed in 1993.

PREEMPTIVE POWER AND NEGOTIATION ACCESS

Fast Track authority for GATT negotiations was scheduled to expire 1 June 1990. The president submitted his request for reauthorization on 1 March; if Congress did not withdraw authorization by 1 June, it would automatically be extended for another two years. The stage was set for a battle over either to halt negotiations or to alter the agenda to satisfy the political demands of its more influential critics. Fast Track's uncertain future had the effect of increasing the political leverage of other groups not traditionally a part of the trade policy agenda nor whose issues were represented in the political monopolies surrounding policy formation. Immigration, religious, human, and animal rights groups all lined up to make an effort to influence the political outcome of the Fast Track debate. The question was which issues had strong enough support to overcome the tendency for trade policy to focus narrowly on economic interests.

Traditional trade-related issues, such as business and agriculture, were important factors shaping the agenda for NAFTA negotiations. But of the nontraditional, trade-related issues, only environmental concerns gained enough attention in the media and in congressional

TABLE 3.1   Preliminary Indicators of Political Interest in Environmental Issues during Fast Track

Newspaper Coverage of NAFTA By Issue*

	Labor	Agricul- ture	Business	Energy	Environ- ment	Immigra- tion	Human Rights
FAST TRACK (6/90–5/91)	.22	.28	.26	.05	.15	.04	.03

Summary of Congressional Hearing Coverage of Some Key NAFTA Issues**

	Environmental Issues	Business/ Economic Issues	Labor Issues
Fast Track (1/91–5/91)	.33	.62	.44

*Percentages reflect total coverage of particular issues pertaining to NAFTA. Coverage of NAFTA based upon NEXIS keyword search of articles appearing in the *Washington Post, New York Times, Wall Street Journal, Los Angeles Times, London Financial Times, Journal of Commerce,* and *The Chicago Tribune.* Each article was counted as many times as individual issues were addressed.
**Classification of hearings based upon *Congressional Record* documentation of hearings on NAFTA. "Coverage of issue" is defined by the presence of one or more panelist at each hearing on NAFTA who spoke on behalf of environmental, business/ economic, or labor issues. Representation of issue can include spokespersons from other sectors, such as the USTR ambassador or representatives of business and economic issues talking about environmental issues. Row percentages do not total to one as a single hearing may have covered more than one issue. For details on classification of hearings, see the list of NAFTA hearings found in Appendix D.

hearings to alter the agenda for negotiations. See table 3.1. Of the traditionally nontrade-related issues, environmental concerns proved to be the linchpin for Fast Track reauthorization. Unlike other NGO communities concerned with immigration or human rights, environmental groups were positioned to pressure members to respond to their concerns related to trade liberalization with Mexico. Why this occurred can be attributed to a number of factors.

Institutional Support for Environmental Protection

Twenty years of environmental activism had institutionalized environmental groups' participation in the politics of policy development. Most national organizations enjoyed access to politicians, either as technical experts on a specific policy issue or because of the political pressure generated by their grassroots lobbying organizations. An additional factor aiding environmental organizations during Fast Track was their image. Unlike other opponents to trade liberalization, environmental groups seemed not to have narrow constituent interests driving their participation. According to one trade official, "With the other groups we knew what they wanted, and could therefore negotiate with them and try to overcome their opposition. Environmentalists were different; they were out to protect the environment, and that is a difficult demand to meet with specific political offers" (Roh, 94). The popular image of the environment and the inability to articulate parochial interests made environmental organizations important allies for groups opposed to Fast Track. Participation of environmental groups in efforts to block Fast Track made it more difficult to promote a conventional protectionist policy agenda. Environmental problems along the Mexico-U.S. border served as a metaphor for the potential problems with unregulated economic integration and reached into the districts of members whose inclination was to support trade liberalization.

Mexico-U.S. Border Environmental Pressures

Since the 1980s border scholars and activists had voiced their concerns over the rapidly deteriorating conditions caused by massive regional industrialization (Texas Center for Policy Studies, 91). Environmental problems, caused by inadequate urban infrastructures, private housing, and nonenforcement enforcement of Mexican environmental regulations, posed threats to the health and safety of these regional cities. Organizations such as the Coalition for Justice in the Maquiladoras, the Texas Center for Policy Studies (TCPS), Arizona Toxics Information (ATI), and the Border Ecology Project (BEP) were created in response to these problems. These organizations had long argued for greater attention to environmental issues related to trade, but they were unable to focus national attention on the problems caused by rapid industrialization and urbanization.

Border health and environmental problems began to receive national attention just as preliminary trade negotiations began. Radio, television, and newsprint focused attention on the plight of *maquiladora* workers living along the border, bringing the human suffering and environmental degradation of this region into homes around the country (*Arizona Daily Republic*, 1990; *National Journal*, 1991). A 1990 American Medical Association report concluded that the border region was a "cesspool of infectious diseases." In their report the AMA implied a direct link with the increased business practices of the *maquiladoras* (*Journal of the American Medical Association*, 1990). It was not, therefore, surprising that Presidents Bush and Salinas discussed environmental issues during their November 1990 trade meeting held in Monterrey, Mexico. During the meeting both presidents pledged to negotiate new bilateral arrangements to address their common concerns related to expanding commerce along their common border.[6]

Coalitions with Anti-Fast Track Interest Groups Amplify Environmental Leverage

While Mexico-U.S. border environmental problems were important, the political leverage for environmentalists did not solely emanate from border environmental problems. Linkages between environmental issues and labor objections to trade policy posed the greatest threat to trade advocates' pursuit of Fast Track authorization. Trade advocates worried that a coalition of labor and environmental opposition to Fast Track could defeat their efforts in the House. A simple majority of members with strong voting records on labor and environmental issues confronted the Bush administration as it approached Fast Track reauthorization. With organized labor already opposed to liberalized trade with Mexico, attention turned toward environmental groups to determine the nature of their demands for Fast Track. Environmentalists were positioned to preempt negotiations but only because they could link their issues with another, more politically salient, trade policy issue. In exchange environmental opposition to NAFTA gave "protectionists" a reason to oppose Fast Track which was less vulnerable to criticism.

NGOs trying to influence GATT joined with Mexico-U.S. border groups' efforts to influence trade discussions between Mexico and the United States as the possibility of formal negotiations became public knowledge (*Arizona Daily Republic*, 1990; Suro, 91; Gregory, 92a; Land, 93).[7] The International Labor Rights Education and Research Fund, with Pharis Harvey as executive director, was one of the Washington, D.C.-based groups to ally with border organizations. Harvey opposed Fast Track reauthorization because of the narrow scope of negotiations.[8] By the winter of 1990, the activities of the smaller groups had attracted the attention of larger national organizations, most especially the National Wildlife Federation (NWF).

NWF's introduction into trade policy matters marks an important point in the history of the preliminary discussions over NAFTA. NWF's formal and informal relationships with elites—officials from the Bush administration and the corporate business community—combined with their concern over the NAFTA negotiating agenda placed them in a strategic position in terms of trade policy. One of the oldest and largest national environmental organizations, NWF enjoyed considerable political influence with both Congress and the administration.[9]

NWF's 5.8 million members are believed to hold "mainstream to conservative" environmental objectives (*Outside*, 1993). NWF also enjoyed strong ties with corporate America through its Corporate Conservation Council, an informal forum where business leaders and environmentalists could discuss topical issues frankly (NWF Corporate Conservation Council, undated [g]). Activity in trade policy negotiations offered NWF the opportunity to gain access to economic policy making in an area of policy essential to ensure long-term efforts at environmental protection.[10]

By the beginning of 1991 Harvey organized a loose coalition of interest groups concerned about trade liberalization with Mexico called the Mobilization on Development, Trade, Labor, and the Environment (MODTLE). Along with NWF, ATI, and BEP, they organized the first congressional briefing on nontrade issues related to U.S.-Mexico Free Trade on 15 January 1991.[11] On 6 February 1991 these same groups authored a document called the "Environmental Agenda for Trade Policy," where they pledged to oppose Fast Track for NAFTA if their issues were not made part of the negotiating agenda.[12]

Environmental concerns expressed by this coalition of local and national environmental groups over the scope of trade policy quickly found their way into the political debate. Arizona Congressman Jim Kolbe acknowledged that, "As we move forward to negotiations, the environment is certainly the number one issue that I think will be on everyone's mind" (House Committee on Ways and Means, 91a). Concern over environment and trade matters also caught the attention of Congressman Ron Wyden (D-OR). Wyden criticized Bush for failing to address environmental issues related to trade. In February he orchestrated a "Dear Colleague" letter sent to President Bush and signed by eleven members of the House, citing the environment as a pivotal issue in their support for Fast Track: "Unless we are confident that environmental concerns will be properly addressed in the proposed trade agreement, we cannot support fast-track negotiating authority" (Wyden, 91d).

Initially, the Bush administration refused to link environmental issues with their request for Fast Track. When asked specifically about environmental issues in trade policy, USTR ambassador, Carla Hills, responded, "I think to attach a condition on trading that talks about similarities of environmental law would not be a good precedent" (Senate Committee on Finance, 91a). The resistance to linkages between environmental issues and Fast Track reauthorization expressed by the Bush administration was severely challenged following a letter from Senate Finance Committee chairman, Lloyd Bentsen, and House Ways and Means Committee chairman, Dan Rostenkowski, on 7 March 1991. Responding to labor and environmental concerns over trade liberalization with Mexico, the chairmen of the two most influential committees on trade policy asked President Bush to respond to congressional concerns regarding labor and environmental issues before they voted on Fast Track (Bentsen and Rostenkowski, 91). The president agreed, promising to submit his response to Congress on 1 May 1991.

Administration Support

Individual actors within the Bush administration also played a critical role. Staff at the EPA's International Program recognized the opportunity to extend national and international policy goals through trade policy (McAlpine, 93). In particular EPA administrator, William Reilly, argued in favor of such linkages and offered both professional and political environmental advice to USTR ambassador, Carla Hills. Reilly used his relationships with high-ranking officials from national environmental organizations to explore the possibility of securing support for environmentally sensitive trade policy. He arranged for Hills to meet privately with leaders of the national environmental organizations to explore their concerns and determine her ability to address these issues within the framework of trade policy negotiations (Esty, 94b; McCloskey, 94; Roh, 94). According to staff officials, Reilly saw linking environmental issues to trade policy as a prime opportunity to increase the political authority of the EPA. He and Ambassador Hills developed a good working relationship that enabled Reilly's staff to attend interagency trade advisory meetings and offer guidance to administrative officials most directly responsible for trade policy development.

To play an important role in negotiations, EPA officials had to overcome numerous institutional barriers. EPA was not a part of the interagency policy dialogue usually formed surrounding trade policy. To help develop its own niche, Reilly developed his own private advisory group to develop policy recommendations that would help overcome the conflicts between the two policy domains (McAlpine and Le Donne, 93). At the time, the USTR had no staff working on environmental issues related to trade and were forced to rely upon EPA officials from the Office of Policy Planning and Evaluation (OPPE) and International Divisions to help them develop responses to environmentalists' concerns. Reilly exploited his relationship with Salinas, his ability to communicate effectively in Spanish, the environmental problems along the Mexico-U.S. border, and his relationships with national environmental organizations to position the EPA as an important component of the U.S. government's negotiating team.

With the problems along the Mexico-U.S. border serving as a backdrop, environmental organizations used their popularity and access to elected officials to position themselves as an important coalitional member for both supporters and opponents of Fast Track. How they would use this leverage to carve their own niche as members of the trade policy regime would be largely determined by their willingness to cooperate with, not confront, trade policy elites.

Accommodating and Aggressive Behaviors Are Key to Environmental Participation in Trade Talks

Bush administration officials were concerned that ties between labor and environmental opponents to Fast Track could stall their effort to negotiate a trade agreement with Mexico. Using Reilly as a conduit, the USTR began to explore the possibility that some environmentalists could be won over for Fast Track.[13] Unlike labor's nearly united opposition to NAFTA, the philosophical differences between environmental organizations and their loosely organized community offered the Bush administration the opportunity to explore possible divisions regarding Fast Track. Both the World Wildlife Fund (WWF) and the Environmental Defense Fund (EDF) were likely supporters of the president's trade initiative. Both organizations are generally supportive of economic growth as a solution to environmental problems.[14] Each organization also enjoyed direct lines of communication between themselves and Bush administration officials.[15] However, support solely from these two environmental organizations was judged to be insufficient to neutralize environmental opposition to Fast Track in the House, especially when grassroots organizations like the Sierra Club were considered likely opponents. The administration sought support from an environmental organization to tip the environmental balance in their favor. The National Wildlife Federation (NWF) and its president, Jay Hair, held the greatest potential for winning support for Fast Track reauthorization.

Until March 1991 NWF was the leading environmental group in the coalitional efforts to block Fast Track. The rhetoric they used was considered "extreme" by representatives at both the EPA and the USTR (Atkeson, 94). In the month immediately after the meeting with Ambassador Hills, NWF withdrew from its role as one of the principal groups involved in MODTLE, arguing that the interests of these groups and NWF were no longer consistent.[16] Its rhetoric shifted away from an aggressive challenge of NAFTA's economic goals toward the potential environmental benefits associated with trade liberalization. The shift in attitude toward Fast Track was so pronounced that, after reading NWF's April 1991 testimony before the House Committee on Banking, Finance, and Urban Affairs, an internal EPA memo concluded "apparently NWF's position on NAFTA has changed."[17]

NWF's shift toward more accommodating politics on Fast Track left vacant the leadership role to argue more aggressive environmental demands. Few organizations had any resources available to staff a new policy issue, and virtually none possessed the technical knowledge to engage in trade policy discussions.[18] Public Citizen emerged as the leading aggressive group to represent environmental issues. Its founder, Ralph Nader, regarded trade agreements as attempts by the administration to circumvent the democratic policy process by using them to pressure members of Congress to remove regulations governing business behavior (Meade, 92). Stopping trade agreements like NAFTA and GATT became a symbol of Nader's efforts to prevent the "undemocratic" erosion of more than twenty years of citizen advocacy in consumer safety, public health, and environmental protection.[19] Public Citizen staff attorney, Lori Wallach, began to attend the weekly MODTLE meetings and argue for a more proactive agenda for defeating Fast Track. By April she organized the Citizen's Trade Watch Campaign (CTWC), comprised largely of the lobbying groups most opposed to Fast Track reauthorization (Wallach, 94; Hudson, 94).

By the end of April 1991, the two different perspectives regarding Fast Track and trade liberalization circulating since the beginning of the year began to crystalize into two distinct political camps within the environmental community. NWF, NRDC, NAS, EDF, and WWF were conditionally supportive of Fast Track. Behind NWF's leadership, they used their relationships with congressional supporters of both trade liberalization and environmental protection to focus political attention on ensuring participation by environmental groups in negotiations. Democrats like Congressman Ron Wyden and Senator Tim Wirth (D-CO) were essential to their efforts to pressure the Bush administration to include environmental issues during negotiations. A second group of environmental organizations, comprised of FoE, Greenpeace, Public Citizen, and the Sierra Club, were conditionally opposed to Fast Track. They developed political alliances with anti-Fast Track legislators such as Congresswoman Marcy Kaptur (D-OH) and Senators Ernest Hollings (D-NC) and Don Riegle (D-MI) to convince Congress to vote against reauthorization. The strength of Public Citizen's opposition to Fast Track combined with their greater human and financial resources to lead the opposition.

These dual roles for environmental groups—accommodators and aggressors—would become the hallmark of their participation throughout negotiations. Aggressive organizations used their ability to focus media attention on environmental concerns to maintain the pressure on Congress to defeat Fast Track. More moderate groups used the political leverage created by this pressure to fight for environmental provisions in Fast Track. As the next section will show, both good cops and bad cops would be essential to gain formal access to negotiations through Fast Track authorization.

Accommodating Groups Control Environmental Agenda during Fast Track Vote

As the deadline for President Bush's 1 May response to congressional concerns over Fast Track approached, environmentalists seemed to be a key stumbling block to Fast Track reauthorization. Congressman Wyden and House Majority Leader Gephardt used environmental concerns related to trade to highlight their apprehensions regarding negotiations (Wyden, 91d; Gephardt, 91). Gephardt directed most of his concern toward labor issues, but Wyden's staff worked more directly with members of the environmental community to enhance the political pressure of their concerns.

In anticipation of the president's 1 May response, NWF tried to organize the environmental community into a unified position. From the last position adopted in February, three broad categories of issues were raised: financial resources to improve enforcement and monitoring of environmental laws, especially within the border region; assessing the potential impact on the Mexico-U.S. border region caused by increased trade; direct integration of some environmental provisions into the trade agreement itself. Working with representatives from EDF, Sierra Club, CNI, NRDC, and the border groups, TCPS, BEP, and ATI, NWF developed a new consensus position designed to signal to the administration the environmental community's willingness to work toward compromise. However, the consensus document failed to gain the approval of the Sierra Club and border groups. In particular, these groups wanted specific reference to the "polluter pays principle" (PPP), financial penalties directed against businesses for noncompliance with environmental law and provisions for civil actions by any citizen of a NAFTA country against a company in its home country as part of the statement. However, both NWF and EDF believed that consideration of their agenda by President Bush meant that certain issues, like PPP and direct fines against companies, could not be a part of the final set of conditions for support. Working with staff in Congressman Wyden's office, and with Senator Tim Wirth, NWF and EDF learned that the administration wished to avoid specific requirements for negotiations, preferring instead to agree on changes to the advisory process surrounding the negotiating process itself. To keep the more specific demands out of the May 1991 consensus position meant that groups like Public Citizen and FoE were not asked to participate, and endorsements by border groups and the Sierra Club were not considered worth the price they had to pay in terms of demands.

On 1 May President Bush released his response to congressional concerns over labor and environmental issues related to NAFTA. Rather than a direct inclusion of environmental issues, Bush proposed a "parallel track" for environmental issues related to NAFTA. Among his proposals were: an emphasis on Mexico's commitment to environmental protection; a commitment to ensure the right to safeguard the environment; the right to exclude any products that do not meet health or safety requirements; the right to impose pesticide, energy conservation, and toxic waste standards; the right to limit trade in products controlled by international treaties; a commitment to work with Mexico to resolve border problems; the inclusion of environmentalists as advisors to trade negotiations; and a commitment to conduct a review of environmental issues.

On 10 May NWF, EDF, NRDC, and NAS released a consensus position regarding President Bush's 1 May response. The document accepted two important elements of Bush's compromise: the idea of parallel environmental discussions and a general environmental review. It still, however, called for financial commitment to environmental remediation and an environmental committee to discuss environmental provisions of the agreement.[20] Despite timing of the 10 May document to respond to President Bush's letter, environmentalists gained little more from the administration during the last stages of these negotiations. Prior to the document's release, the EPA administrator, Reilly, confirmed to the administration he had secured enough support from the environmental community to neutralize its opposition.[21] Apparently he was correct; on 17 May, with no real changes to the 1 May response, NWF endorsed Fast Track (*The New York Times*, 17 May 1991). Without additional changes to the compromise offered by President Bush, formal support for Fast Track came from NWF, NAS, and EDF.[22]

As is evident from this discussion, the initial debate about trade liberalization with Mexico was characterized by classical interest group politics. Most businesses supported greater trade liberalization in Mexico, attracted by an untapped market of potential consumers, low-cost labor, and a safer investment environment. Labor organizations regarded any trade agreement with Mexico as a means to accelerate job relocation to a nearby, low-cost production center. The U.S. government saw negotiations as an opportunity to exploit Mexico's desire to increase investment, reduce investment barriers, open Mexico's market to U.S. goods, and promote democratic reform. Finally, trade negotiations with Mexico might bolster the administration's desire to keep alive interest in trade liberalization through GATT.

It was under these political circumstances that environmentalists found their way into U.S. trade policy. The differences in circumstances between their failed effort to engage the Uruguay Round and NAFTA reveal the important role institutional factors play in shaping policy outcome. Environmentalists began with a history of popular support for environmental protection and with access to elected officials earned as a result of their popularity. Growing problems facing border communities legitimated their concerns regarding trade policy despite their lack of access to the monopoly surrounding trade policy. The perceived political need for Fast Track negotiating privileges gave environmental organizations an opportunity to modify NAFTA's negotiating agenda to include environmental concerns. However, because trade policy was not part of their policy domain, and because of the stiff resistance they faced from traditional trade policy elites, environmental organizations had to threaten the success of negotiations in order to gain access to those negotiations. The threat came in the form of an alliance with influential anti-Fast Track interest groups, namely, organized labor.

What environmental organizations offered both pro- and antitrade advocates was "legitimate" political protection. The Bush administration sought to neutralize its political potential without harming its overall goals in negotiations, while antitrade advocates sought the cover offered by "green protectionism." It would be a mistake, however, to regard the relationship between labor and environmental groups in excessively strategic terms. Each understood that, in the interests of their own constituents, they would pursue the political course that promised the highest probability of political success. In fact, prior to the Fast Track vote, the AFL had already determined they could *not* defeat it, choosing not to "spend our political chits on a lost battle" (Anderson, 94).

President Bush and his trade policy staff used their ability to influence the political agenda surrounding trade to minimize the impact of including environmental groups as part of the political coalition required for its passage. They counted on support from key trade policy elites in Congress, business, academia, and in the media to support their effort to liberalize trade in North America. Opponents to Fast Track were hampered by public criticisms of protectionism that made it difficult to overcome political opposition from leaders in both parties to change the political agenda for negotiations and to integrate social and environmental issues on a par with trade objectives. However, public concern over the environmental implications of more trade with Mexico created an opportunity for elites to use environmental issues as political cover for their objections to NAFTA.

Positioning environmental issues in a preemptive position for Fast Track required both accommodating and aggressive behavior on the part of environmental groups. Initially, NWF led aggressive efforts to threaten Fast Track, but following overtures by the Bush administration to include environmental issues as part of negotiations, they led efforts to develop common ground between trade and environmental objectives. In this sense the preemptive power enjoyed by environmental groups was collectively shared but disproportionately generated. Pre-emptive power was maintained by more aggressive groups like Public Citizen, FoE, and the Sierra Club, but it was better used to gain accept-able compromises by NWF, EDF, and others than to defeat Fast Track.

The Bush administration's ability to satisfy political demands re-garding environmental issues with a parallel track for the environment reveals a number of important consequences for the normative frame-work and rules that characterized the trade and environment intersec-tion in NAFTA. First, the administration was able to minimize the conflict created by environmental issues over trade by targeting key environmental groups willing to accommodate President Bush's eco-nomic objectives. Second, accommodating environmental organiza-tions controlled conflicts among these organizations over the set of conditions for environmental support for Fast Track. A comparison of the collective demands made by the environmental community in February 1991 and those accepted by some members of the environmen-tal community in May indicate the degree to which environmentalists were willing to compromise. See table 3.2.

Obviously, a great many of the compromises made by environmen-tal groups between February and May were due to the interactions between government officials and business and environmental interest groups. Environmental organizations were quickly learning the practi-cal limitations of addressing the full range of environmental concerns they brought to negotiations under the agenda of trade conventions policy negotiations.

Members of the accommodating coalition used their access to trade policy elites to learn where to moderate their demands for Fast Track. They were concerned that too aggressive a position would jeopardize their inclusion in negotiations or that overly aggressive demands would defeat reauthorization in Congress. As a result of their concern, they began to shift their positions toward those advocated by the admin-istration, creating distance between themselves and the members of the aggressive environmental coalition. Because the more aggressive groups were unwilling to moderate their demands, groups like NWF and EDF enjoyed the political space to negotiate compromises accept-able to the administration. In this sense, the preemptive power enjoyed by the environmental community was collectively generated but dis-proportionately exploited.

A Delicate Balance: Environmental Issues and Trade Reform

One of the implications of this analysis suggests that, had environmen-talists remained united or had they advocated stronger inclusion of their issues in negotiations, they may have gained more concessions

TABLE 3.2   Demands Made by U.S. Environmental Groups during Fast Track*

February 1991	May 1991	Compromise Accepted by Congress
Public hearings during negotiations	**	Public hearings on issues pertaining to Border Plan; congressional oversight over proceeding (Fast Track)
Community right to know	**	No explicit promise
Participation by environmental groups in negotiations	Independent working group on the environment	Environmental advisors included as part of existing advisory proceedings
National Environmental Policy Act (NEPA) review	Environmental Review, "consistent with NEPA guidelines"	Environmental review without conditions
Polluter pays principle (PPP)	**	No specific commitment
Trade sanctions used for violations of international environmental laws	**	Rejection on principle
Tort damages	**	No specific commitment
Compensating investment for environmental protection, cleanup	Same	No specific commitment
"Sustainable agenda," including long-term management of natural resources, point source reduction, subsidies for sustainable agriculture, and oil investment prohibition	**	Rejection as beyond scope of trade policy
Creation of trilateral commission for the environment	**	No specific commitment
Preserve right of national, state, and local government to set high environmental standards	Same	Preserve commitment, consistent with international standards for environmental protection

*Information here based upon three documents: 6 February 1991, "Environmental Agenda," 8 May 1991, "Consensus Position," and 1 May, "Response to Concerns Expressed Over the North American Free Trade Agreement."
**Indicates no specific mention of issue.

from President Bush in exchange for their support. However, care should be used when speculating along these lines. Just as the circumstances and sequence of events prompted environmental organizations to preempt negotiations, pressuring the administration for greater demands may have overplayed their hand. Evidence exists to suggest that too few members of Congress were concerned enough about the environmental implications of NAFTA to block an "environmentally insufficient" Fast Track.

Following the splintering of the environmental community in early May, FoE, the Sierra Club, and Public Citizen campaigned to oppose reauthorization. Lobbying efforts were directed at members in the House of Representatives where they felt Fast Track was most vulnerable (Wallach, 94). Their efforts to defeat reauthorization were dealt a serious blow when House Majority Leader Gephardt endorsed Fast Track on 16 May. On 17 May Congressman Byron Dorgan's (D-ND) bill to revoke Fast Track was defeated by a vote of 231 to 192; six days later the Senate defeated similar legislation proposed by Ernest Hollings (D-NC) by a vote of 37 to 13.

Content analysis of the floor statements made by House members suggests that they were not as interested in environmental issues as they were concerned about the impact of trade on jobs and investment (*Congressional Record*, 23 May 1991). Of the 422 total votes cast, 112 members expressed their views on the floor of the House. Twenty-five percent of the members supporting Fast Track expressed an interest in the environment, while twenty percent of those opposing made reference to the environment as a reason not to support reauthorization. In comparison, eight-five percent of both supporting and opposing statements made reference to the economy and jobs.

There is one more piece of evidence that suggests environmental groups could hardly have expected more from the leverage they enjoyed during Fast Track. Jules Katz, former assistant U.S. trade representative under USTR Ambassador Hills, indicated that had environmental groups been unwilling to accept the compromise offered by President Bush, they were prepared to negotiate NAFTA without them. Had this occurred, environmentalists would not have enjoyed the same formal access granted to organized labor and may have been forced to gain access solely on the basis of whether or not Congress would have halted negotiations because of environmental issues (Katz, 94).

Fast Track reauthorization formalized environmental interests in U.S. trade policy negotiations. The nature of that formalization is best explained by the institutional factors just described and by focusing on the individual behavior of environmental groups who reacted to this political opportunity. While the divisions between the organizations would become one of the legacies of the debate, they may also have been the means by which the organizations translated preemptive leverage into substantive policy alternatives. It may also have been fortunate that the moderate coalition was able to neutralize the opposition's response to the compromise offered by President Bush or environmental groups may not have found themselves part of negotiations at all.

ENDNOTES

1. For information on Codex, see Avery, Drake, and Lang, 93.
2. Canada's interest in NAFTA negotiations was largely defensive. Many Canadians argued that the passage of the U.S.-Canada Free Trade Agreement was directly responsible for the economic downturn suffered in Canada during the late 1980s. Fearing similar political fallout from United States efforts to extend trade liberalization to include Mexico, Canadian officials expressed formal interest in negotiations in February 1991.
3. Other scholars argued for liberalized trade for other reasons. Mexicanist Sidney Weintraub of the University of Texas at Austin, economist Rudiger Dornbush at MIT, and Canadian trade scholar Peter Morici of the University of Maine were early proponents of trade policy, arguing for greater linkages for political, economic, and cultural reasons. By April 1991 more than one hundred academics would lend their reputations to support expanded trade with Mexico (*The Wall Street Journal*, 19 April 1991).
4. With the notable exception of the Economic Policy Institute which argued against liberalized trade with Mexico.
5. In 1991 there were 208 members of Congress with voting records indicating strong support for organized labor (AFL-CIO, 92). Scores of more than seventy (out of a total one hundred) were considered "strong supporters" of labor.
6. Esty reported that an important official from General Motors remarked that the two issues that could stall trade liberalization between Mexico and the United States were labor and the environment. See Esty, 94b.
7. According to interviews with AFL-CIO officials, the *Coalition for Justice in the Maquilas* was funded by monies from AFL. They also stated that early newsprint coverage of border issues by the *New York Times*, and regional papers such as the *Phoenix Gazette*, was initiated (in part) by their encouragement.
8. ". . . an agreement that deals only with narrowly defined trade and investment rules may have serious adverse effects on the environment, on labor standards, on human rights, agricultural interests and consumers. . . ." Testimony by Pharis Harvey (House Committee on Ways and Means, 91a).
9. See Appendix A for details on individual environmental organizations.
10. According to Stewart Hudson of NWF, ". . . we needed to go where the money was, and trade is where money is made." See Hudson, 94.

11. *U.S.-Mexico Free Trade—Opening Up the Debate,* 15 January 1991. The briefing was sponsored by Congresswoman Marcy Kaptur (D-OH) and was endorsed by twenty organizations including the AFL-CIO, the Community Nutrition Institute, the United Methodist Board of Church and Society, the Development Group for Alternative Policies (D-GAP), and the Arizona Toxics Information Project.

12. *Environmental Agenda for Trade Policy,* 6 February 1991. The endorsing groups included: NWF, BEP, TCPS, CNI, the Institute for Agriculture and Trade Policy (IATP), Natural Resources Defense Council (NRDC), the National Toxics Campaign, Arizona Toxics Information, and Friends of the Earth (FOE).

13. Hills met with representatives from NWF, WWF, NRDC, EDF, Sierra Club, and NAS; groups considered fundamentally opposed to trade, such as Greenpeace and FoE, were not contacted. See Esty, 94.

14. See Appendix A for detailed information describing the national environmental organizations.

15. EDF's president, Fred Krupp, served as President Bush's advisor to the Council on Environmental Quality (CEQ), and EPA administrator Reilly was former president of WWF.

16. Interview with Stewart Hudson, of NWF, 1994.

17. Internal EPA memorandum, no date.

18. At this time, only NWF had received any foundation support for trade policy work. In 1991, they received a one-year, $100,000 grant from the Pew Charitable Trust to share jointly with CNI and IATP.

19. In a 21 February 1991 memorandum from Lori Wallach to Joan Claybrook, president of Public Citizen: "Fast track thoroughly undermines our ability to fight both international preemption of our most basic domestic health and safety standards as well as our ability to promote environmental and other consumer standards in trade agreements. This is the case because fast track is undemocratic." See Wallach, 91.

20. Consensus position, 10 May 1991. These same positions were reiterated in a letter from Senator Wirth to EPA administrator Reilly, sent on 7 May 1991.

21. Clark urged the groups not to agree to any White House pledges regarding Fast Track and the environment without discussing the position with other members of the environmental community. He expressed alarm over Reilly's statement to the Senate Finance Committee that he had secured support for Fast Track from the environmental community. See Clark, 91b.

22. In response to earlier versions of this manuscript, NRDC's Justin Ward argued that his organization did not take a formal position on the Fast Track vote (Ward, 96). While this may be true, a review of NRDC's public statement released upon the completion of Fast Track suggests that NRDC was supportive of the president's efforts. The 1 May 1991 press release was subtitled "Administration Proposal Called Positive Step in Need of Additional Environment and Review Measures"; it goes further to indicate that ". . . NRDC today responded favorably to the Bush Administration's 'action plan' for a North American Free Trade Agreement" (NRDC 91). EDF's support for Fast Track based upon an evaluation of the organization's position by Tom Wathen (Wathen, 92).

4

NAFTA Negotiations

From June 1991 through September 1993, representatives from Canada, the United States, and Mexico negotiated the terms of the North American Free Trade Agreement and its Supplemental Agreements on Labor and on the Environment. When the "NAFTA Package" was completed, every living U.S. president would declare it a watershed event in the history of environmental policy. But while the terms of the NAFTA Package would be enough to satisfy Congress, they would leave the U.S. environmental community bitterly divided.

This chapter analyzes the political events that shaped both the original NAFTA text and its Supplemental Agreements. There are three central points. First, *trade policy elites used formal and informal rules and relationships to minimize the impact of environmental interests on negotiations.* The ability to control conflicts with environmental groups centered within the Bush administration during NAFTA negotiations, then broadened to include the business community and members of Congress supportive of trade liberalization during the Clinton administration. Second, *the ability of environmental groups to maintain a credible threat to NAFTA's success and to compromise with trade policy elites were central to the nature of NAFTA's environmental provisions.* Environmental groups formed two coalitions—one willing to accommodate demands made by protrade elites, the other allied with other anti-NAFTA groups to oppose the agreement—and the combination of adversarial and accommodating roles sustained political interest in environmental issues relative to trade. Finally, *accommodating environmental groups controlled the environmental agenda and moderated their demands in exchange for formalized roles in trade policy.* Accepting NAFTA's basic goal to liberalize trade enabled accommodating environmental organizations to forge relationships with protrade policy elites that kept them a part of the political process surrounding negotiations. In exchange for this new role, these groups moderated environmental demands, making it possible to endorse the NAFTA Package in September 1993.

FORMAL RULES AND INFORMAL RELATIONSHIPS CONSTRAIN ENVIRONMENTAL INFLUENCE DURING NEGOTIATIONS

Congressional reauthorization of Fast Track and acceptance of the "parallel track" for the environment gave the Bush administration a relatively specific set of requirements for integrating environmental issues into trade negotiations. To satisfy the commitments made in President Bush's 1 May 1991 response to Congress, the administration was required to include environmental advisors during negotiations; negotiate the Mexico-U.S. Integrated Border Environmental Plan (IBEP); conduct a Review of Environmental Concerns (Environmental Review) related to NAFTA; and keep its promise not to harm existing environmental health and safety standards during negotiations. The administration relied upon the formal rules characterized by Fast Track and on their ability to control access to negotiators to minimize the political influence of environmental issues during negotiations.

Selection of Environmental Advisors

President Bush selected representatives from five national environmental organizations, plus one state-level environmental director, to participate as members of the USTR's public advisory committee. The selection of these advisors from among the environmental groups involved in trade negotiations reveals an effort to incorporate environmental groups most likely not to oppose negotiations. Emphasis was also placed on selecting groups with stronger informal ties to the administration; for example, the EPA administrator, Reilly, was a former WWF official and a close personal friend of the NWF President, Jay Hair. Both organizations expressed greater willingness to reconcile their differences between environmental goals and trade policy (Advisory Committee for Trade Policy, 92). Emphasis on friendliness toward the administration over active interest in trade negotiations was obvious; of the environmental groups selected as advisors, only NWF and NRDC participated in Fast Track issues.[1] None of the organizations opposed Fast Track, while NWF, NRDC, and NAS supported President Bush's parallel compromise.

Another factor that influenced the effectiveness of the environmental advisors was their small number. The six environmentalists joined a team of 1,000 advisors, divided into seventeen different negotiating committees. Ideologically, most advisors supported trade liberalization in North America; they were opposed to complicating the advisory process with environmental issues (Advisory Committee for Trade

TABLE 4.1   Environmentalists Selected as Trade Advisors for USTR

Name	Organization	Appointment
Russell E. Train	World Wildlife Fund	Advisory Committee for Trade Policy Negotiations
John C. Sawhill	The Nature Conservancy	Industry Policy Advisory Committee
John H. Adams	Natural Resources Defense Council	Services Policy Advisory Committee
Jay D. Hair	National Wildlife Federation	Investment Policy Advisory Committee
Peter A. A. Berle	National Audubon Society	Agriculture Policy Advisory Committee
James M. Strock	California EPA	Intergovernmental Policy Advisory Committee

Policy, 92). The comparatively small number of environmental organizations complicated the task of convincing other trade policy advisors of the importance of including environmental issues in trade policy.[2] Finally, the environmental advisors were not formally appointed and cleared until November 1991. A six-month delay in their appointment gave the administration ample time to agree with Mexican and Canadian officials about the scope of discussions surrounding the environment.

The IBEP and Environmental Review

The Review of Environmental Concerns (Environmental Review) and the Integrated Border Environmental Plan (IBEP) were two specific policy instruments responsible for framing the formal introduction of environmental issues into NAFTA. The IBEP separated border environmental problems from direct influence over negotiations but was linked to NAFTA through President Bush's 1 May commitment to Congress and by the politics of the trade and environment debate in the United States. By negotiating border issues and trade policy separately, the administration insulated NAFTA negotiations from the potentially destructive implications of correcting trade-related border environmental problems prior to expanding trade. The Environmental Review defined which environmental issues were relevant to the negotiations themselves.

Both the EPA and the USTR collaborated on negotiations responsible for the Environmental Review and IBEP, and despite its lack of experience, the USTR took direct responsibility for developing the Environmental Review.[3] When it was completed, the Environmental Review argued that NAFTA would improve environmental quality because it would increase economic activity in Mexico, thereby increasing the level of available resources for environmental protection. It also argued that NAFTA would encourage investment throughout Mexico, dispersing industry concentration on the Mexico-U.S. border and alleviating environmental stress suffered by border communities. Without NAFTA, industry concentration along the Mexico-U.S. border would continue with no federal revenues for environmental protection. In effect, the USTR used the Environmental Review to argue that a failed NAFTA would actually harm the environment.[4]

The content of the Environmental Review offered by the Bush administration illustrates the significance of decoupling it in two areas from the requirements of the National Environmental Policy Act (NEPA). A NEPA review requires EPA officials to assess the potential for environmental damage resulting from proposed federal action. The Environmental Review submitted by President Bush argued solely from the point that NAFTA would improve the quality of the environment and offered no specific estimates as to the degree of improvement. Second, an NEPA review involves public comment during the preliminary stages and following the release of a draft before it is finalized. The administration sought comments during the drafting stage but used the document as their negotiating position before the draft was circulated for public comments. The final draft was released in February 1992, but the USTR used it during the 26 October 1991 Trade Ministerial Meetings in Zacatecas, Mexico, where the scope of environmental issues were agreed to by all three countries.[5] Environmental groups were highly critical of the draft Environmental Review. NRDC and Sierra Club spokespersons argued that there was no guarantee that any increases in government revenue resulting from NAFTA would be directed toward improving the level of environmental protection (Ward, 91a; Mikesell and McCloskey, 91; NWF, n.d.[a]). Dispersing polluting industries throughout the country rather than concentrating them on the border was no solution to environmental problems. But due to the timing of the release of the draft Environmental Review, these comments weren't circulated until after the October meeting. USTR ambassador Hills, Mexican negotiator Jaime Serra Puche, and Canadian minister Wilson agreed to the framework for including environmental issues in negotiations suggested by the draft Environmental Review, thereby finalizing the agenda for addressing environmental issues during negotiations. Following the Zacatecas meeting, USTR counsel Charles Ries, testified to Congress:

> In general, I think the Ministers, while acknowledging . . . very clearly that the environmental issues themselves were not specifically part of the negotiations of the NAFTA . . . are very much interested in them and have now taken stock of the progress in this area at each one of their ministerial meetings. (House Committee on Energy and Commerce, Subcommittee on Commerce, Consumer Protection and Competitiveness, 31 October 1991).

Careful selection and placement of environmental advisors and control over the manner in which environmental issues were framed within trade policy negotiations enabled the Bush administration to minimize the influence of formally incorporating environmental issues into negotiations. The Environmental Review effectively focused the NAFTA trade and the environment debate in terms which argued in favor of trade liberalization as a means of environmental protection. The IBEP kept difficult environmental problems, already caused by trade liberalization, away from NAFTA, avoiding difficult political battles with Congress over regional environmental issues.

Despite this level of influence over the framing of the trade and environment debate during the early stages of NAFTA negotiations, the Bush administration was not able to win support from the advisors they selected. In July 1992 the environmental community sent a letter to President Bush warning him of their continued dissatisfaction with the progress of negotiations (NWF, 92a); NRDC president, John Adams, indicated in a letter to USTR Carla Hills that his organization would not support NAFTA as negotiated (Adams, 92). When the Agreement was finally made public in September 1992, the Sierra Club, Friends of the Earth, and Public Citizen called for renegotiation, arguing the president had not met the conditions of his 1 May letter to Congress (Sierra Club, 92a). President Bush chose not to submit NAFTA for congressional consideration at this time; but it wasn't just environmental opposition that determined his course of political action.

Additional Institutional Factors Shape NAFTA's Future

A number of institutional factors made it difficult for President Bush to present NAFTA to Congress in September. Led by House Majority Leader Richard Gephardt's opposition to the agreement, rank and file Democrats opposed NAFTA as negotiated in September. Their opposition was supported by a coalition between anti-NAFTA groups and the more adversarial environmental groups actively involved in trade negotiations.[6] But of all the mitigating factors, the presidential election scheduled for the fall of 1992 was the most significant.

Election years have never been a good time to vote on trade policy; public concern over the impact on employment tends to be uppermost in the minds of voters (Audley and Uslaner, 96; Destler, 92). NAFTA was an exceptional case because not only was the public concerned, but presidential politics created an opportunity for opponents of President Bush to use the Agreement as a reason to voice opposition to his reelection. A staff person with Congressman Ron Wyden (D-OR) suggested that environmental issues were particularly valuable at this time because a member could be supportive of trade liberalization yet object to Bush's negotiations on the grounds that environmental concerns were not properly addressed.

The situation amplified the leverage environmental groups enjoyed at this stage of negotiations. In an effort to secure some support from environmentalists, Ambassador Carla Hills announced her intention to negotiate the creation of a North American Commission on the Environment, an announcement that won the public support of the National Wildlife Federation.[7] But presidential politics and President Bush's failure to win the support of environmental groups meant the most leverage was with the Democratic presidential candidate, Bill Clinton. While President Bush entered the 1992 presidential campaign as a strong supporter of NAFTA, Bill Clinton's support for the Agreement was tempered by his party's concerns over organized labor and environmental community opposition. Instead of adopting a strong position, he vacillated on support for the Agreement itself (Clinton/ Gore Campaign Committee, undated). President Bush exploited Clinton's uncertainty by labeling Clinton an old-style "protectionist" of narrow labor interests. The pressure to clarify his position on NAFTA compelled Clinton to seek policy recommendations from environmental groups and labor organizations to enable him to refute the protectionist accusations.

At the same time the presidential politics amplified the leverage enjoyed by environmental groups, other institutional factors continued to limit their ability to dramatically redefine trade negotiations. The specific issues surrounding NAFTA and its labor and environmental provisions were complex, but the politics were simple: should Clinton endorse the Agreement as negotiated, or should he argue that he could negotiate a better Agreement once elected? Friends of the Earth, the Sierra Club, and Public Citizen all argued for renegotiation, while the environmental advisors to the USTR, and in particular NWF and WWF, argued for the existing Agreement. To resolve this dilemma, Clinton campaign political advisor, Barry Carter, selected representatives from NWF and WWF to work with him and staff from the House Ways and Means Committee and the Senate Finance Committee to develop a position on NAFTA.[8] On 4 October 1992, during a speech at North Carolina State University, Clinton pledged not to renegotiate the text initialed by President Bush on 18 September, but instead promised to address the weaknesses of the basic Agreement in supplemental negotiations on labor, environment, and import-surge issues (Clinton, 92; *The Washington Post*, 5 October 1992).

The politics surrounding Clinton's position on NAFTA suggest he understood the need to sustain the support he drew from interest groups not usually supportive of a Democratic candidate who wanted to see NAFTA pass. The tenuous support Clinton received from business groups during his campaign could not be risked in an effort to satisfy Democratic supporters of Clinton who opposed NAFTA. Adopting a position arguing for renegotiations would have implied that Clinton was too closely allied with organized labor, too willing to yield to "old Democratic" temptations of protectionism.[9] In fact, opposing such strong recommendations from labor and other anti-NAFTA interests gave Clinton the opportunity to appear outside the influence of a strong Democratic constituency. By relying on the policy recommendations offered by NWF and WWF on NAFTA, Clinton could also claim support for his agenda for NAFTA from environmental groups without demanding renegotiations that would offend core NAFTA supporters.[10] Environmental groups opposed to NAFTA would not turn on Clinton to support Bush during the presidential campaign season, and he could avoid their opposition by rejecting the Agreement without the Supplemental Agreement attached.

Clinton Administration Expands Environmental Agenda

Between September 1992 and January 1993, political attention shifted away from the terms of the Agreement itself and onto the Supplemental Agreement agreed to in principle by President Bush (the Commission), and explicitly by President-elect Clinton. While sensitive to U.S. politics, neither Canada nor Mexico wanted to renegotiate the text initialed by their governments in December 1992. Combined with Clinton's stated unwillingness to revisit the Agreement, the door to renegotiations was apparently shut. In the words of a Senate Finance Committee staffer, "While not completed, the cement is drying quickly around the terms of the North American Free Trade Agreement" (Beil, 93).

The task of negotiating Supplemental Agreements capable of satisfying the conflicting demands of both supporters and opponents of

NAFTA fell to the new USTR ambassador, Mickey Kantor. Unlike his predecessor who had no history of working directly with labor and environmental interest groups, Kantor brought to his job an appreciation of the difficult balance between pro- and anti-NAFTA supporters in the Democratic party (Senate Committee on Finance, 93a). His professional background included working on progressive social causes, where he developed working relations with activists such as Public Citizen's Ralph Nader and AFL-CIO treasurer, Tom Donahue.[11] As the president's 1992 campaign manager, he was also aware of Clinton's commitment to business leaders supportive of NAFTA and of Clinton's general support for liberalizing trade. Mindful of the difficult politics surrounding the Supplemental Agreement, Kantor was committed to arbitrating differences of opinion between opponents and supporters of NAFTA.

In response to demands made by environmental groups, Kantor used the Supplemental Agreement negotiations to address concerns related to nonenforcement of national environmental laws, financial issues related to the environmental problems along the Mexico-U.S. border, and the expanded role for public participation in policy decisions surrounding implementation of the Supplemental Agreements (Senate Committee on Finance, 93b; House Committee on Ways and Means, 93a; Senate Committee on Environment and Public Works, 93a; House Committee on Agriculture, 93a). His willingness to negotiate strong provisions in the Agreement was tempered by opposition from business associations and pro-NAFTA members of Congress who objected to any effort to use trade sanctions to enforce environmental regulations or linkages between environmental remediation and a commerce tax (The Business Roundtable, 93). Congressional Republicans threatened to withdraw their support for the Agreement if the administration succeeded in their efforts to generate revenues for environmental cleanup or to establish sanctions that might deter trade. Democratic supporters of Clinton's trade agenda also warned that too much emphasis on environmental issues could jeopardize the success of the Agreement itself (Wyden and Matsui, 93; Danforth, 93).

Environmental organizations benefited from stronger Democratic commitment to their concerns and broader access to trade policy decision makers. But whether or not the Clinton administration, or other trade policy elites, had the greatest influence over the nature of the response to environmental demands for NAFTA, it is clear that NAFTA's own history and sequence of events limited the options available to Clinton as he completed negotiations. Clinton inherited an Agreement already endorsed by leaders from all three countries, and he realized that neither Mexico nor Canada was interested in returning to the original text. While sensitive to environmental and labor concerns voiced by his core constituency, Clinton could not risk NAFTA's core supporters to satisfy all of these concerns.

The parallel track for environmental issues originally established by President Bush produced a trade agreement with few linkages between trade and the environment. Ambassador Hills used the Environmental Review and the IBEP to limit the scope of environmental issues in negotiations. Clinton used the same parallel track format to expand the agenda for environmental issues within the framework of the Supplemental Agreement as long as it did not interfere with the progress toward trade liberalization already made in the NAFTA text. In reality Clinton had no alternative but to agree *not* to renegotiate NAFTA and use the Supplemental Agreement framework already suggested by his predecessor as a vehicle to increase the level of support for NAFTA in the United States.

ENVIRONMENTAL "GOOD COPS AND BAD COPS"

The classic police detective movie often includes an interrogation scene where the "bad cop" uses aggressive interview tactics while the "good cop" takes advantage of the fear generated by his/her partner to obtain information from a (now) more forthcoming suspect. Similar to the roles played during the Fast Track debate, the political leverage used by members of the environmental community to gain concessions from both the Bush and Clinton administrations was the result of their ability to both threaten NAFTA's passage and accept the policy compromises offered by pro-NAFTA policy elites. Maintaining a credible threat to NAFTA's success by a willingness to compromise with protrade policy elites was fundamental to the nature of the trade policy regime change that incorporated environmental issues in trade policy. Playing these two roles required two coalitions of environmental groups within the national environmental community.

Significant Events Amplify Environmental Leverage

At the start of NAFTA negotiations U.S. environmental organizations were poorly staffed to meet the expanding political demands of trade negotiations. In 1991 and 1992 the USTR simultaneously worked to complete Uruguay Round negotiations and initiate NAFTA. Other discussions linking trade and the environment were also under way at the Organization for Economic Cooperation and Development (OECD). Environmental issues surrounding NAFTA included the Environmental Review, the IBEP, the terms of the Agreement itself, and eventually its supplemental documents. Among the national environmental organizations involved in NAFTA, there were fewer than six staff people dedicated to trade and environment issues.[12] The disarray felt by environmental groups as they tried to organize to participate in trade negotiations was exacerbated by their split over Fast Track.

Two exogenous political events—the completion of the GATT Tuna/Dolphin and the Uruguay Round Decision—invigorated environmental leverage on NAFTA, increasing their ability to pressure Congress to pay greater attention to environmental issues in trade and helping to overcome differences of opinion over the direction of trade policy negotiations. In September 1991 a GATT dispute panel decision found that portions of the U.S. Marine Mammal Protection Act (MMPA) were inconsistent with GATT trade rules (Christensen and Geffin, 92). The second event was the release of a draft of the Uruguay Round GATT Agreement. In December 1991, GATT director, Arthur Dunkel, released a "Final Draft Act" of the Uruguay Round on his own authority in the hope of accelerating the completion of negotiations. Failure to address any of the concerns raised by environmental groups during these negotiations resulted in nearly unanimous opposition to United States approval by the U.S. environmental community.[13]

The Tuna/Dolphin Decision and the release of the Final Draft Act text were important events for a number of reasons. First, they increased the number of environmental organizations concerned about trade policy, thereby increasing the leverage enjoyed by environmental issues during negotiations. Linkages were made between the GATT decision and NAFTA negotiations by publicizing Mexico's role as the principal complainant in the dispute and by suggesting that the complaint was a good example of Mexico's insensitivity to environmental issues (*The New York Times*, 2 October 1991). Second, environmental concerns raised during each of these events sparked media coverage that enabled environmental groups to keep pressure on Congress; the once arcane world of trade policy began to invade the world of citizens who cared about protecting dolphins. Finally, both the Tuna/Dolphin Decision and the Uruguay Round Final Draft alerted some members of Congress to the potential restrictive impact current trade negotiations might have on their right to make laws in the United States (House Committee on Energy and Commerce, 91b).

Differentiated Behavior of Environmental Organizations

While public responses to the Dunkel Draft and to the Tuna/Dolphin Decision gave the appearance of an environmental community united on trade policy at the start of 1992, the two coalitions resulting from the split over Fast Track reauthorization continued. Each coalition used their unique political resources to develop and implement different political strategies they believed would achieve their goals for trade policy negotiations. I will differentiate their behavior during negotiations by examining each coalition's relationship with Congress and other political elites, coverage by the media, and response to significant events.

Relations With Congress

Dissatisfied with the outcome of Fast Track, FoE, the Sierra Club, and Public Citizen became the core of the adversarial environmental coalition. Political alliances were formed with anti-NAFTA coalition leaders such as Congresswoman Marcy Kaptur (D-OH), House Majority Leader Richard Gephardt (D-MO), and Majority Whip David Bonior (D-MI). Of particular significance was their relationship with Gephardt. As Majority Leader, Gephardt exerted a great deal of influence over Democrats in the House. But his ability to lead any challenge to NAFTA was complicated by a number of factors. Gephardt's eleventh hour support for Fast Track may have been the key to producing enough Democratic support to enable President Bush to begin negotiations. His longstanding relationship with organized labor and his support for aggressive trade legislation made him an easy political target for accusations of protectionism (Bhagwati and Patrick, 91). Environmental issues in trade provided Gephardt with important political protection to deflect charges of protectionism as he criticized the Agreement, so he linked both labor and environmental issues in the positions he took regarding NAFTA.

In a 1 March 1991 letter to President Bush, Gephardt outlined his concerns for labor and the environment. Gephardt's particular concerns regarding trade with Mexico focused on his understanding of the *maquiladora* program.[14] Gephardt worried that the failure of the Mexican government to enforce its own environment and labor standards would give industries in Mexico an unfair cost advantage in the competition for U.S. market share (Gephardt, 91). He argued that the administration should negotiate both labor and environmental provisions in NAFTA to avoid creating an incentive for plant location in Mexico to reduce labor and regulatory costs. His position on labor and environmental issues resulted in his opposition to the September 1992 NAFTA. When Clinton became president, Gephardt's public criticisms of the Agreement were muted. With very little public shift in approach to the completion of NAFTA expressed by candidate Clinton, Gephardt expressed confidence in Clinton's ability to correct NAFTA's weaknesses (Gephardt, 92). Despite his earlier call for renegotiations, he accepted

Clinton's Supplemental Agreement solution and refrained from public criticisms against the progress of negotiations until September 1993.

Beyond alliances with key policy entrepreneurs, members of the adversarial coalition testified before committees unfriendly toward NAFTA to help give congressional supporters a public forum to criticize the terms under negotiation and to pressure other members of Congress to oppose the Agreement. But their testimony before these committees is indicative of the relative lack of influence they enjoyed over negotiations. While their testimonies were important, these committees did not have jurisdiction over the terms of the Agreement. Therefore, to expand their level of influence over negotiations, the adversarial coalition tried to change the rules surrounding negotiations. House Concurrent Resolution 246 and the NEPA lawsuit provide two important examples of their efforts.

Following the GATT Tuna/Dolphin Decision, the adversarial coalition turned to Congressman Henry Waxman (D-CA) for support for their efforts to influence NAFTA. Waxman was a good candidate to act as a spokesperson for adversarial groups; his strong labor and environment voting record and his support for Fast Track reauthorization shielded him from direct accusations of protectionism. Coauthored by Majority Leader Gephardt, Waxman sponsored a resolution designed to remind President Bush ". . . not to submit to Congress any trade agreement that does not preserve existing environmental, health, and labor laws (House Concurrent Resolution 246-100). As a nonbinding sense of Congress, H.C.R. 246 had no direct authority to dictate future behavior. Its more important role was to mobilize grassroots organizations opposed to NAFTA and pressure members of Congress to eventually oppose the Agreement (author's personal notes; Wallach, 94; Blackwelder, 94). It was not, however, endorsed by most members of the accommodating coalition. The NWF president, Jay Hair, argued that H.C.R. 246 unnecessarily diverted attention away from negotiations (Hair, 92e).[15] More importantly, H.C.R. 246 was opposed by both the Bush administration and by Democratic elites in Congress. The House Ways and Means chairman, Dan Rostenkowski, used his committee's jurisdiction over HCR 246 to postpone its move to the floor for a vote until just prior to the 1992 summer recess. By then the Resolution was endorsed by more than 180 members, and the Bush administration had taken steps to weaken its message by endorsing it themselves.

The NEPA case filed by Public Citizen on behalf of the Sierra Club and Friends of the Earth was another attempt to change the formal rules surrounding negotiations. In a suit filed against the USTR, Public Citizen argued that a trade agreement constituted a formal act by the federal government and, therefore, required the government to submit a NEPA environmental impact assessment prior to implementation. While the case was eventually decided in favor of the government, the prolonged legal trial acted as a lightning rod, drawing attention to the potential conflict between efforts to liberalize trade and to protect the environment. Anti-NAFTA groups used the case to broaden the scope of their opposition coalition and to lobby members of congress to support HCR 246 (Snape, 95).

NWF, EDF, and WWF constituted the core of the accommodating environmental coalition. The coalition worked directly with pro-NAFTA policy entrepreneurs such as Congressman Ron Wyden (D-OR) and Senator Max Baucus (D-MT). As chairman of the Senate Committee on Finance, Subcommittee on Trade and the Senate Committee on Environment and Public Works, Baucus had direct authority over NAFTA's environmental provisions. He used his position as chairman of these two influential committees to facilitate a dialogue between accommodating environmental organizations and the USTR.[16] Baucus arranged two significant meetings between environmental groups and the administration. In May 1992, USTR ambassador Carla Hills met with representatives of WWF, NWF, EDF, NRDC, and Defenders of Wildlife to discuss concerns related to the NAFTA text; one year later Ambassador Mickey Kantor met with officials from WWF, EDF, NRDC, FoE, NWF, and the Sierra Club. The first meeting with Hills did not produce the level of support from environmental groups Baucus hoped for, but the 1993 meeting marked an important moment of support from members of the accommodating coalition. Originally scheduled for late April, it was postponed at the request of the accommodating group to provide them time to complete a compromise position developed by pro-NAFTA environmental groups that positioned them to accept Clinton's NAFTA package in September 1993.

Congressman Ron Wyden also played a significant role as an entrepreneur for environmental issues.[17] During the first two years of negotiations, Wyden used his support for greater trade and environmental protection to press the Bush administration for greater inclusion of environmental issues in negotiations.[18] He argued that environmental protection deserved the same kind of attention given economic issues such as intellectual property and merited similar enforcement mechanisms under consideration for property rights protection:

> How are rules governing intellectual property and investment more relevant to business operations, and thus a NAFTA issue, than rules governing, for example, industrial emissions, hazardous waste disposal and worker safety? (Wyden, 20 October 1991).

TABLE 4.2 NAFTA Environmental Coalition Leaders*

Member	Role	LCV Score**	Environmental Group(s) Associated with during NAFTA***
Pro-NAFTA Coalition Leaders			
Ron Wyden (D-OR)	Early proponent of environmental issues in trade.	0.94	NWF
Bill Richardson (D-NM)	Mexico-U.S. Border Representative; supportive of trade policy with environmental provisions; Whip for Clinton's vote for NAFTA	0.83	none
Robert Matsui (D-CA)	Organized NAFTA support for Clinton	0.78	NWF, WWF
Senator Tim Wirth (D-CO)****	Early supporter of environmental issues in trade; developed compromise position during Fast Track	0.91	EDF, NWF
Senator Max Baucus (D-MT)	Chair, Environment and Public Works; Chair, Subcommittee on Trade; mediated differences of opinion between environmental groups and USTR	0.32	NWF, NRDC
Anti-NAFTA Coalition Leaders			
Richard Gephardt (D-MO)	House Majority Leader; active critic of NAFTA throughout process	0.83	Sierra Club, Public Citizen
Marcy Kaptur (D-OH)	Early opponent of NAFTA; co-founded "Fair Trade Caucus"	0.78	Public Citizen
David Bonior (D-MI)	Led NAFTA opposition fight during vote	0.83	Sierra Club, Public Citizen

*Concept of "coalition leader" adapted from R. Doublas Arnold, *The Logic of Congressional Action*. New Haven: Yale University Press, 1990. The term means any member of Congress who used enviornmental issues to define problems, initiate agenda, develop alternatives, and mobilize other members. Selection based upon authorship of significant documents, speeches, and information provided during interviews.
**Voting record based upon a 0 to 100 scale prepared by the League of Conservation Voters, 1707 L Street NW, Suite 550, Washington, D.C. 20036. Scores are based on a weighted average of LCV evaluations from 1989 to 1992.
***Relationship ties based on interviews with member's staff and with representatives of each environmental organization.
****Did not vote on NAFTA because of appointments to President Clinton's administration.

Wyden's effort to convince the administration of the need for environmental protection in NAFTA was supported by Congressmen Bill Richardson (D-NM) and Robert Matsui (D-CA), both strong supporters of NAFTA with good environmental voting records.[19] Because of their voting records on both trade and environmental policy issues, these Democratic proponents of NAFTA were able to use environmental issues to pressure the administration to consider stronger policy alternatives during negotiations, yet avoid the "protectionist" label. With the change to a Democratic administration in 1993, Wyden shifted his position on the environment. In a January letter cosponsored by Matsui, he urged the administration to pursue the Supplemental Agreement but not at the risk of jeopardizing the Agreement's success (Wyden and Matsui, 93).

Both pro- and anti-NAFTA coalition leaders in Congress used environmental issues to gain political leverage during negotiations. Anti-NAFTA members used the environment to shield them from protectionist attacks by media and others. Pro-NAFTA environmental coalition leaders used the environment to attack a Republican president, then shifted their position to support Clinton's efforts to complete environmental negotiations within the mold created by Bush. Both uses of the environment suggest that environmental issues may have been important to members but were not the key issues that determined their position on NAFTA. For some, it is clear that environmental issues were used as pawns to achieve other goals during negotiations.

Coverage by the Media

Evidence of differentiated behavior can also be found by examining media attention directed at different environmental organizations. Analysis of newsprint coverage of environmental groups suggests that members of the accommodating coalition minimized negative exposure to environmental issues during negotiations, especially after Clinton was elected president. Using print media as the gauge for all media coverage, a clear pattern can be detected. As negotiations progressed, newsprint attention increasingly focused on environmental groups critical of the Agreement, while attention on supporting organizations began to drop. The gap in coverage between adversarial and accommodating groups broadened following Clinton's election; coverage of pro-NAFTA environmental groups dropped to less than 10 percent of all coverage. This trend contrasts with newsprint attention during the Fast Track stage when attention was evenly distributed among the three groups most active during that period (labor, agriculture, and business).

Some of the shift in attention to anti-NAFTA groups probably occurred because of the media's tendency to focus on conflict in news.

TABLE 4.3 Newspaper Coverage of NAFTA by Issue*

Adminis-tration	Period	Labor	Agricul-ture	Business	Energy	Environ-ment	Immigra-tion	Human Rights
Bush	FAST TRACK (6/90–5/91)	.216	.283	.264	.047	.147	.039	.025
	NAFTA I (6/91–9/92)	.193	.322	.285	.054	.096	.018	.022
Clinton	NAFTA II (10/92–9/93)	.210	.310	.292	.034	.101	.026	.020
	VOTE (9/14/93–11/24/93)	.216	.321	.302	.040	.060	.034	.020

*Percentages reflect total coverage of particular issues pertaining to NAFTA. Coverage of NAFTA based upon NEXIS keyword search of articles appearing in the Washington Post, New York Times, Wall Street Journal, Los Angeles Times, London Financial Times, Journal of Commerce, and The Chicago Tribune. Each article was counted as many times as individual issues were addressed.

However, the timing of the shift in coverage coincides with strategic decisions made by officials representing members of the accommodating coalition. While WWF and EDF were never spotlighted by the media, NRDC decided to avoid future conflicts with the administration by downplaying conflicts in the media.[20] The tendency by accommodating groups to avoid negative media coverage was especially true under the Clinton administration, which enjoyed the support of most members of the environmental community.

Participation as Members of Broad-Based Coalitions

Members of the adversarial coalition allied themselves with other interest groups in loose coalitions to enhance their efforts to defeat NAFTA. Two coalitions—Mobilization on Development, Trade, Labor, and the Environment (MODTLE) and Citizen's Trade Watch Campaign (CTWC)—were most important. MODTLE established a trinational dialogue among activists from all three NAFTA countries in the hope of mobilizing opposition to NAFTA's narrow economic agenda. Their principal political vehicle was the passage of a "social charter" for trade policy, championed by Congressman George Brown (D-CA) (MODTLE, 92). But MODTLE played a relatively minor role in negotiations for two reasons. Their agenda calling for the creation of a social charter within NAFTA was outside the agenda for negotiations outlined during Fast Track reauthorization. Second, most of its membership came from small groups with little political leverage in Congress.[21] Lacking the leverage enjoyed by constituency-based groups, they did not have as strong an impact on congressional attitude. Unlike most interest groups active with MODTLE, CTWC was composed largely of membership organizations capable of lobbying Congress.[22] CTWC coordinated its Washington, D.C. lobbying emphasis with the Fair Trade Campaign (FTC), headquartered in Chicago, Illinois, and Minneapolis, Minnesota. FTC organized anti-NAFTA lobbyists in thirty-three states; they devoted their attention to converting the complexities of trade policy into political action at the grassroots level. Both CTWC and its field ally, the FTC, adopted a political strategy designed to prepare voters to mobilize against NAFTA, pressuring their members of Congress to vote against the Agreement if it were ever presented to Congress for a vote.

But perhaps the most important coalition involving aggressive environmental organizations was one that did not develop as publicly as either MODTLE or CTWC. Through its individual member organization, both MODTLE and CTWC were loosely allied with organized labor.[23] Both labor and environmental groups were conscious that too many linkages between interest groups would be difficult to sustain, in part because of pressure against "protectionist" policies but also because of historical differences of opinion between labor and environmental groups over other policy issues. Pursuing individual interests and avoiding protectionist pressures kept labor and environmental groups tenuously linked throughout negotiations. One important event orchestrated by labor and environmentalists was a September 1992 conference called "Trade in the 21st Century," a conference designed to influence the position taken by the Democratic presidential candidate on NAFTA.[24]

Members of the accommodating coalition did not participate as members of coalitions outside the environmental community. Instead, they concentrated their associations on other national environmental organizations or with regional environmental groups who provided technical or regional expertise, such as TCPS, the BEP, or ATI. In particular, most accommodating organizations refused broad association with labor organizations, considering their "protectionist" position harmful to their own interests. But the divisions between environmental organizations also affected their ability to remain coordinated. By the summer of 1992, NWF avoided formal association with clearly antitrade factions who might harm its ability to negotiate compromises with protrade policy elites and leave them relatively isolated from smaller, non-Washington, D.C.-based organizations focused on trade policy. Both NWF and NRDC seemed to formally disassociate themselves from more adversarial environmental organizations, in particular Public Citizen and Greenpeace, as evidenced by the different positions endorsed by coalition papers.[25]

Different Responses to Significant Events

Table 4.4 compiles the significant events of the NAFTA period and evaluates the responses of eleven key environmental organizations. Notice that three of the formal advisors to the USTR avoided critical comments on the release of the Dunkel Draft of GATT and the Tuna/Dolphin Decision and avoided public comments on the USTR Review of Environmental Concerns and the Integrated Border Environmental Plan. However, these same events prompted strong negative reactions by adversarial groups.

Analysis of the relationships established among the political actors involved in NAFTA negotiations, shifts in the media coverage of key environmental groups, and responses to significant events during negotiations show a clear pattern of both accommodating and adversarial behavior. Adversarial groups used their resources to fight an aggressive campaign against NAFTA's passage, while accommodating groups positioned themselves to avoid confrontations that might threaten their

TABLE 4.4   Significant Events Involving National Environmental Organizations

	Advisors to Administration						Adversarial Groups				
	WWF	EDF	NWF	TNC	NRDC	NAS	DoW	SC	FoE	PC	GP
8/91 GATT Tuna Dolphin Decision											
10/91 USTR "Review of Environmental Concerns"	N	N	N	N	–	–	–	—	—	—	+
12/91 GATT "Dunkel Draft"	N	N	–	N	–	N	N	—	—	—	–
2/92 Integrated Border Environmental Plan	N	N	–	N	–	–	–	—	—	—	—
8/92 NAFTA	+	N	+	N	–	N	–	—	—	—	—
6–8/93 NEPA Decisions	+	N	N	N	–	–	—	—	—	—	N
9/17/93 NAFTA Package	++	++	++	N	+	+	N	—	—	—	—

Key: — Strong Public Negative Reaction
— Public Negative Reaction
N No Public Position Taken
+ Public Support
++ Strong Public Support

Evaluations based upon review of numerous public documents offered by each organization during the period 1991 to 1993. For a review of these documents, please refer to the bibliography.

relationship with negotiators. Accommodating groups controlled the conflicts within the environmental community to shape the policy demands associated with environmental issues and remain part of the negotiating agenda for NAFTA.

Accommodating Coalition Defines Terms of Environment Policy Recommendations

While adversarial environmental organizations were principally responsible for establishing and maintaining preemptive power during negotiations, members of the accommodating environmental coalition were better positioned to exploit political leverage to gain political concessions from trade policy elites. Accommodating environmental organizations used their own formal and informal resources to define the environmental agenda for negotiations and present a more moderate set of policy demands than were being made by adversarial organizations. An examination of NWF's role during NAFTA negotiations is instructive.

NWF's own policy of constructive engagement with industry elites convinced them that a dialogue between business and responsible environmental organizations could result in effective changes in investment patterns and improve the chances for environmental quality through trade (Hudson, 94). NWF president, Jay Hair, was confident that his position as Investment Policy Advisor (INPAC) would provide him access to economic elites central to negotiations.[26] In November he outlined the relationship between investment patterns and environmental degradation and offered policy recommendations to address the problem, challenging the assumption that increased economic activity *necessarily* results in higher levels of environmental protection. Instead they suggested that environmentally conscious trade policy focuses equally on net increase in pollution, social and community costs, and the presence of environmental infrastructure as well as increases in economic output (Hair, 91a). They urged the USTR to forge direct linkages between trade and environmental goals by negotiating standards for new investments that required the use of pollution prevention technologies and the generation of revenues for environmental remediation and protection by placing a "green tax" on increased trade. However, their attitude toward direct linkages in negotiations changed; in a letter to Ambassador Hills in January 1992, Hair indicated:

> Our interest is not to stop trade expansion, or stop trade liberalization . . . with some conscious effort trade policies and trade negotiations can assure that we get the maximum economic benefits, and reduce or avoid the environmental costs. . . . Certainly, a parallel approach to environmental issues does not *necessarily* rule out linkages between the two (Hair, 92e).

Ambassador Hills responded to NWF's policy recommendations in February 1992. She dismissed both the recommendation for a "green tax" and for direct linkages between trade and environmental goals:

> I think we agree that more rapid economic growth which we expect to follow implementation of a NAFTA in all three countries, would, through the tax structure, provide increased revenues to governments at all levels for environmental infrastructure investment. . . . Having said that, however, we do not consider it advisable for the NAFTA to venture into the realm of taxation. . . . (R)equirements (to) make new investors internalize the direct environmental costs of economic development . . . are best met by general taxation and spending decisions made in a democratic fashion (Hills, 92).

NWF did not publicize the USTR's rejection of their position to the press or to other members of the environmental community. Instead, they moderated their own demands for negotiations and attempted to influence the demands made by other organizations. Remaining actively a part of negotiations (they believed) offered the best chance of influencing negotiators; of the two active advisors, Hair had most access and, arguably, the greatest opportunity for influence.

Not all environmental advisors to the USTR were willing to make similar compromises in their agenda for trade policy. Despite a similar commitment to participate in negotiations, the NRDC president, John Adams, was unwilling to modify their agenda for trade to accept negotiations made by President Bush (Adams, 92).

Preferred access to protrade policy elites and willingness to avoid public conflicts between trade officials and their own organizations positioned accommodating groups to exert greater influence over the tone and content of the environmental demands for NAFTA than was enjoyed by adversarial organizations. Table 4.5 aggregates the documents produced by environmental organizations during negotiations. With the exception of the Sierra Club's letter supporting the Waxman/ Gephardt Resolution 246, documents authored by adversarial organizations were not endorsed by accommodating groups. However, four out of seven documents authored by accommodating groups were endorsed by one or more adversarial organizations. On a number of occasions, such as the letter from Senator Tim Wirth to EPA administrator Reilly in May 1991 and during the drafting of the 9 May 1993 "Group of Seven" letter, accommodating groups did not inform adversarial organizations of their efforts but worked directly with administrative officials to reach compromises on environmental issues. I will detail the events surrounding two significant documents here.

May/June 1992 "Consensus Position"

In March 1992 NRDC began an effort to organize environmental demands into a set of policy recommendations for negotiators. On 18 March senior policy analyst, Justin Ward, circulated a draft document designed "... to translate some of the environmental community's NAFTA recommendations into agreement language" (NRDC, 92e). The tone of the document captured the level of optimism held by NRDC regarding NAFTA's success:

> The negotiators have taken the basic position that, with limited exceptions, environmental safeguards belong outside the trade agreement. . . . Unfortunately, current government actions do not inspire confidence that NAFTA implementation will proceed with adequate environmental safeguards (NRDC, 92e).

Groups discussed various policy alternatives under five categories: enforcement of environmental laws; trade dispute settlement; environ-

TABLE 4.5 Documents Prepared by National Environmental Organizations

Environmental Organizations	WWF	EDF	NWF	TNC	NRDC	NAS	DoW	SC	FoE	PC	GP
2/6/91: "Environmental Agenda"	N	N	AE	N	N	N	N	N	PE	N	N
5/7/91 Letter from Senator Wirth to EPA administrator Reilly	N	AE	AE	N	N	N	N	N	N	N	N
5/9/92: "Consensus Position"	N	PE	AE	N	PN	E	N	P	N	N	N
10/91 Letter critical of Tuna/Dolphin Decision	N	N	N	N	N	N	N	PE	PE	AE	N
2/92 Letter critical of GATT "Dunkel Draft"	N	N	N	N	E	N	N	PE	AE	PE	N
2/92 Support for HCR 246	N	N	N	N	E	E	E	AE	PE	PE	N
5/28/92: "Minimum Environmental Safeguards"	N	PE	AE	N	P	N	N	P	N	N	N
6/92: "Environmental Safeguards"	N	PE	P	N	AE	E	N	PE	PE	PE	N
7/20/92 Letter to Ambassador Hills	N	E	AE	N	PE	E	E	E	E	E	N
2/93 "NAFTA Threatens Environment"	N	N	N	N	N	N	N	E	E	E	AE
3/93 Recommendations for North American Commission on the Environment	N	AE	N	N	AE	N	N	N	N	N	N
3/12/93: Letter to Ambassador Kantor	N	P	P	N	N	N	AE	PE	PE	PE	E
4/29/93 Letter to Congress regarding NAFTA	N	N	N	N	N	N	N	E	E	AE	E
5/8/93: "Group of Seven" letter	AE	PE	AE	PE	PE	PE	E	N	N	N	N
9/12/93 CTC letter to Ambassador Kantor	N	N	N	N	N	N	N	E	E	E	E

Key: A = Principal Author; P = Participated in Deliberations; E = Endorsed; N = Nonparticipant

mental standards; environmental program funding; and energy. By May the list of categories had expanded to include recognition of all international environmental agreements that use trade sanctions, with specific recommendations for investment criteria. Specific reference to energy concerns had been replaced with a general reference to the principles of sustainable development. Concerns raised over the sanitary and phytosanitary language from Uruguay Round text into NAFTA prompted detailed recommendations for food safety. References to border environmental funding were also added, along with a specific section for hazardous material treatment and disposal (NRDC, 92e). Policy recommendations on border taxes and sanctions were included, even if the likelihood of their acceptance was slim.

The timing of the final draft of the May document upset officials at NWF, who believed that a final version of "the green language in NAFTA" would be completed by the end of May. To ensure that recommendations would be ready for the USTR by the end of May, NWF began their own effort to develop a consensus position. NWF produced its own set of guidelines, more general in scope and content than those being developed by NRDC. The vagueness of the recommendations concerned the groups involved in the NRDC process, causing them not to endorse the document when NWF released it on 25 May (NRDC 92e). The NRDC paper was completed in June, signed by the Sierra Club, Public Citizen, CIEL, CNI, Defenders, EDF, FoE, IATP, NAS, TCPS, ATI, and BEP.

Although the two documents differed in style and detail, each shared a similar set of policy recommendations:

- *Direct Inclusion of Policy Recommendations in the NAFTA*, rather than in parallel agreements not linked to the final NAFTA text.
- *Creation of a Trinational Environmental Commission.* The NRDC paper stressed the creation and activities of an environmental commission, outlining its reporting and investigative powers. The NWF document spoke generally of the creation of a committee "that assists the signatories in implementing environmental provisions" (of the agreement).
- *Relationship to International Environmental Agreements.* Specific attention was given to NAFTA's relationship to international environmental agreements.
- *Protection of the Right to Set National Standards for the Environment, Consumer Health, and Safety.*
- *Public Participation in Dispute Proceedings and General Implementation of NAFTA.*
- *Funding for Environmental Remediation along Mexico-U.S. Border,* as well as future environmental regulatory needs by "recapturing" a fraction of the revenues associated with trade (Audley, 93a).

The two consensus documents were important because they strengthened the environmental community's leverage in negotiations by unifying their recommendations. But the form these recommendations took shaped in response to the progress of negotiations to date, progress shaped largely by the agenda for trade liberalization and a reluctance to include environmental concerns. Knowledge of possible consensus positions was known more intimately to those environmental groups acting as advisors to the administration, and it is likely that this information helped to shape the consensus positions advocated by the accommodating coalition. While there was more resistance expressed by presidential advisors under the Bush administration, a willingness to compromise was much more evident under President Clinton.[27]

But the documents were also important because they reflected which organizations had greatest influence over the content of the policy recommendations that shaped the environmental community's position. With the exception of the Sierra Club, none of the organizations from the adversarial coalition were involved in the early formation of the recommendations. They were invited to participate toward the end, after the document had taken shape, but most of their more aggressive recommendations were not included in the final consensus position.[28]

It is also interesting to note that NWF was willing to provide a more general set of recommendations to meet the USTR's timeline for negotiation, while NRDC and most other groups preferred to make their recommendations more specific to avoid ambiguities. From the negotiators' perspective, the NRDC document was a more valuable contribution to their efforts, but from a political perspective the more generally worded document gave each organization political room to argue that the administration had met the objectives outlined in the policy recommendation.[29] The reluctance to include politically infeasible policy alternatives and the willingness to offer recommendations open to broad interpretation suggests the overall willingness of the most influential organizations to keep the environmental community within political reach of accepting the policy alternatives negotiated in NAFTA.

May 1993 "Group of Seven" Letter
NWF's public support for the original Agreement weakened its ability to act as the principal force for shaping policy recommendations from the environmental community. With President Bush's departure, WWF CEO Russell Train stepped down as advisor to the USTR to be replaced by WWF's president, Kathryn Fuller. Fuller's participation in negotiations was important for a number of reasons. First, she was concerned that much of the criticism focused on Mexico's environmental record was unjustified and that Mexican officials deserved recognition for efforts to protect endangered species and diverse ecosystems. Second, her organization believed that economic growth was an essen-

tial element of any campaign to urge developing countries to protect their own environment. Efforts by more adversarial environmental organizations to focus attention on Mexico's environmental record, or to impose stiff environmental penalties on Mexico as part of the Supplemental Agreement, might jeopardize the success of the Agreement itself.

Moderate and adversarial environmental organizations took advantage of Clinton's willingness to consider a broader range of environmental issues during the Supplemental Agreement negotiations and produced a letter in March 1993 detailing their concerns.[30] With a framework agreed upon by the majority of environmental organizations working on trade in January 1993, the consensus document was an attempt address NAFTA's impact on International Environmental Agreements, problems related to language in the negotiated Agreement itself, the absence of language to address production process standards, and a failure to include public participation in the dispute settlement process (author's personal notes). Specifically, the letter called for negotiations to:

- Provide a secure source of funding for infrastructure development, environmental enforcement, investigation, and cleanup for all NAFTA-related environmental programs. Funding for these projects should originate from penalties levied because of nonenforcement of environmental laws, phased-out tariffs, or the creation of a development bank for environmental projects.
- Provide public access and accountability for all activities related to NAFTA implementation and enforcement.
- Clarify rights of countries to set tariff restrictions based upon production processes.
- Clarify rights of local, state, and federal governments to set independent food, environment, and health safety standards.
- Provide a means to ensure that industries internalize environmental costs.
- Recognize all international environmental agreements that use trade measures as a means of enforcement.
- Preserve right to restrict exports of energy and energy resources to promote global environmental quality.
- Preserve right to employ government incentives to promote sustainable agricultural practices.
- Allow governments to establish purchasing policies that promote use of green technologies.
- Clarify the meaning of "necessary to protect the health and human safety" and "sound science" in terms of standard setting.

The demands made by environmental organizations in the 4 March letter came at an important time in the process of negotiations. The USTR and its counterparts in Mexico and Canada had not yet finalized the agenda for discussions. The letter offered a more detailed outline of the commitment the Clinton administration made to address environmental concerns in the Supplemental Agreement negotiations. But the accommodating coalition was afraid that the environmental recommendations for the Supplemental Agreement embodied in the 4 March letter jeopardized the chances for any environmental provisions in the Agreement. Instead of endorsing this set of recommendations, they developed a new, less aggressive set of policy recommendations for the administration.

The WWF president, Kathryn Fuller, employed Kenneth Berlin, a partner at the Washington, D.C., law firm of Winthrop, Stimson, Putnam and Roberts, to examine the demands of the environmental community and try to establish a politically feasible position.[31] Berlin organized meetings among trade staff from NWF, NRDC, EDF, and NAS to review the set of environmental demands for the Supplemental Agreement in the early part of April 1993. Participants agreed to two things. First, they agreed to keep their deliberations secret to better control the list of recommendations and avoid those offered by adversarial environmental groups.[32] Second, they agreed to offer a compromise within reach of negotiators. According to Berlin, "Our objective was to offer a politically feasible position for NAFTA that kept us players in the policy debate" (Berlin, 94).[33]

The 4 May letter was organized around seven policy areas: organization and structure of the North American Commission; enforcement of environmental regulation; funding for border and conservation projects; clarification of environmental standards; dispute settlement procedures; public participation; and international environmental agreements. Each set of policy recommendations was developed to allow for broad interpretation of the requests made to the government in exchange for their support of NAFTA. Where the environmental advisors knew that no environmental provisions were possible (such as in the energy and agriculture chapters), demands were dropped from their agenda. Drafters avoided direct confrontation with the NAFTA text by recommending a protocol that stated each country's commitment to public access and to the processes that guarantee environmental experts would hear cases.[34]

By late April Berlin began circulating a draft document to other members of the environmental community. While interested in broadening support for their recommendations, they rejected requests by other groups to make the policy recommendations "nonnegotiable"

(Wallach, n.d.), to qualify the legal status of the Supplemental Agreements,[35] or to include sanctions for both business noncompliance and government nonenforcement (Sierra Club, 92a). Minor modifications were made to accommodate recommendations made by The Nature Conservancy to provide funds for environmental conservation and ecosystem protection. When the final letter was prepared on 4 May 1993, it was endorsed by WWF, NWF, NRDC, EDF, Defenders, TNC, and NAS.

Signed by mainstream environmental groups that represented approximately 80 percent of the membership of the entire environmental community, the 4 May letter signaled the end of particular focus on environmental issues in trade negotiations. Accommodating environmental groups positioned themselves to endorse the Supplemental Agreement negotiated by Ambassador Kantor by creating enough leeway in their demands to accept the final settlement between Mexico, Canada, and the United States. The momentum created by adversarial groups who capitalized on Democratic discontent with the Agreement was derailed.

Again, groups in the middle of the adversarial/accommodating continuum offer constructive insights. Unlike other accommodating groups, NRDC both publicly opposed the Uruguay Round and supported the NEPA. Critical of the original Agreement, they nonetheless continued to offer constructive comments on the development of the Supplemental Agreement and the Integrated Border Environmental plan. Their dissatisfaction with the technical barriers and sanitary and phytosanitary language in NAFTA resulted in a personal letter from Ambassador Kantor assuring NRDC officials that the United States would not interpret the terms of the Agreement in any way that would jeopardize the right to set and maintain high environmental standards. Yet the fact that they were willing to accept a written explanation by Ambassador Kantor regarding this language, a letter which is not recognized by the government of either Mexico or Canada, is evidence of their willingness to support the final terms of the Agreement.

It is also interesting to note that two of the most significant environmental groups were not as publicly involved in the debate surrounding NAFTA. During interviews with congressional staff, negotiators, and administrative officials, it is clear that both WWF and EDF were instrumental in creating the NAFTA provisions. However, based upon media coverage, congressional testimony, and participation in significant events or documents, these two groups did not play a significant role in the public dialogue on NAFTA. An examination of the organizational structure and informal relationships between organizational staff at WWF and EDF shows that these two groups have the strongest ties to

Republican party elites (see Appendix A) and have strong relationship ties to industries supportive of growth-oriented trade policy. WWF's role in NAFTA only became public when they orchestrated the 8 May "Group of Seven" letter that dramatically redefined the environmental agenda for Supplemental Agreement negotiations. That they played such an important role despite the lack of public attention suggests that the informal ties among trade policy elites are as important as the formal ties in influencing policy outcomes.

On 17 September 1993 President Clinton endorsed the Supplemental Agreement to NAFTA in an elaborate ceremony at the White House. In attendance were representatives from the World Wildlife Fund, Environmental Defense Fund, the National Wildlife Federation, the Natural Resources Defense Council, the National Audubon Society, and Conservation International. On Capital Hill, Majority Whip David Bonior (D-MI) held his own media event in opposition to the Agreement. Representatives from the Sierra Club, Public Citizen, and Friends of the Earth spoke out against the environmental provisions of the Agreement. What had begun in January 1991 as a unified effort to include environmental issues into trade policy, ended in bitter disagreement among those organization most actively involved in negotiations.

To dwell solely on the differences of opinion over NAFTA among environmental groups would obscure the manner in which environmental issues found their way into negotiations. Adversarial and accommodating roles played by two different coalitions within the environmental community helped to maintain the preemptive threat created during Fast Track, but it also positioned environmental issues within the political reach of both the Bush and Clinton administrations. Each coalition used its own private resources differently; grassroots, broad-based coalition efforts on the part of the anti-NAFTA environmental coalition, and "inside-the-Beltway," narrowly defined environmental efforts by pro-NAFTA environmental coalition. Each used media attention and congressional concern for the environment to its own advantage. Together, their efforts produced enough leverage to institutionalize environmental issues into U.S. trade policy.

It is difficult to assess the level of interest shown by members of Congress regarding the environment. Apparently both pro- and anti-NAFTA members used environmental issues as part of their overall strategy to pass or defeat NAFTA. Up to this point, the strength of their commitment to the environment is difficult to measure. If Wyden can be used as some kind of gauge for environmental interest in NAFTA, his shifting position on the environment following Clinton's presidential victory suggests that concern for the environment was opportunistic at best. The concern for environmental issues expressed by anti-NAFTA members of Congress seems less genuine, used primarily as a shield to protect themselves from criticism by pro-NAFTA elites. The next chapter will explore this observation more fully, as the analysis shifts to the voting stage of the Agreement.

ENDNOTES

1. NAS endorsed the *May Consensus* position but was not actively involved in trade policy discussions at this time. See Rogers, 94.

2. Personal interview with Justin Ward, NRDC. NRDC filed criticisms of both the Environmental Review and the NAFTA agreement as negotiated by President Bush.

3. Responsibility for the Environmental Review and the IBEP were divided between the Office of International Affairs at the Environmental Protection Agency and the USTR. The EPA assistant administrator for international affairs, Timothy Atkeson, was placed in charge of negotiating a new binational accord with Mexico, while the USTR deputy assistant trade representative for North American affairs, Charles Ries, was placed in charge of the Environmental Review. USTR staff relied heavily upon the expertise offered by EPA officials regarding an Environmental Review, as they did not have staff adequately trained to conduct such a review.

4. The Environmental Review concluded, "When coupled with environmental sensitivity, however, policies which stimulate economic growth are an indispensable element in improving environmental protection." See Office of the United States Trade Representative, 1991.

5. NEPA requirements for an environmental impact statement state that federal officials must respond to public comments before an Environmental Review is used for policy guidelines. Both the EPA and USTR held public hearings during the summer of 1991 to provide an opportunity for public comment. See *Federal Register* Document no. 91-32456; *Federal Register* Document no. 91-21672. Drafts of both documents were made available to the public in October 1991. See United States Environmental Protection Agency, 91a; Office of the United States Trade Representative, 91. Both drafts were severely criticized by the environmental community for their limited scope and weak analysis. In particular, see Mikesell and McCloskey, 91; Ward, 91b. Following the release of the draft Integrated Border Environmental Plan, the EPA provided a second review period and incorporated many of the recommendations into their final Agreement in February 1992. See *Federal Register* Document no. 92-5593. While it was not unanimously embraced by environmentalists, it was met with lukewarm support and a willingness to explore the possibilities contained in the Plan. See United States Environmental Protection Agency, 92.

6. A conference called *Trade in the 21st Century* was organized by the AFL-CIO, Public Citizen, the Sierra Club, Friends of the Earth, and American Family Farms Coalition and was scheduled to take place 7 September 1992 in Washington, D.C.

7. The endorsement of the Commission suggested by Ambassador Hills will be discussed later in this chapter.

8. Clinton campaign representatives began contacting the environmental community regarding positions on trade policy in late July 1992. See Baum, 92. Memoranda were sent from environmental groups to the campaign beginning in August. See Audley, 92d; Biel, 94; Hudson, 94; Siglin, 94.

9. Mark Anderson, director, International Trade Program, AFL-CIO, acknowledged that they never expected Clinton to oppose the Agreement. See Anderson, 94.

10. President Bush had already agreed to negotiate a Supplemental Agreement to NAFTA on the environment. See Samuel, 94.

11. During his professional career as an attorney in Florida and California, Kantor worked as an advocate for migratory workers and other civil rights organizations, as well as consumer groups like Ralph Nader's organizations (Senate Committee on Finance, 93a).

12. See Appendix A for details on involvement of national environmental organizations.

13. A phrase coined by Mr. Dunkel when describing the draft UR-GATT document. In January 1992 a letter objecting to the GATT text was circulated on Capitol Hill by the Sierra Club and endorsed by twenty-four organizations: ". . . we urge you to join us in rejecting the proposed GATT text, and in sending the message to the White House that no GATT agreement is better than a bad GATT agreement. . . ." (*Inside U.S. Trade*, 17 January 1992). NRDC sent its own letter urging Congress to reject the UR-Draft, as did NWF. However, NWF's criticisms of the Final Draft Act text was tenuous: In a January 1992 letter from Jay Hair to Carla Hills, Hair detailed NWF's concerns regarding the Draft, focusing on the creation of the World Trade Organization, GATT's impact on domestic health and safety standards, and the lack of democratic transparency in decision making at GATT. Hair does not indicate that NWF is opposed to the Draft, but that he hopes ". . . in the Administration's response to this text, you reserve the time needed to address the problems that we and other groups in the environment community have raised." See Hair, 92a.

14. Gephardt visited the Mexico-U.S. border at least five times during the NAFTA debate. Accompanying him on trips were other members of Congress, including Karan Shepard (D-UT), Ron Wyden (D-OR), Sander Levin (D-MI), and Karan English (D-AZ).

15. Hair, 92e. NRDC endorsed HCR 246 in early 1992, with NAS endorsing the resolution by the summer of 1992. See Ward, 94; Rogers, 94.

16. Baucus proposed tariffs on goods from nations with lower environmental norms to offset unfair lower production costs (*Inside U.S. Trade*, 20 September 1991).

17. Wyden's record and district can be found in the *American Almanac Profile* of Congress, 1993.

18. Wyden coauthored six letters in 1991 to the Bush administration arguing on behalf of environmental issues in NAFTA: 29 July; 19 August; 20 August; 13 September; 20 October; and 23 October.

19. Over the past three years, Richardson has an average score of 81 percent from the League of Conservation Voters; Robert Matsui averages 72 percent.

20. Representatives from NWF indicated that they consciously avoided negative coverage on NAFTA, especially following the release of the September 1992 NAFTA text. See Ward, 94; Hudson, 94. Officials from the Sierra Club, FoE, and Public Citizen acknowledged that they actively sought media coverage to heighten tension surrounding negotiations (author's personal notes). See Wallach, 94; Hittle, 94.

21. Principal organizations included the Development Gap and the Institute for Policy Studies. Friends of the Earth, Sierra Club, and Greenpeace were also members of MODTLE; only Greenpeace devoted most of its time working with MODTLE members during the NAFTA negotiations stage (author's personal notes).

22. Initially, CTWC executive committee consisted of representatives from FoE, the International Ladies Garment Workers Union, Amalgamated Clothing and Textile Workers Union, National Farmers Union, National Family Farm Coalition, International Union of Electricians, Sierra Club, and Public Citizen. Most of the information pertaining to the CTWC and Fair Trade Campaign (FTC) is taken from the author's personal notes while acting as the Sierra Club's director for trade and the environment. The Sierra Club was active in both CTWC and FTC activities.

23. Author's personal notes taken during meetings between AFL-CIO secretary-treasurer, Tom Donahue, and Sierra Club chairman, Mike McCloskey (1992, 1993). The situation was different outside Washington, where CTWC's field ally, the Fair Trade Campaign (FTC) worked closely with AFL-CIO.

24. Author's notes taken during meetings between representatives of FoE, Sierra Club, AFL-CIO, the National Family Farm Coalition, and Public Citizen.

25. NRDC's Justin Ward disagrees with this interpretation. In a 12 December 1996 letter to the author, Ward argues that each organization was advocating its own position relative to the progress toward environmental provisions in NAFTA (Ward, 96).

26. NWF founded the Corporate Conservation Council to provide a friendly forum for discussion among members and for the creation and implementation of policy statements. Members include: Asea Brown Boceri, AT&T, Bank of America, Browning-Ferris Industries, Ciba-Geigy Corporation, Dow Chemical, Duke Power Company, DuPont Company, Johnson and Johnson, 3M, Merck and Company, Monsanto, Pacific Gas and Electric, Proctor and Gamble, Shell Oil, USX, and Waste Management (NWF Annual Report, 1994).

27. A draft of the NAFTA document was leaked in February 1992. For an analysis of this document, see Audley, 92a.

28. Ward explains why he is unwilling to consider substituting the word "recommendations" for "demands" in the document. ". . . I don't want to foreclose the possibility of alternative (different, not necessarily weaker) and supplementary formulations that may satisfy our underlying principles and objectives." See Ward, 92c.

29. This was one of the reasons border groups and NRDC did not endorse the NWF proposal; "Regrettably, ATI will not be signing onto the Trinational Declaration you [Stewart Hudson, NWF] circulated last week. Although we all seem to be in general agreement on most points, we feel that language of

the Declaration leaves too much room for misinterpretation by the negotiators" (Arizona Toxics Information, 92). ". . . we prefer not to join the safeguards declaration. Our main concern is that the generalized document leaves room for the negotiators plausibly to claim concessions on most issues raised." See NRDC, 92e.

30. Defenders of Wildlife, Center for International Environmental Law, Sierra Club, Friends of the Earth, Public Citizen, Humane Society of the United States, Humane Society International, Institute for Agriculture and Trade Policy, Center for Rural Affairs, National Family Farm Coalition, Earth Island Institute, Marine Mammal Fund, Animal Protection Institute, Rainforest Action Network, Whale and Dolphin Conservation Society, Performing Animal Welfare Society, Fund for Animals, Environmental Investigation Agency, Environmental Solutions International Primate Protection League, N.Y. Public Interest Research Group, Community Nutrition Institute, National Toxics Campaign, World Policy Institute, Greenpeace U.S.A., 4 March 1993.

31. Berlin's law firm was well acquainted with both the environmental community and the trade community: Jeff Lang, another partner with Winthrop, once worked as chief counsel to the House Ways and Means Subcommittee on Trade and had authored a number of articles on trade and the environment. Berlin himself was a former partner of USTR legal counsel, Ira Shapiro, and had worked on a number of environmental issues representing the environmental community. Interview with Ken Berlin: Berlin had worked full-time for the National Audubon Society on a project to protect the Endangered Species Act from efforts by the Reagan administration to drastically reduce its protection. He and Fuller met when they both worked at the Department of Justice.

32. According to participants in the meetings, a great deal of deliberation focused on whether or not to include the Sierra Club. NRDC advocated including the Club, but fears over the close ties between the Sierra Club and Public Citizen on NAFTA, and a statement made by Sierra Club executive director, Carl Pope, regarding the "need to kill a bad trade agreement before getting a good one," eventually resulted in their exclusion (Ward, 96; Hudson 94, Berlin, 94; author's personal notes).

33. Mr. Berlin was in the employ of the World Wildlife Fund to establish a compromise position within the environmental community that would not be rejected by the Clinton administration. Berlin also sat on the Board of Directors of Defenders of Wildlife.

34. The first draft of the letter shared with other members of the environmental community was on 26 April 1993. However, versions of the letter had been circulating at the USTR and EPA earlier than this. See Berlin, 94; Hudson, 94.

35. Questions regarding the legal relationship between the NAFTA text and the Supplemental Agreements were of great concern to environmental groups. If the Supplemental Agreement did not have the same legal status as the Agreement, some feared the original Agreement would take precedence over the Supplemental Agreement.

5

Voting Stage

On 22 November 1993 the United States House of Representatives voted in favor of implementing legislation enacting the North American Free Trade Agreement. By a 234 to 200 vote, the House successfully concluded three years of contentious trade policy negotiations.[1] But while the NAFTA vote portended many things, what is interesting to this analysis is the lack of attention paid by members to environmental issues during the floor debate prior to the vote. Examination of the political speeches made by members of Congress shows that NAFTA's effect on jobs and economic performance dominated their thinking.[2] Of the 308 floor statements, only thirty-two NAFTA supporters—slightly more than 20 percent of those voting in favor—cited NAFTA's environmental provisions as one reason for support. Fifty-eight members—29 percent of those voting against NAFTA—used the environment as an issue to justify their opposition. Further examination of the records of those members citing the environment suggests that NAFTA supporters and opponents may have been less than sincere in their concern for the environment. Fourteen of the thirty-two members citing environmental reasons as a basis for their vote for NAFTA had voting records indicative of strong support of environmental legislation.[3] Fifty-two votes cast against NAFTA on environmental grounds—89 percent of the members who spoke out against NAFTA for environmental reasons—were made by members with strong labor records, only half of whom were supporters of environmental legislation.[4] But perhaps the most telling evidence of a shift in fortune for environmental issues in the NAFTA debate can be found in the speeches made by members of Congress who led the fight against NAFTA. While pro-NAFTA coalition leaders like Congressmen Robert Matsui (D-CA) and Bill Richardson (D-NM) extolled the Agreements' environmental provisions, not one of the leading opponents of NAFTA mentioned the environment as part of their justification for opposing NAFTA.[5] After holding court as one of the most contentious aspects surrounding negotiations, environmental issues drifted out of the center of political discourse as Congress deliberated NAFTA in the fall of 1993.

Had anyone been monitoring news coverage of environmental issues in trade policy, perhaps the shift away from the environment might have been noticed. Throughout negotiations, news coverage of environmental issues related to NAFTA made up about 10 percent of all newsprint coverage in the major national newspapers. Following NAFTA's signing on 14 September, coverage dropped to 6 percent.[6] For some reason trade policy elites showed little concern for the environment as the NAFTA vote approached.

Two factors explain why the political decks surrounding NAFTA were cleared of environmental hazards prior to the vote. First, environmental issues were neutralized as a reason to oppose NAFTA prior to the beginning of the voting stage. Resolution of major environmental issues as part of the supplemental negotiations, strong support from most national environmental organizations, and the political in-fighting among environmental groups made casting a vote on NAFTA based on environmental issues politically irrelevant for members of Congress. The second explanation is more speculative than the first. Perhaps environmental issues weren't important to members when they considered trade policy. Perhaps environmental issues had always been a pawn in a larger game of trade policy. When environmental issues were neutralized in September 1993, members could no longer use the environment for political gain, so it dropped out of their voting logic.

NEUTRALIZED ENVIRONMENTAL ISSUES ELIMINATE POLITICAL LEVERAGE

By the end of the summer 1993, the U.S. environmental community could no longer sustain the outward appearance of unified concern for the environmental implications of U.S. trade policy. The May 1993 letter initiated by WWF made permanent the divide between groups begun during the Fast Track period. The strong divisions among environmental groups over NAFTA's environmental provisions created a "no win" situation for members of Congress. If a member's vote on NAFTA was premised on the environmental aspects of the Agreement, some portion of their environmental constituency would be upset.[7] It, therefore, made little sense for members to use environmental issues as a reason for supporting or opposing NAFTA. An examination of the votes cast by House members, targeted by both environmental opponents and supporters of NAFTA during the voting stage, suggests such a scenario took place. By September 1993, both the anti- and pro-NAFTA environmental coalitions had reduced their list of "undecided" members of the House of Representatives influenced by environmental concerns to forty people.[8] These forty were targeted by environmental groups because of their individual histories of support for environmental protection. Twenty-four of the forty targeted members supported the Agreement. Six of the twenty-four used environmental issues in support of their vote. Of the sixteen that opposed NAFTA, only two specifically mentioned the environment to support their opposing vote. A total of eight out of forty members, targeted by environmental groups because of their historical support of environmental issues, mentioned the environment when they voted on NAFTA.

A number of factors help explain so dramatic a change in the fortune of environmental issues in NAFTA.

Environmental Groups Won Concessions before Voting Stage Began

On 14 September 1993 President Clinton held a signing ceremony at the White House formally marking the completion of the NAFTA Package. Representatives from NWF, WWF, NAS, NRDC, and EDF—environmental organizations that endorsed NAFTA—were invited to kick off the administration's push to pass NAFTA. The following day Senator Max Baucus (D-MT) held a press conference with representatives from the supporting organizations, Vice President Al Gore, USTR ambassador Kantor and EPA administrator Browner.[9] At the press conference, six national environmental organizations expressed support for the environmental virtues of the NAFTA, the Supplemental Agreement creating the North American Commission on Environmental Cooperation, and the bilateral agreement with Mexico creating the Border Environmental Cooperation Committee.

These two political events were orchestrated by the administration to highlight the NAFTA Package's environmental provisions. They staged these events in the first days of the administration's push to pass NAFTA because USTR officials had resolved most of the differences of opinion between environmental groups and the administration during negotiations of the Supplemental Agreement.[10] Supporting environmental groups could not guarantee the administration their ability to deliver more support from undecided members on the basis of unresolved environmental issues; the Administration had no incentive to focus side-payments on outstanding environmental issues. Free from pressure from environmental groups for greater concessions, Clinton officials focused the administration's efforts to win undecided votes on other members of Congress and their issues.[11]

Neutralizing environmental issues only required support from "some," not all, national environmental organizations. What constituted "enough" organizations is uncertain; for example, support for

TABLE 5.1   Targeted House Members by Pro- and Anti-NAFTA Environmental Organizations

Name	Floor Speech	Reference to Environmental Provisions	NAFTA Vote
Castle, Mike (R-AL)	✓	N	S
English, Karan (D-AZ)	–	—	S
Lambert, Blanche (D-AR)	✓	Y	S
Farr, Sam (D-CA)	–	—	S
Pelosi, Nancy (D-CA)	✓	Y	S
Eshoo, Anna (D-CA)	✓	Y	S
Roybal-Allard, Lucille (D-CA)	✓	Y	S
Waxman, Henry (D-CA)	✓	Y	O
Deal, Nathan (D-GA)	–	—	O
Gutierrez, Louis (D-IL)	–	—	O
Yates, Sidney (D-IL)	✓	Y	O
Slattery, Jim (D-KS)	–	—	O
Markey, Ed (D-MA)	–	—	O
Kennedy, Joe (D-MA)	–	—	S
Studds, Gerry (D-MA)	–	—	S
Andrews, Tom (D-ME)	✓	Y	S
Upton, Fred (R-MI)	–	—	S
Minge, David (D-MN)	✓	Y	O
Vento, Bruce (D-MN)	✓	Y	O
Skelton, Ike (D-MO)	–	—	S
Hoagland, Peter (D-NE)	–	—	S
Saxton, Jim (R-NJ)	–	—	O
Zimmer, Dick (R-NJ)	–	—	S
Hamilton, Fish (R-NY)	✓	Y	S
Gilman, Ben (R-NY)	–	—	O
Schumer, Chuck (D-NY)	–	—	O
Lancaster, Martin (D-NC)	–	—	O

Sources: "Swing Members With Enviro Concerns," document created by WWF, 10/6/93; "Democratic Members of Congress—Target List Conflicts," Citizens' Trade Campaign, undated.
✓ gave floor speech
Y reference made to NAFTA's environmental provisions
·N no reference made to NAFTA's environmental provisions
S voted in favor of NAFTA
O voted in opposition to NAFTA

President Bush's NAFTA from EDF, WWF, and NWF may or may not have been enough to resolve the environment as a political obstacle for a Democratically controlled Congress. But President Clinton's willingness to expand environmental provisions as part of the Supplemental Agreement negotiations enabled him to secure the support from each of the environmental advisors, representing about 80 percent of national environmental organizations.

Lobbying Efforts Caused Questions in the Minds of Members

Lobbying by both pro- and anti-NAFTA environmental coalitions may also have contributed to the demise of environmental issues before Congress. Two equally strong, yet diametrically opposed, perspectives on NAFTA from the "same" constituency may have "canceled one another out," making it difficult for members to form decisions on the basis of their views.

NAFTA supporters defined political success in the voting stage as the absence of NAFTA opposition for environmental reasons.[12] The theme of their lobbying message was that the status quo between Mexico and the United States was unacceptable; improvements in environmental regulations resulting from the NAFTA Package made passing the Agreement better than maintaining the status quo (NWF, n.d. [a][b][d][e]; Berlin, n.d.). Environmental groups opposed to NAFTA defined victory in more formidable terms than did its supporters. To defeat NAFTA, opponents believed they had to convince Congress that the environmental provisions within the NAFTA Package would actually do more harm to environmental quality than no NAFTA at all. Yet because they believed that this message alone would not convince members to oppose the Agreement, their lobbying message adopted a more complicated theme. Opposition environmental groups tried to convince members that NAFTA's impact on democratic procedures would damage the environment. Instead, they urged Congress to defeat "this NAFTA" and negotiate a new, more broadly focused, trade agreement.

Perhaps because anti-NAFTA environmental groups felt they had a more difficult task than their pro-NAFTA counterparts, opponents adopted very strong rhetoric to deliver their message. NAFTA's anti-democratic theme was pursued by the Sierra Club's chairman, J. Michael McCloskey, during the 14 September press conference when he stated that NAFTA would lead to the "end of democracy in America." NAFTA opponents also associated the Agreement with environmental, health, and human safety issues on the border by linking trade liberalization to hepatitis and breast cancer (Public Citizen, n.d.).

But the strong rhetoric used by anti-NAFTA organizations made them vulnerable to political attacks by NAFTA supporters. McCloskey's attack on NAFTA prompted strong criticism of the Sierra Club by Congressmen Robert Matsui, Sam Gibbons, and Richard Armey during testimony by Sierra Club executive director, Carl Pope, before the House Subcommittee on Trade.[13] To imply support for trade liberalization was somehow undemocratic and was unacceptable for undecided members to consider. According to interviews with congressional staffers working for "undecided" members, the extreme scenarios suggested by anti-NAFTA groups actually undermined the more substantive criticisms of NAFTA offered by its opponents.

Anti-NAFTA groups may also have damaged their message through association with nationally recognized anti-NAFTA citizens. By the middle of 1993, Public Citizen's Ralph Nader; conservative Republican pundit Pat Buchanan; ex-California governor Jerry Brown; and Texas billionaire Ross Perot began to coordinate their attacks against NAFTA (*The New York Times*, 23 August 1993 and 16 September 1993; *USA Today*, 3 September 1993; *The Washington Post*, 5 September 1993, 19 October 1993, 7 November 1993). As these men became the most prominent spokespersons for anti-NAFTA interests, the credibility of the entire anti-NAFTA movement was increasingly associated with them. In particular, Perot became the *de facto* leader of the anti-NAFTA campaign, even though most interest groups opposed to the agreement had not selected him to act as their spokesperson.[14] Association with Perot meant access to his vast financial resources, but it also imposed political costs to be associated with his style and credibility. For many anti-NAFTA activists who hoped to use the debate to amplify their message to members who were home just prior to the NAFTA vote, Perot's disrespectful attitude toward Vice President Al Gore during a nationally televised debate heralded their defeat (*The Washington Post*, 20 August 1993, 13 September 1993, 15 September 1993; *Boston Globe*, 23 August 1993; *The Christian Science Monitor*, 16 September 1993).[15]

Good Cops and Bad Cops Institutionalized Group's Positions on Final NAFTA Package

The institutional factors discussed throughout the book—organizational philosophy toward trade, shared norms, and relationship ties between environmental groups and other trade policy elites—suggest that support or opposition may have been dictated long before the NAFTA negotiations were completed. Two years of playing "good cop–bad cop" roles actually predicated the final positions of national environmental organizations regarding NAFTA's environmental provisions and institutionalized the role played by certain environmental organizations.

Table 5.2 organizes four institutional traits along a continuum that characterizes eleven national environmental organizations. For the most part, environmental groups that acted as formal advisors to either the USTR or to President Bush supported the Agreement, while those that did not play a formal advisory role opposed NAFTA. Groups that had better relations with protrade policy elites tended to support NAFTA, while those who worked with anti-NAFTA trade policy elites opposed the Agreement. The informal norms that shaped attitudes shared within each group fostered both formal and informal avenues of access and influence, making it difficult to untrack organizations once they became part of one group or the other.

Four organizations deviated from the pattern of support and opposition suggested by these characterizations. Each case provides an interesting example of how institutional ties and historical events shape behavior.

Sierra Club

While national environmental organizations informally supported Clinton's presidential candidacy, the Sierra Club's nontax-exempt status enabled it to formally support Clinton's presidential campaign and contribute financial and human resources through its political action committee (author's personal notes). As discussed in Chapter 3, the relationship between Clinton and the Sierra Club resulted in a number of changes in the organization's behavior, including formal separation from membership in the Citizen's Trade Campaign and increased interaction with USTR officials. Therefore, the Club's opposition to the Agreement was the focus of considerable political attention on the part of Clinton officials. Prior to the September signing ceremony, State Department assistant secretary of state, Timothy Wirth; EPA administrator, Carol Browner; and Office of Management and Budget chairperson, Alice Rivlin, tried once again to convince Sierra Club leaders to change the organization's position on NAFTA (author's personal notes). Despite this pressure, officials felt that they had established a solid basis from which to evaluate NAFTA, and the final Agreement failed to meet minimum requirements (author's personal notes).

Despite new avenues of influence through stronger relationship ties with the Clinton administration, Sierra Club officials believed they were committed to defending the demands they made throughout negotiations. By the summer of 1993 they mobilized their grassroots members to oppose the agreement through individual lobbying efforts and in conjunction with the CTC and organized labor events. Officials

TABLE 5.2 Institutionalized Behavior of National Environmental Organizations

Organization	Position on NAFTA	Trade Philosophy	Role as Advisor to Administration	Relations with Trade Policy Elites*
World Wildlife Fund	Supported	Endorsed growth-oriented trade policy	USTR	Pro-NAFTA congressional, administration, business elites
Environmental Defense Fund	Supported	Endorsed growth-oriented trade policy	Council of Environmental Quality	Pro-NAFTA business, administration, congressional elites
National Wildlife Federation	Supported	Endorsed growth-oriented trade policy	USTR	Protrade business, congressional, administration elites
The Nature Conservancy	Took no position on NAFTA	Accepted growth-oriented trade policy	USTR	Was not an active participant
Natural Resources Defense Council	Supported	Accepted growth-oriented trade policy	USTR	Pro- and anti-NAFTA congressional, business, administration elites
National Audubon Society	Supported	Accepted growth-oriented trade policy	USTR	Pro-NAFTA congressional, administration, business elites
Defenders of Wildlife	Took no position on NAFTA	Accepted growth-oriented trade policy	None	Pro-NAFTA congressional, administration, business elites
Sierra Club	Opposed	Opposed growth-oriented trade policy	None	Anti-NAFTA congressional elites; Clinton administration
Friends of the Earth	Opposed	Opposed growth-oriented trade policy	None	Anti-NAFTA congressional, labor elites, anti-NAFTA grassroots coalition
Public Citizen	Opposed	Opposed growth-oriented trade policy	None	Anti-NAFTA congressional, labor elites; anti-NAFTA grassroots coalition
Greenpeace	Opposed	Opposed growth-oriented trade policy	None	Anti-NAFTA grassroots coalition

More Accommodating

More Adversarial

*For additional information describing these relationships please refer to the Appendix.

believed that to withdraw from their position on NAFTA was considered backing away from a principled position on trade policy. Whether principles were driving their position or not, consistent hostility toward growth-based trade policy, relationships with other anti-NAFTA organizations, and participation in significant events that challenged the administration's trade policy agenda made it difficult for the Sierra Club to change its course despite numerous requests from the administration.

NRDC

Perhaps more than any other organization, NRDC staff contributed substantive recommendations and critical comments regarding the scope and direction of negotiations. Based upon their own interpretation of the environmental provisions negotiated by President Bush, NRDC staff felt compelled to oppose the September 1992 Agreement but were committed to devoting time and resources to craft alternatives that would meet their environmental demands. With Clinton's election as president, NRDC staff redoubled their efforts, taking great care to avoid negative public and private statements concerning the Agreement. Their willingness to cooperate with both administrations yet remain steadfast in their criticisms of specific aspects of the Agreement enabled them to remain part of negotiations up to the completion of negotiations. As evidence of their steadfast participation, USTR ambassador Kantor directly responded to their specific concerns regarding "sound science" and "risk/benefit analysis" language in the Agreement, a response which eventually became part of the administration's Letter of Administrative Intent (Kantor, 93b).[16]

Avoiding formal associations with anti-NAFTA coalitions, and remaining steadfast in their commitment to produce an environmentally acceptable trade agreement, NRDC was compelled to support the final Agreement. To endorse the Agreement, Washington, D.C., staff overcame internal differences of opinion between themselves and some board members.[17] Given the level of influence exerted over the technical components of the Agreement, it is clear that NRDC's own reputation was greatly invested in NAFTA.

Defenders of Wildlife and The Nature Conservancy

Two organizations—Defenders of Wildlife and The Nature Conservancy—did not take a formal position on the NAFTA Package. In part, they were able to avoid doing so because they did not have as much invested in the NAFTA process itself. While formally appointed the Conservancy was never actively involved as an advisor to the USTR, and board members discouraged staff attorneys from engaging in the potentially damaging political debate surrounding the last months of NAFTA. In exchange for a commitment to seek funds for securing environmentally sensitive land along the Mexico-U.S. border, the Conservancy agreed to sign the 8 May 1993 letter organized by Ken Berlin for WWF. However, following the split between environmental organizations and no specific commitment by Mexico and the United States regarding their request for targeted resources, they decided not to publish any position on the final NAFTA (Snape, 94). Defenders was philosophically predisposed to accept growth-oriented trade policy, but staff attorneys were concerned about NAFTA's impact on wildlife laws and its inability to address production process issues. NAFTA's failure to address these issues led staff to recommend opposition. However, many members of its board were supportive of the final NAFTA Package; led by board member Ken Berlin, who negotiated the May 1993 compromise for WWF, they urged the organization to endorse the final Agreement. Their inability to resolve the internal conflicts resulted in no position on NAFTA. Both Defenders and the Conservancy were able to avoid stating a final position on the Agreement, in part, because they did not have long track records of participating in political events or associations with other pro- and anti-NAFTA organizations.

Conservation International

Finally, one other organization not active during negotiations offered their support for the Agreement in September. Based in Washington, D.C., Conservation International (CI) is a medium-sized environmental organization with no real "constituency" other than its staff, board members, and contributors. Dedicated to scientific understanding of environmental matters, it devotes most of its time to national and international environmental projects, some of which involve Mexico's environmentally sensitive rain forests and desert ecosystems (Conservation International, 93). CI had not actively participated in negotiations but had maintained lines of information and communication open between themselves and representatives from WWF, NWF, EDF, and the Sierra Club. They were worried that Mexican President Carlos Salinas was being wrongly criticized by anti-NAFTA environmental organizations. Their own projects in Mexican environmental initiatives lead them to believe that Salinas and the Mexican government were committed to both economic growth and environmental preservation. When asked by Clinton administration officials to support the final NAFTA Package, they felt they were adequately knowledgeable of the issues to support NAFTA. Relations with Mexican officials and sustained contact with pro-NAFTA environmental organizations justified their support for an Agreement they personally invested neither time nor energy to develop.

The values inherent in each organization, the historical roles each played during NAFTA negotiations, plus their individual formal and informal relations with other trade policy elites hard-wired some organizations to support and others to oppose the NAFTA Package. It is impossible to tell which factor had the greatest impact on their positions on NAFTA; had the Bush administration included Sierra Club officials in their negotiations, it seems doubtful that they would have endorsed the final Agreement without some change in their organizational philosophy toward trade policy. Nonetheless, taken together, institutional issues apparently played an important part in determining the final support or opposition.

Early victories on environmental issues, two years of history behind their lobbying positions, conflicting messages, and extreme lobbying tactics helped to neutralize environmental issues for members of Congress as they prepared to vote on NAFTA. Adopting a position on NAFTA that knowingly put a member at odds with his or her constituency, and which was not fundamental to the Agreement's success or failure, was political suicide. The choice for most members was to steer clear of the environment and focus on more traditional trade-related issues.

ENVIRONMENTAL ISSUES WERE NOT IMPORTANT TO NAFTA'S OUTCOME

We have seen that environmental issues may not have been relevant to the outcome of Fast Track. We have also seen that both pro- and anti-NAFTA trade policy elites used environmental issues as a foil to obscure other objectives. A similar theme of strategic use of the environment also runs through events occurring during the voting stage. As discussed earlier, both Congressional supporters and opponents of NAFTA cited the environment in defense of their positions, despite limited interest or historical support for environmental issues. More importantly, the political entrepreneurs opposed to NAFTA— Richard Gephardt, David Bonior, and Marcy Kaptur—made no references to the environment in their floor speeches against NAFTA. Instead they focused on job loss in the United States, corruption in Mexico, and the loss of congressional authority over the formation of domestic policy. Pro-NAFTA entrepreneurs like Robert Matsui and Bill Richardson extolled NAFTA's environmental provisions, and interviews with their staff confirm their commitment to environmentally sensitive trade. But when their staff was asked whether the absence of effective environmental components would have prevented them from supporting the Agreement, staff from both offices indicated they could not answer. Perhaps more telling than these interviews was the behavior of Congressmen Wyden and Gephardt.

According to members of Wyden's staff working on trade policy, Wyden considered environmental issues an effective issue to criticize President Bush's trade policy yet remain a supporter of trade liberalization. When the Democrats won the presidential election, Wyden no longer needed an issue to attack the president. Instead of continued efforts to press for stronger environmental provisions in the Agreement, he shifted his position toward outright endorsement of NAFTA as early as January 1993. Wyden argued that NAFTA could not be defeated and that environmental organizations would have to be content with the gains they made in negotiations.

Because of his long-standing concern for environmental issues in NAFTA, Wyden should have become a spokesperson on behalf NAFTA's environmental provisions during the final months of negotiations. However, following his stated support for Clinton's supplemental negotiations approach in January 1993, Wyden expressed little public interest in environmental issues in 1993. In part, his limited interest can be explained because he believed NAFTA's environmental provisions were enough to justify support for the final Agreement; in meetings with the author, Wyden argued that environmental organizations had gotten all they could expect and should not risk losing their gains by opposing the Agreement.[18] His absence from the public debate, however, is better explained because of the opposition he faced in his home district. Oregon was among the most organized of the Fair Trade Campaign regions, and FTC members pressured Wyden to reconsider his position on NAFTA. Despite the prominence Wyden brought to environmental issues in trade policy, he did not mention them as part of his floor speech when NAFTA was passed in November.

Gephardt had also made environmental issues part of his conditions for supporting NAFTA. In each of his formal speeches on trade policy, he included some concern for the environment. However, his floor speech on NAFTA did not include any references to the environment; instead, he focused on NAFTA's impact on jobs in the United States. When staff members were asked why the environment was absent, their response was that the differences of opinion over NAFTA's environmental provisions made it politically difficult to mention the environment.

While environmental issues were an important component of the pre-August strategies surrounding NAFTA, they were not significant to the post-August strategies. By the end of August, NAFTA task force chief, William Daley, had decided that the administration should stop spending political resources trying to expand its list of environmental supporters beyond the core group of USTR trade advisors and instead focus their political energy on other issues that blocked NAFTA's passage (author's personal notes). During the final push to pass NAFTA, the administration initiated a high-profile campaign focused on the economic aspects of the Agreement. Launched by unprecedented support from every living president, the NAFTA team returned to traditional trade policy themes, emphasizing job creation and the political-economic implications of expanding regional trade (*The Washington Post*, 15 September, 18 September, 19 September, 19 October 1993; *The New York Times*, 15 September 1993; *USA Today*, 15 September, 17 September 1993).

House Majority Whip David Bonior's staff was responsible for organizing NAFTA opposition. While they were comfortable with attacking NAFTA on labor grounds, they were uncertain how to address environmental issues in October and November. Divisions within the environmental community over NAFTA made it difficult for members of Congress to approach environmental issues without fear of criticism from either the pro- or anti-NAFTA environmental groups.

Congress Rejects Linkages between Trade and Environment after NAFTA

But perhaps the most important indication of the strategic nature of environmental issues during NAFTA can be seen by reviewing congressional action on environment and trade after NAFTA was passed. USTR officials hoped to extend the environmental progress made in NAFTA into other trade agreements considered by the administration (Kantor, 94). Working with representatives from WWF, NWF, EDF, NAS, FoE, and the Sierra Club, they included environmental issues as part of their request for Fast Track reauthorization and in the completion of the Uruguay Round of GATT. Environmental organizations accepted the fact that major revisions in the Round were not possible; instead, they offered to accept an agreement that committed member nations to future discussions and to declare a moratorium on trade disputes involving environmental regulations.[19] While Kantor rejected such a moratorium, he agreed to establish permanent linkages between trade and environment in future negotiations by establishing a committee to study trade and the environment within the World Trade Organization and to make environmental issues a permanent component of all Fast Track negotiations. But the responses to environmental demands to further the linkages between trade and the environment alarmed business interests and Republicans in Congress. Senator

John Danforth (R-MO) wrote the president opposing such linkages and threatening to vote against the Round's passage if the linkages were a part of its implementing legislation (Danforth, 94). Pressure from Danforth, from House Minority Whip Newt Gingrich (R-GA), and from business coalitions such as the Business Roundtable, the U.S. Council for International Business, and the American Chamber of Commerce compelled the administration to remove the language from GATT's implementing legislation in July.[20] Environmental organizations ultimately opposed the passage of the Round, but their lobbying efforts could not convince members of the importance of environmental issues in the passage of the Round.

The New Republican Congress further decoupled any linkages forged between trade and environmental goals in December 1994. Republican Speaker of the House-elect Gingrich stated in a letter to Ambassador Kantor that

> ... the lack of consensus on the relationship between trade agreements and labor and environmental issues has frustrated efforts to embark on new market-opening negotiations. We believe that this hurdle can be overcome by limiting fast-track authority to trade legislation, excluding changes to domestic labor or environmental laws in trade bills, and abandoning any use of trade sanctions tied to labor or environmental objectives. The economic benefits resulting from comprehensive trade disciplines and market reforms will prove to be a tremendous boon to both environmental protection and working conditions (Gingrich et al., 94b).

Whether environmental issues were neutralized during the voting stage, or whether environmental issues were never considered fundamental to voting decisions of members of Congress, the lack of concern for environmental issues during the voting stage reveals that most of the political leverage enjoyed by environmental organizations came from their ability to create and sustain a credible threat to NAFTA's passage. Endorsement of NAFTA by the majority of national environmental organizations neutralized any threat posed by environmental opponents to the Agreement because such endorsement gave the administration, members of Congress, and other protrade policy elites solid support for their defense of NAFTA on environmental grounds. Extreme rhetoric and unholy alliances between anti-NAFTA environmental groups and other anti-NAFTA trade policy elites such as Ross Perot and Patrick Buchanan made alliances between undecided members and anti-NAFTA environmental groups difficult because of the anticipated political costs associated with membership in "protectionist" coalitions. Pro-NAFTA environmental groups were well within the mainstream of NAFTA's popular debate by offering support for trade policy that was both "protrade" and "proenvironment," a winning policy position for the majority of members of Congress who held concerns for the environment.

ENDNOTES

1. H.R. 3450, A Bill To Implement the North American Free Trade Agreement. There was no real concern that the Senate would defeat NAFTA. Seven days later, the Senate passed S. 1627.

2. 308 of the 434 members who cast a vote on H.R. 3450, A Bill To Implement the North American Free Trade Agreement, gave statements in defense of their positions. All references to the floor debates are based upon information provided in the *Congressional Record*, 22 November 1993.

3. "Environmental supporters" based upon voting record evaluations done by The League of Conservation Voters, 1992 Scorecard. Overall scores of more than 75 percent were considered "strong supporters of environmental policy."

4. Evaluation based on AFL-CIO, *How They Voted, 1992*.

5. See floor speeches by Richard Gephardt (D-MO), David Bonior (D-MI), Marcy Kaptur (D-OH), and Duncan Hunter (R-CA).

6. Chapter 4 includes a table with a complete breakdown on newsprint coverage of environmental issues during NAFTA.

7. Conclusion drawn from interviews with congressional staff working for both pro- and anti-NAFTA members of the House of Representatives (1994). For a more theoretical argument, see Arnold, 90.

8. List of House members was compiled from documents obtained from environmental groups during NAFTA's voting stage. In particular, see WWF, 1993c, Citizen's Trade Campaign 93a.

9. The White House signing ceremony was attended by Jay Hair, NWF; Katheryn Fuller, WWF; John Adams, NRDC; and Peter Krupp, EDF, 14 September 1993.

10. NRDC was not satisfied with the language regarding sanitary and phytosanitary and technical barriers, particularly surrounding the terms "sound science" and the use of economic cost-benefit analysis. Ambassador Kantor resolved these differences in a letter to NRDC executive director, John Adams, the content of which was also a part of the Letter of Administrative Intent from the administration. See Kantor, 93b.

11. Among the concessions made by the Clinton administration to gain support from undecided members: military purchases (*The Journal of Commerce*, 8 November 1993); the location of a research study center in Texas (NAFTA text, vol. 1, Sec. 219); bridges built in Texas (*Houston Post*, 1993); reduction of proposed increase of tobacco tax to pay for health care (*The Washington Times*, 1993); airline routes to Mexico to benefit tobacco states (*The Wall Street Journal*, 1993); accelerated tariff reduction on Maytag products for the Iowa delegation

(*Iowa Filibuster*, 14 November 1993); changes to the tariff schedule to reduce the impact of competition with Mexican produce on the Florida sugar and citrus industries (*The London Financial Times*, 1993; *The Washington Post*, 14 November 1983; *The New York Times*, 28 October 1993).

12. Conclusions drawn here based upon author's interviews with representatives of each environmental organization actively involved in NAFTA, plus staff of key members of Congress involved in trade negotiations (1994).

13. During the hearing, Thomas, Matsui, and Gibbons launched an aggressive challenge to the anti-NAFTA argument. According to Mr. Gibbons, "You are against it, you are dreaming, I have forgotten about you, you are irrelevant, I have written you off" (House Committee on Ways and Means, 93d)

14. One exception was a press release by Friends of the Earth, stating that Ross Perot did not act as a spokesperson for the organization or for their issues (Friends of the Earth, 1993c).

15. With the exception of Public Citizen, none of the national interest groups opposed to NAFTA were supportive of the role played by Perot as the leader of the NAFTA opposition. Public Citizen staff briefed Perot on positions related to NAFTA and helped prepare him for the debate against Vice President Gore (Wallach, 1994).

16. The *Letter of Administrative Intent* is part of the President's formal presentation of NAFTA to Congress.

17. Jack Sheehan, President of the United Auto Workers, is a member of NRDC's board and an opponent of NAFTA. NRDC's San Francisco Office was opposed to the agreement, but its staff in Washington, D.C., who had invested their own time and energy into negotiations, were convinced that the environmental provisions were adequate to support (Ward, 1994).

18. Author's personal notes 1993. Wyden indicated that, although he felt strong ties to the Sierra Club, there was a need to "agree to disagree" and go on to other issues.

19. Letter from eighty-one members of the House of Representatives to Ambassador Mickey Kantor, as published in *Inside U.S. Trade*, 2/18/94.

20. "It is not appropriate to use fast track procedures for legislation approving unlimited environmental and labor goals" (Gingrich, Richard Armey [R-TX], and David Drier [R-CA], 94).

6

Institutionalizing Environmental Interests in NAFTA

Three years of political pressure from national and local environmental organizations forced changes to the existing U.S. trade regime to incorporate environmental interests into the trade policy agenda. New rules and procedures for making trade policy, permanent advisory positions for environmental representatives, and language in the text of the Agreement itself institutionalized the role environmental interests would now play in trade policy. This chapter describes both the formal and informal components that characterize this new environmental role and provides a brief summation of environmental organizations' response.

Although the focus of this study has been on the scope of U.S. trade policy, the linkages between trade rules and environmental protection forged in NAFTA extend beyond the U.S. Linkages that can trace their roots back to the NAFTA debate can be found in the new environmental provisions of the World Trade Organization (WTO), the policy dialogue at the Organization for Economic Cooperation and Development (OECD), and other regional policies designed to liberalize trade. While it is not the purpose of this project to explore the environmental implications of all of these institutions, it is important to discuss them briefly to capture a sense of the broader implications of the trade and environment nexus forged by NAFTA.

NAFTA PACKAGE

The environmental provisions of the "NAFTA Package," passed by Congress and signed into law by President William J. Clinton in January 1994, are divided into three parts: the administration's Letter of Administrative Action, the NAFTA Agreement, and the Supplemental Agreement on the Environment. Together, this package of environmental provisions represents an unprecedented inclusion of environmental issues in U.S. trade policy.

112

TABLE 6.1 Reforms to Trade Policy Regime Resulting from NAFTA

NAFTA Package	USTR	Environmental Protection Agency
NAFTA Agreement *Commitment to sustainable development *Sensitivity to some domestic and international environmental laws *Investment language discourages weak laws *Disputes require challenging party to prove strength of their case **North American Agreement on Environmental Cooperation (NAAEC)** *Commission on Environmental Cooperation (CEC) *Joint Policy Advisory Committee (JPAC) *Independent dispute mechanism *Financial penalties for persistent pattern of nonenforcement *Promotes transparency **Bilateral Mexico-U.S.** *Border Environmental Cooperation Commission *North American Development Bank (NADBANK)	*Permanent representatives on USTR Advisory Committee for Trade Policy and Negotiations (ACTPN) *Trade and Environment Policy Advisory Committee (TEPAC) —Includes thirty-five advisors —Coordinated with EPA *Office of Environment and Natural Resources *Expand interagency advisory process includes EPA *NAFTA Report on Environmental Issues	*NAFTA Task Force *BECC Staff *Implementation of IBEP *Create National Advisory Committee (NAC) including two environmental advisors *International Programs Division *Office of Policy Planning and Evaluation —Permanent member of Interagency Advisory team for trade policy. —Ongoing trade and environment work at OECD, WTO, and other international forums.

The Letter of Administrative Action

The Letter of Administrative Action serves two purposes. First, it articulates NAFTA's terms and identifies the changes to national laws considered by the administration to be inconsistent with the terms of the Agreement. Second, the Letter is used by the administration to stipulate the goals for negotiations and to clarify the position of the U.S. negotiators on difficult or unresolved issues left over from negotiations. One of the areas where issues were unresolved involved the legal status of the Supplemental Agreement. Since it was not negotiated under congressional "Fast Track" authority, and it was not voted on simultaneously by either the Canadian or Mexican governments, environmental groups expressed concern that environmental provisions included in the Supplemental Agreement and meant to address specific problems with the NAFTA text lacked the legal authority to withstand challenges by other NAFTA Parties. The Clinton administration used the Letter to stipulate that both NAFTA and the Supplemental Agreement have the same status in U.S. law (NAFTA, 93).[1] Environmental groups were also concerned about NAFTA's direct implications for landmark environmental laws that may have implications for trade. The Letter grandfathered twenty-one environmental laws—including the Clean Air Act; the Federal Insecticide, Fungicide, and Rodenticide Act; the Comprehensive Environmental Response, Compensation, and Liability Act; and the Superfund Amendments and Reauthorization Act—in an effort to overcome these concerns (NAFTA). Finally, the administration clarified the meaning of controversial terms that alarmed environmental groups throughout negotiations. Terms such as "risk assessment" and "scientific principles" were defined in such a way as to minimize the potential for conflict between environmental laws and NAFTA trade principles by emphasizing that, "The NAFTA provisions are designed to preserve the ability of governments, which include state and local government, to act in this area while guarding against the unjustified use of these types of measures as a way to protect domestic industry" (NAFTA, Chapter 7[B]).

While politically important in the United States, the Letter has questionable effects on other NAFTA Parties. Neither Canada nor Mexico, nor the new institutions created by NAFTA, are bound to recognize the clarifications to language or jurisdiction stipulated in the Letter. For example, virtually every Chapter in NAFTA defines terms used therein, definitions agreed upon by the other NAFTA Parties. Clarifications to these terms, such as those introduced by Ambassador Kantor to clarify the U.S. position on sanitary and phytosanitary laws, have no bearing on the Canadian or Mexican use of those provisions. Therefore, grandfathered environmental laws may still be challenged by NAFTA

Parties if Parties believe them to be inconsistent with the terms of the Agreement. What it does do, however, is put the administration on record that their intention is to use these definitions as their guidelines for interpreting NAFTA and to resist any effort to modify the grandfathered laws under the auspices of the NAFTA. The Letter does very little to establish any legal relationship between NAFTA and the Supplemental Agreement. Concerns about provincial authority over environmental laws has been cited as one of the principal reasons that only one Canadian province has ratified the Supplemental Agreement as of this date.[2] The Supplemental Agreement remains a text negotiated in addition to the principal document, and inconsistencies between the two documents would be resolved through future negotiations among Parties, either informally or formally through the dispute resolution processes.

NAFTA Text

The heart of the formal relationship between trade and the environment is found in the NAFTA text. It begins with the Preamble, where Parties agree to "PROMOTE Sustainable Development," and "STRENGTHEN the development and enforcement of environmental laws and regulations" by expanding their economies in a manner "... consistent with environmental protection and conservation" (NAFTA). While the Preamble carries no obligation on the part of Contracting Parties, it does reflect increased sensitivity to the complex relationships between both policy domains. The level of sensitivity suggested by the language in the Preamble is uncertain, however. For example, Article 102, NAFTA Objectives, is binding; while it makes specific references to the principles of expanded trade and trade barrier elimination, it does not reiterate the importance of environmental quality or of developing the economy in an ecologically sustainable fashion. Instead, the NAFTA Objectives section establishes a pattern between trade rules and environmental goals which requires countries to prove that the goals and procedures embodied in national environmental laws are not inconsistent with the terms of the Agreement. A number of examples taken from the text will help illustrate.

In a limited fashion, NAFTA recognizes that some international environmental agreements (IEAs) can and do legitimately use trade measures. The trade restrictions in three existing IEAs—the Convention on International Trade in Endangered Species of Wild Fauna and Flora (CITES), the Montreal Protocol on Substances that Deplete the Ozone Layer (Montreal Protocol), and the Basel Convention on the Control of Transboundary Movements of Hazardous Wastes and Their Disposal (Basel Convention)—are recognized by NAFTA Parties as legitimate constraints on trade.[3] Recognizing the right of sovereign nations to establish and enforce environmental laws and regulations that use trade restrictions was an important issue to environmental organizations engaged in the NAFTA debate. To that degree, formal recognition of the trade provisions contained in these IEAs is an important shift in the normative principle of unrestricted trade liberalization. However, the nature of this recognition is framed within the procedural rules of trade liberalization. First, relying upon international consensus as a guide to restricting national behavior is consistent with the consensus principles discussed in Chapter 1. Under other circumstances NAFTA Parties had already agreed to the trade constraints found in these agreements. Trade constraints in any additional multilateral environmental agreements (MEAs) recognized by NAFTA would require agreement by all of its Parties, a task that complicates the already difficult task of national MEA ratification by institutionalizing trading partner pressure on Congress. Second, any restrictions on trade applied within the guidelines of these IEAs must be done in a manner that is "least inconsistent" with the terms of the Agreement (Article 104.1). At this point, the term "least inconsistent" lacks its own legal history, leaving the interpretation of the term to future trade disputes resolved under NAFTA's dispute process.[4] Again, MEAs whose enforcement requires some component of national legislation (which almost all do) will again face both domestic and international political pressure, given greater weight by the terms of the Agreement. In essence, NAFTA rules impose upon national environmental law the assumption that trade liberalization, under all circumstances, is optimal, then requires governments to prove that environmental regulations that do compromise trade are consistent with the terms stipulated in the Agreement.

A relationship between environmental laws and trade rules that requires other international consensus or evidence that the policy tool can be shown to be least inconsistent with trade principles requires national environmental laws challenged under the Agreement to defend themselves using normative guidelines not usually associated with their legitimization. For example, NAFTA recognizes that local, state, and federal governments have the right to set appropriate levels of environmental protection in the areas of food safety and product standards.[5] Yet while governments retain the authority to set and implement food safety and product standards law, their efforts may be challenged by trading partners if they feel such standards negatively impact trade. To avoid challenge, national standards must meet NAFTA's exceptions test. First, Parties are required to use international standards for food safety and technical standards to avoid inconsistencies between national policies (Articles 713 and 905). If no such standard exists, or if a national or local government wishes to set a higher standard for protection, the standard must survive scrutiny under NAFTA's risk assessment and sound science criteria (Articles 715 and 907). The risk assessment procedure requires NAFTA Parties to take into account a wide variety of factors, including those adopted by national standard-setting bodies, relevant scientific testing methods, and the loss of production or sales that may result from the pest or disease (Article 715.1[a–g] and 715.2[a–c]; Article 907.1[a–d] and 907.2[a–c]). In each instance, Parties must conduct themselves in a manner that "minimize(s) the trade effects" of taking such actions (Article 715.3), and must assume that differing standards among NAFTA Parties are "equivalent" to their own (Articles 714 and 906).

A number of questions are raised by the language found in NAFTA's sanitary and phytosanitary and technical barriers discussion. First, to what degree will existing environmental provisions be challenged by NAFTA conditions for legitimate constraints on the policy tools used for environmental protection? To date, no one has explored this question, but the revisions to the Marine Mammal Protection Act (MMPA) under the authority of the GATT offer some indication. Political pressure generated by trading partners in opposition to the "dolphin-safe" tuna provisions of the MMPA resulted in attempts by Congress to reconcile these differences to make the provisions "GATT-consistent."[6] The first attempt to reconcile these differences was rejected by the countries who brought the case to GATT, resulting in a second dispute filed against the U.S. government. As of this writing, efforts are under way in Congress to modify the MMPA to conform to international trade principles.[7]

Another related question is, will there be laws that are not promulgated because they appear to be "trade inconsistent"? Answering this question is more difficult than the first because any answer would rely upon an analysis of political innuendo and unconfirmed reporting about what did *not* occur. At this time, there is no evidence to suggest that proposals to environmental laws are in some way constrained by the provisions for legitimate trade restrictions imposed by NAFTA. However, the net effect of trade jurisprudence's influence on environmental policy is twofold. First, if challenged under trade rules, environmental regulations must justify themselves using criteria not normally associated with environmental protection. These new criteria compel legislators to consider a more limited range of policy tools to implement environmental goals, tools that do not restrict trade liberalization between countries. These criteria also encourage national legislators to use newly emerging international standards for environmental protection, such as the ISO 14000 Environmental Management Series, as guidelines for the scope and tools used in national environmental policies (Audley, 96). If national standards are consistent with internationally recognized guidelines for environmental protection, then no conflict between trade and the environment exists. But if a national standard is higher than international guidelines, or if guidelines do not exist, then the assumption is that any constraint to trade created by national environmental regulations is "guilty" until proven innocent under the provisions of the Agreement itself. Second, the language negotiated into the Agreement, designed to mitigate environmental concerns in this area, will remain ambiguous until an adequate body of legal decisions establishes precedent for future decisions.

While NAFTA's formal interaction with environmental laws is shaped by the norms and rules of trade policy, it departs from trade procedures in the area of dispute settlement. In the event of a dispute between NAFTA Parties involving environmental laws, the burden of proving alleged violations lies with the Challenging Party (NAFTA, 2005[3]). If a NAFTA Party wishes to avoid the GATT/WTO dispute procedures, in the event that the dispute falls under the jurisdiction of either Agreement, the Responding Party may select which venue they feel is most appropriate for their defense. This shift in the burden of proof is directly related to environmental organizations' concerns related to the dispute settlement process. Disputes involving environmental laws taught environmental groups to both fear the "guilty until proved innocent" assumption used in GATT/WTO proceedings and resist the practice of relying solely on "trade experts" as dispute panelists. While NAFTA did not alter the practice of using trade experts as panelists, panel members may now call upon experts from the environmental community to provide them information relevant to the case.

Finally, NAFTA takes the first step toward establishing guidelines for environmentally responsible business investment. Negotiators rejected environmentalists' demands for investment criteria that encouraged the use of environmentally appropriate technologies, and instead negotiated language that discourages industries from taking advantage of governments who have difficulty establishing and maintaining strict environmental standards. NAFTA Parties agree that "it is inappropriate to encourage investment by relaxing domestic health, safety, or environmental measures . . . a Party should not waive or otherwise derogate from . . . such measures as an encouragement . . . of an investment or investor" (NAFTA, 1114[2]). If such a finding occurs, Parties are remanded to discuss their differences of opinion with the goal of preventing a repeat of such occurrences. While language discouraging governments from attracting businesses by creating a less onerous regulatory environment fell considerably short of environmental demands for responsible business behavior, the language contained in this section becomes an important standard used by environmental groups to encourage the adoption of similar provisions in other trade agreements such as the Uruguay Round of GATT and the Asia-Pacific Economic Cooperation (APEC).

By remaining consistent with the precedent established by other trade agreements, NAFTA framed the intersection between trade and environmental policies using norms, rules, and procedures consistent with contemporary efforts to liberalize trade. Some changes were made in the rules to recognize the legitimacy of environmental protection efforts, but these efforts must either be consistent with internationally recognized standards or meet NAFTA guidelines for acceptable constraints to trade. The dispute process shifts the burden of proving a NAFTA violation to the challenger, but the tests used to determine whether a violation exists were themselves written from the perspective that trade liberalization is the accepted principle; obstacles to trade must be eliminated.

The Supplemental Agreement

The NAFTA Agreement described above was inherited by the Clinton administration under conditions that made it politically impossible to scrap and restart negotiations. With only the public support of the NWF for its environmental provisions, the administration sought the support of the balance of the environmental community by using the Supplemental Agreement to fulfill Clinton's October 1992 campaign promise to increase the level of environmental and labor protection in the NAFTA Package. The North American Agreement on Environmental Cooperation (NAAEC) commits Parties to foster protection and improvement of the environment, promote sustainable development based upon cooperation and mutual support, avoid creating trade distorting barriers, promote procedural transparency and public participation in the development and implementation of environmental laws, and promote pollution prevention policies and practices (Article 1[a–j]). To achieve these objectives, each Party commits to periodical publication of reports on the state of their environment, develops environmental emergency programs, promotes education in environmental matters, and promotes the use of economic instruments for the efficient achievement of environmental goals (Article 2.1[a–f]).

NAAEC establishes the Commission for Environmental Cooperation (CEC), composed of three distinct components. The Council oversees a permanent Secretariat who is charged with implementing NAAEC. The Council is chaired by the environmental ministers from each NAFTA Party, while the Secretariat is headed by an independent executive director. This structure was meant to balance environmentalists' desire to give the Secretariat as much independence from political pressures as possible with pressure from governments to keep the Secretariat responsive to their demands. While the executive director is selected by the Council to serve one or two three-year terms, they are employed by the Secretariat and not by any NAFTA Party.

The Secretariat's duties are broadly defined. It must provide the Council with reports on issues of concern identified by its members, administer the daily activities of the CEC, and prepare its annual program and budget. To achieve this task in a manner consistent with its constituents' interests, it is advised by a fifteen-member Joint Public Advisory Committee (JPAC). The JPAC is comprised of five presidential appointments from each Contracting Party.[8] The JPAC is charged with providing information and advice regarding the establishment of priorities for NAAEC and with acting as a formal avenue for input from citizens in all three countries.

The record of the CEC's first three years of performance reflects that of a newly created trinational institution charged with an ambitious, yet ambiguous, set of political demands. The first two years were devoted to establishing procedures designed to help the Secretariat realize its objectives, what the CEC Secretariat, Victor Lichtenger, described as "mostly brainstorming and planning meetings" designed to prepare specific methodological papers, and in seeking a balance of public interests in its daily activities (CEC Annual Program Budget, 1995 and 1996). The 1996 work plan outlined in the annual budget reflects a more serious attempt to address the substantive issues pertaining to the trade and environment intersection. Early published reports helped to establish a baseline of information available to measure NAFTA's effects on the environment and provide information to the public.[9] In 1996 the CEC initiated a project designed to evaluate these effects on North American environmental quality. A research team comprised of academics, businesspeople, and activists began a project designed to assess the current state of knowledge about NAFTA's existing and anticipated environmental effects. They identified main predictors, outcome variables, and preliminary patterns and developed criteria for measuring relevant economic and environmental variables to help forecast emerging relationships and identify linkages for further analysis (CEC, 96a). Finally, in an attempt to address continuing concerns raised by NGOs related to sustained participation in CEC activities, the Secretariat created the North American Environment Fund (NAEF) to provide means to support projects in Canada, Mexico, and the United States that address the CEC's work program (CEC, 96a). Grants totaling $2 million (Canadian), were awarded by August 1996 (CEC, 96a).

Formal analysis of performance of the CEC has not yet been conducted, but stakeholders involved in the process are of two opinions.[10] Most are generally supportive of the efforts made by the Secretariat to develop procedurally transparent decision-making processes and to address some of the broader trade and environment concerns as outlined in the Secretariat's annual budgets. At the same time environmental NGOs feel frustrated by the lack of concrete progress in reconciling trade and environment conflicts since the CEC began its work in 1994. An example from the discussions with the participants will help illustrate. Under Article 14, Factual Submission on Enforcement Matters, NGOs petition the CEC to take action or make recommendations to Contracting Parties for failing to meet their obligations to protect the national environment. Recommendations from NGOs were solicited by CEC officials to develop procedures for filing complaints against NAFTA Parties who shows a "consistent pattern" of failure to enforce their laws (CEC, 95). The outcomes of disputes resolved under Article 14 have not yet met with the satisfaction of environmental groups.

Four petitions have been filed with the CEC under Article 14. One petition (Mr. Aage Tottrup) was terminated because the petitioner had also taken action against the Canadian and Alberta governments. Two cases (Sierra Club on the "Salvage Rider" Provision of the Rescissions Act [P.L. 104-19] and Biodiversity Legal Foundation on the "Hutchinson Rider" [P.L. 104-6]) were dismissed because the petitioners asked the CEC to take action against a NAFTA Party for changing domestic environmental laws; CEC officials argued that there was no evidence to suggest the laws were modified to attract international investment, but rather the modification of existing laws was the result of national democratic processes. One case (the Cozumel case) resulted in a formal request for investigations into the activities of the Mexican government, a request reluctantly complied with by Mexico.[11]

The performance of the CEC operating under Article 14 disputes is indicative of two institutional aspects that threaten its future. First, CEC has very little jurisdiction over the content of national environmental policy. In the Tottrup, Sierra Club, and Biodiversity Legal Foundation cases, the CEC was asked to take action against a NAFTA Party beyond the interpretation of its mandate. Issues of national sovereignty complicate efforts by the Secretariat to become a tool to be used by environmental NGOs to act as a counterbalance to NAFTA's trade-oriented criteria for legitimate environmental regulations. The burden placed upon panelists—to determine a "consistent pattern of non-enforcement,"—makes the Article 14 dispute process more of an exercise in moral persuasion than punishment. The Cozumel case is an example of just such a kind of persuasion; CEC officials apparently hope that public knowledge of the poor implementation of existing laws will convince officials to act in a manner more consistent with those stipulated. Indeed, no one supportive of the Supplemental Agreement ever envisioned a strong enforcement mechanism to be a part of the Supplemental Agreement; now the Secretariat must adapt to the circumstances created by its own institutional form (NAAEC [5]).[12]

The other implication, stemming from the anecdotal evaluation of the CEC's performance, is political. CEC officials expressed concern over making too dramatic a decision at a time when their political support has not yet been firmly established. CEC officials are aware that they do not as yet have the broad support of legislators in any of the NAFTA countries. Fear that their actions may result in a reduction or elimination of their budgets compels officials to operate with a great deal of caution until they have established more solid relationships with political decision makers who have influence over their own institutional future.

The Border Environmental Cooperation Commission (BECC) was created in direct response to concerns expressed by NGOs over the effect expanding trade would have on the Mexico-U.S. border region. BECC is charged with coordinating regional, state, and local governments and local citizens in their efforts to develop and implement solutions to environmental problems.[13] It is comprised of a ten-person *Board of Directors* whose responsibility it is to make decisions over the environmental projects approved by BECC staff. The daily operations of the BECC are under the authority of the General and Deputy Assistant Manager, both appointed by the Board of Directors.[14] An eighteen-member Advisory Board made up of residents of the border region are integrated into the decision-making procedure to ensure that interests of state and local communities affected by BECC decisions are represented.

BECC's mandate is very narrow; officials work directly with local government, private organizations, and NGOs to develop solutions to environmental problems affecting communities within sixty-two miles of the international boundary. Much of their work involves assessing the technical and financial feasibility of proposed environmental projects and organizing, developing, and arranging public and private financing to help realize such projects. Preference is given to projects relating to the development and implementation of basic community infrastructure: wastewater treatment, pollution prevention, and solid waste management.

While its scope and regional impact are narrowly construed, the BECC's mandate shares the CEC's commitment to integrate public stakeholders into its daily operation. During their first year of operations, BECC officials worked with border residents to develop the Guidelines for Project Submission and for Certification Criteria (Criteria), circulating more than one thousand drafts of the guidelines and responding to comments made by more than 150 individuals and organizations (BECC, 96). Stage One is a preliminary proposal where general information is provided the BECC. Submissions are reviewed by the Board; those accepted are requested to submit detailed project proposals. Projects approved by the Board must meet rigorous requirements for location, relevance to environment and human health issues, and transboundary effects and must include an environmental impact evaluation. In addition, each proposal must provide evidence that communities affected by the proposed project were involved in its development. Routine meetings are held by BECC officials to provide citizens with the opportunity to offer comments on projects submitted for approval. In 1995 BECC received forty-six project proposals, the majority of which were submitted by Mexican border communities. Three projects were approved, all involving wastewater treatment or reuse.[15]

To realize its objectives BECC coordinates its activities with those previously existing binational institutions. The International Boundary and Water Commission (IBWC), a binational organization charged with maintaining groundwater quality in the border region, is involved in many of the BECC activities. The IBWC is operated under the auspices of the 1944 Treaty on International Boundary and Water and is, therefore, a component of the U.S. Department of State. To encourage interaction, two of BECC's Board members are officials with the IBWC. BECC must also coordinate its activities with the Environmental Protection Agency and SEDESOL, Mexico's environmental protection agency. As with the IBWC, BECC's Board of Directors includes the directors of both the EPA and SEDESOL.

To assist the BECC in its efforts to coordinate and implement environmental projects, the North American Development Bank (NADBANK) was created to act as the financial component of the binational accord. The primary purpose of the NADBANK is to assist in the funding of environmental infrastructure, emphasizing water treatment, waste management, and the supply of potable water.[16] NADBANK acts as an investment bank, organizing the financial needs of projects which have been approved by the BECC. NADBANK operates with capital provided by both the Mexican and U.S. governments. When fully capitalized, NADBANK will have $450 million in paid-in capital and $2.55 billion in callable capital.[17]

A review of BECC and NADBANK proceedings points out a number of issues. First, the BECC was much slower getting started than the CEC, prompting criticisms from those who were concerned that the bilateral agreement was more political window dressing than substantive policy (Costanza et al., 95). Board members were finally recommended in February 1995, with the full set of members and community advisors not resolved until the end of that year (BECC News, 95).

Conflicts over appointments and community participation point to the second issue; it appears that the BECC is struggling to realize its goal of blending public input with its desire to prioritize and fund environmentally related border projects. For example, the BECC developed a set of Project Criteria to help the board determine which projects submitted by border residents merit their support. Among other things the Criteria stipulate that any submission to the BECC must demonstrate the ability to repay loans and guarantees, use technology in a cost-effective and environmentally sensitive manner, and show evidence of public participation in the development of the proposal (BECC, 95, 96b). BECC recommendation of a project acts as a screen for loans considered by the NADBANK, but the same level of public input guaranteed by the BECC Project Criteria is not a part of the NADBANK decision-making process. Arguing that loan decisions require greater confidentiality, NADBANK officials developed lending procedures that restrict public access to limited public comments prior to a final loan decision (NADBANK, 95). Border residents were frustrated by what they perceived to be ineffective or restrictive loan-making procedures designed to block their ability to influence lending decisions (Gregory, 96; Kelly, 96). At this point it is difficult to determine whether their objections reflect a difference of opinion over organization or reflect more deeply rooted differences in the goals each has for the institution's future. One report recently released by the General Accounting Office indicated that the NADBANK has failed to realize its own mandate for improving the environmental infrastructure in the border region, hampered by inadequate scope, poor organizational structure, and a complex decision-making structure involving citizens, elected officials, and other agencies that often have competing interests (GAO, 96).

CHANGES AT USTR AND EPA

Beyond the changes to the nature of the U.S. trade regime created by the NAFTA Package, the Clinton administration authorized a number of other formal changes that reflect the institutionalization of environmental issues in trade policy. In the spring of 1993, the USTR created the Office of Environment and Natural Resources (ENR), formalizing their attention to environmental issues begun in 1991. The ENR has responsibility for coordinating environmental interests with all U.S. trade negotiations. The USTR also expanded participation by environmentalists as advisors to U.S. trade policy. Representatives from national environmental organizations now hold two positions on the permanent Advisory Committee on Trade Policy Negotiations (ACTPN).

The administration also relies on trade advice from environmental organizations participating in policy discussions surrounding NAFTA's Supplemental Agreements through two advisory organizations. The Trade and Environment Policy Committee (TEPAC) was created to provide advice to the U.S. Trade Representative on issues involving trade and the environment. Thirty-five CEOs and senior-level executives were appointed from industry, agriculture, consumer, and environmental groups (Office of the President, 94). Along with the JPAC, the National Advisory Committee (NAC) was created to advise the EPA on issues related to the implementation of the CEC and BECC. Working with the JPAC, the NAC sponsored a series of trinational hearings on guidelines for Article 14/15 submissions, which resulted in the adoption of the guidelines currently used by the CEC.[18]

Changes at the EPA also reflect the movement toward integrating trade and environmental policy. Under the Clinton Administration the EPA director acts as a permanent member of the Interagency Advisory Committee for Trade Policy. EPA was charged with operationalizing many of the components of NAFTA's Supplemental Agreements. Under the authority of the Office for Policy Planning and Evaluation (OPPE), a NAFTA team was organized to implement the Integrated Border Environmental Plan (IBEP) and coordinate EPA activities with both the CEC and the BECC. EPA officials rely upon the NAC to ensure environmental NGO input in their trade policy deliberations. The EPA's International Division continues to participate in trade policy discussions surrounding activities at the Organization for Economic Cooperation and Development (OECD), the World Trade Organization (WTO), and the Asian Pacific Economic Cooperation (APEC). The EPA also played an active role in the negotiations of the International Standards Organization, 14000 Environmental Management Series (ISO 14000) (Audley, unpublished). ISO 14000 represents one of the first attempts by private interests to negotiate and implement universal standards to environmental regulation (Cascio, 96). Designed to both reduce compliance costs and facilitate trade, the standards reflect the movement away from government regulation, command, and control toward less intrusive and more voluntary guidelines for environmental management (Audley, unpublished). EPA staff was active in the negotiations of the standards and in establishing guidelines for their implementation in the United States.

NAFTA FUELS INTERNATIONAL EFFORTS TO LINK TRADE AND ENVIRONMENT

While NAFTA was initially a North American policy issue, it had profound effects on other international trade regimes. This section offers a brief sketch of the "ripple effects" of the environmental debate within NAFTA.

WTO

The Uruguay Round of GATT did not include a mandate to address environmental issues (Esty, 94a). Environmental organizations opposed the final version of the Uruguay Round after they failed in their efforts to secure substantial changes to its language.[19] In response to concerns expressed by NGOs, GATT officials accepted a proposal offered by the GATT Subcommittee on Trade and the Environment to create a Committee on Trade and Environment (CTE) of the World Trade Organization. The CTE was made a permanent component of the WTO in January 1995.[20] The CTE embodies the formal recognition of the linkages between economic and environmental policies as reflected in the WTO's preambular commitment to protect the environment and promote sustainable development. The goal of the CTE is to "identify the relationship between trade measures and environmental measures in order to promote sustainable development and to make appropriate recommendations on whether modifications of the provisions of the multilateral trading system are required" (WTO, 94: 36). While focused on the relationship between trade rules and environmental protection, the Subcommittee's chief allegiance is to trade liberalization. As a trade organization, the WTO recognizes that its competency in the field of environmental protection is limited to trade and that any conflicts between these two policy domains would be resolved in a manner that ". . . upholds and safeguards the principles of the multilateral trading system" (WTO, 94: 36).

The preeminence of trade over the environment is embodied in the CTE implementation of its mandate. CTE's work was structured around ten items outlined in Annex I of the Marrakesh Ministerial Decision on Trade and the Environment. The report of the CTE to WTO Ministers prepared for the 1996 WTO meeting in Singapore concluded that WTO provisions were intended to balance a member's right to adopt or enforce measures in pursuit of important public policy objectives for the protection of their environment with the need to protect

other members from arbitrary or unjustifiable restrictions on trade
(WTO, 96: 6). While this effort to balance trade and environmental
goals was emphasized, the criteria for justified environmental policies
was written in accordance with trade principles: restrictions on unilateral action, the avoidance of trade measures as tools for environmental
protection, and greater consideration of trade disciplines when negotiating MEAs (WTO, 96 [Section II]).

Beyond the trade and environment dialogue taking place within the
Committee, most interactions between trade rules and environmental
protection occur in the form of trade disputes between WTO member
nations. Three cases, in particular, exemplify the concerns raised by
many environmental groups relative to the trade and environment
nexus. In all three instances, U.S. environmental laws were found to
be in violation of GATT/WTO equal treatment provisions (Article III)
and that the discriminatory nature of the laws was inconsistent with
Article XX guidelines for acceptable constraints to trade (Charnovitz,
94a, 94b, 96). See Table 6.2. The impact of these decisions on policy
makers is not lost; according to UNEP executive director, Elizabeth
Dowdeswell, ". . . national governments are finding that when playing
by liberal trade rules, their autonomy is increasingly constrained by
what amounts to a principle of non-interference in the sovereignty of
the marketplace" (Charnovitz, 96: 191).

OECD

Of particular importance to the trade and environment debate was
a process begun at the OECD in September 1991. Joint meetings between the Trade Committee and the Environment Committee resulted

---

TABLE 6.2   Multilateral Trade Disputes Involving Environmental Regulations

Case	Brought By	Affected U.S. Law	Decision Date/Venue
Standards for Reformulated and Conventional Gasoline	Venezuela and Brazil	Clean Air Act	1/17/96 (WTO)
Taxes on Automobiles	European Union	Corporate Average Fuel Economy of Clean Air Act	9/30/94 (GATT)
Restriction on Imports of Tuna	European Union and Netherlands	Marine Mammal Protection Act	5/20/94 (GATT)

in a set of guidelines meant to improve the mutual compatibility of trade and environmental policies (OECD, 93). OECD experts recommended five procedural guidelines to govern future dialogue: transparency and consultation; trade and environmental examination, reviews, and followup; international environmental cooperation; and dispute settlement. Each of these guidelines is consistent with trade principles. For example, the OECD recommended that governments should "provide for transparency and for consultation when potential national policies may conflict with trade principles" (OECD, 93). In this sense, the term "transparency" is used in trade terms—transparent policies have no "hidden" nontariff trade implications. Environmental organizations urged the OECD to consider "transparent" proceedings—proceedings which allowed nongovernmental actors to participate in the discussions that shaped policy. Officials demurred, arguing that external influences would harm the open and frank nature of conversations held between officials (OECD, 93).

APEC

To help coordinate economic expansion in the Asia-Pacific theater, fifteen nations joined to form the Asia-Pacific Economic Cooperation (APEC).[21] Initiated in 1989, APEC provides a forum for discussion of a broad range of economic issues. APEC is headed by a permanent Secretariat located in Manila, Philippines.

Environmental concerns were first raised during the 1993 Summit. In response to a call for integrating environment and trade policies, APEC ministers agreed to a Vision Statement that said, "Our environment is improved as we protect the quality of our air, water and green spaces and manage our energy resources and renewable resources to ensure sustainable growth and provide a more secure future for our people" (APEC, 96b). Following up on this statement, Canada invited APEC ministers to a meeting in 1994 where they adopted the Environmental Vision Statement and a Framework of Principles for integrating economic and environment issues. At the following ministerial meeting, APEC ministers endorsed the integration of environmental issues into ongoing APEC activities, basing their approach on "embracing the three pillars of sustainable growth, equitable development, and national stability" (APEC, 96a).

To operationalize this commitment, two additional environmental experts meetings were held in 1994 and in 1996. At the ministerial meeting on sustainable development, held in July 1996, the leaders discussed sustainable cities/urban management, clean production and technology, the marine environment, and approaches toward environmental sustainable development (APEC, 96b). The commitments made by the ministers at the conclusion of this meeting included facilitating technological exchanges in the area of environmental protection, developing specific strategies for industrial and agricultural sectors that promote dissemination of these technologies, promoting the adoption of the ISO 14000 Environmental Management Series, and continuing a dialogue focused on establishing a cooperative approach to realizing sustainable economic development by the year 2010.

With this kind of outward commitment to integrating environmental issues into economic development, it is somewhat surprising that NGOs following APEC activities have expressed their disappointment in the performance of APEC. According to an NWF paper, while they recognize the important formal steps taken by APEC ministers toward integrating trade and the environment, ". . . taken as a whole, APEC's attention to environmental issues has been inadequate to the forum's own stated goal of promoting sustainable development in the region. Integration of environmental concerns in the working groups, and ideas put forth in the thematic areas described above, amount to rather vague statements of intent, with little to suggest that actual work products will be delivered within a given period of time" (NWF, November 95). At the 1995 ministerial meeting, an NGO "Peoples Forum" called on APEC to raise environmental standards and ensure effective implementation throughout the region, protect biodiversity, and protect the intellectual property rights of indigenous peoples (NGO Forum, 95). In preparation for the 1996 ministerial meeting to be held in Manila, NGOs organized another forum to facilitate a dialogue among themselves in an effort to address issues related to the APEC process; economic, environmental, social and human rights policies; concerns related to deregulation; and indigenous property rights.[22]

ISO 14000

Evidence of the trade and environment debate formalized in NAFTA can also be found in a recently completed effort by private organizations to harmonize worldwide environmental standards. Under the auspices of the International Organization for Standardization (ISO), business leaders and some government officials and NGOs collaborated to produce a set of voluntary standards for business performance. The ISO 14000 Environmental Management Systems employs a systems approach to environmental protection where private organizations internalize environmental "cradle to grave" thinking in all their business decisions. Companies seeking ISO certification voluntarily submit to a private, third-party audit of their activities, committing to "implement, maintain, and improve an environmental management system" (ISO 14001.1). Concerns were raised by environmental organizations as to the effectiveness of such a voluntary approach to environmental protection.[23] Standards adopted by a company must take into consideration relevant national environmental standards, but compliance is not required to receive certification. The systems approach to environmental protection breaks the links between performance-based standards and compliance with national environmental laws. Information provided to third-party auditors is not necessarily available to the public, thereby restricting interest groups from access to performance data normally used to watchdog industry performance. Finally, environmental organizations express concern that the structure of the ISO is not conducive to public participation in standard-setting efforts. Voting membership in the ISO is restricted to one organization per country, compounding environmental NGOs efforts to overcome technical and financial constraints that already greatly limit their participation in meetings.

United Nations

While many observers mark the U.N.'s Rio Conference as a watershed event in the trade and environment dialogue, since Rio, U.N. agencies have adopted a cautious approach to the nexus of these two policy domains. In particular, the United Nations Environmental Program (UNEP) is the principal participant in the trade and environment debate. UNEP has sponsored a number of papers (Vaughan, 96; Stonehouse and Mumford, 96; Repetto, 96; Hunter, Sommer, and Vaughan, 96; Housman, 96), but they have not yet developed any recommendations beyond those made in Rio.

NATIONAL ENVIRONMENTAL
ORGANIZATIONS' RESPONSE

The internalization of environmental interests in NAFTA, the WTO, and the other trade regimes responding to the trade and environment debate created opportunities for environmental organizations to become full-time members of the U.S. trade policy monopoly. The collective response of the organizations was twofold. First, organizations supporting NAFTA were rewarded with a higher number of advisory appointments, thereby facilitating long-term participation in trade policy monopolies. Second, these same organizations received a greater share of monies awarded by philanthropic foundations for trade and environment work. The net effect of these two trends was to facilitate institutionalizing a long-term commitment to the trade and environment issue for members of the accommodating coalition.

TABLE 6.3 Institutionalized Commitment to Trade Policy Made by National Environmental Organizations

Organization	Position on NAFTA	Advisory Committees	Foundation Support for "Trade and Environment"		Human Resource Commitment*	
			1991–1993	1994	1993	1994
WWF	Supported	ACTPN JPAC NAC	$300,000	None	1	1.5
EDF	Supported	JPAC TEPAC ACTPN BECC	None	None	1	1
NWF	Supported	NAC JPAC TEPAC ACTPN	$350,000	None Reported	3	2.5
TNC	No Position	None	None	None	0.5	0
NAS	Supported	JPAC	None	$85,000	1	1.5
NRDC	Supported	ACTPN TEPAC JPAC	$50,000	$75,000	2	1.5
Defenders	No Position	None	None	None	0.5	0.3
Sierra Club	Opposed	TEPAC	$143,000	$20,000	1	0.8
FoE	Opposed	TEPAC	$70,000	$25,000	1.5	0.3
Public Citizen	Opposed	None	$240,000	$115,000	3	3
Greenpeace	Opposed	None	None	None	.75	.10

*Human resource commitment based upon interviews with national environmental organizations. Attention was given to whether trade staff was paid through "hard" (organization) or "soft" (foundation support) monies, presence of organization leadership on advisory panels, and a self-evaluation of time spent on trade policy both during and after negotiations.

NWF and WWF have become the most involved organizations in trade policy development during the post-NAFTA period. NWF staff continue to be active in the CEC and in international policy forums such as the APEC and the WTO. Of the two organizations, NWF has perhaps internalized participation in trade and environment matters to a greater extent; beyond staff work on these matters, its Corporate Conservation Council continues a dialogue with business leaders about the importance of continued emphasis on reconciling these problems. Neither organization, however, has made their commitment to trade and the environment permanent; staff assigned to this policy area are funded with foundation support. In the event that foundations turn their attention to other policy issues, both organizations would have to consider paying for these positions out of their internal budgets. Through 1995 NAS remained actively involved in CEC work, due in part to the appointment of Peter Berle as chairman of the NAC. With Berle's departure from NAS toward the end of 1995, routine participation in meetings has diminished.

Of the national organizations involved in NAFTA, EDF alone has kept staff actively involved in Mexico-U.S. border activities. Perhaps this happened because of EDF's regional office in Austin, Texas; while the Sierra Club, NAS, and NWF have affiliates or chapters in the border region, they have not dedicated full-time staff to BECC/NADBANK activities to the same degree. One reason for their lack of attention is resources; none of these organizations felt they had the financial support necessary to maintain active participation in border issues when their staff was trying to remain effective in so many other trade and environment policy forums. Another reason is structure. Both Sierra Club and NAS rely on volunteer activists for involvement in most local environmental issues. Of the members of the adversarial coalition, Public Citizen has done the most to make trade and the environment part of its long-term political strategy. Obtaining information on the source of their funding was not possible.[24] In 1994 they organized the Trade Watch, an independent organization operating under the umbrella of Public Citizen's Washington, D.C., office.

What is most striking about the post-NAFTA period is the absence of many of the national groups from the trade and environment dialogue. Defenders, NRDC, TNC, and FoE have, for all practical purposes, stopped active participation in the daily activities of the trade and environment nexus. For Defenders and NRDC, the reason may be due to financial constraints; neither organization received much of the foundation support in the post-NAFTA period to remain active. Staff who once worked on the details of NAFTA's Supplemental Agreement and on the nature of the BECC can no longer justify working on these issues because they lack the foundation support. FoE continues to receive small contributions from foundations such as the Charles Stewart Mott Foundation, but staff there devote little time or energy to maintaining their participation in the dialogue.[25] Over the past year, Sierra Club staff has shifted its focus away from daily participation in the activities of these institutions and instead has focused attention on raising the level of interest in trade policy among its members.

Two trends may help to explain the diminished interest in trade and the environment. The first is resources. Even among the organizations that were appointed to the most number of advisory boards, there is little money to maintain the same level of participation in trade and environment debates. Each organization involved in trade and the environment relies on foundation support for its work; none have moved its staff off "soft" money and onto the more permanent "hard" money associated with an organization's internal budget. As foundations begin to shift their attention away from trade and the environment toward other issues of greater topical interest, their ability to sustain their own interest in participating is jeopardized.

The second trend can be explained by the overall feeling that little progress continues to be made on their issues. Without exception, those organizations with staff who continue to participate feel frustrated by their inability to generate leverage to "make things happen." Their desperate feelings can perhaps be explained by a number of factors. First, the number of forums where the dialogue continues has flourished. Maintaining active participation in these dialogues takes time, human resources, and money. None of the organizations has the resources to sustain such a high level of commitment. The large number of forums also serves to dissipate focused interest in the dialogue itself. The absence of any particular policy issue for consideration—both NAFTA and GATT are completed, as are the discussions at the OECD—means that actors must focus attention on the mundane activities of a day-to-day dialogue. Some efforts to sustain such a dialogue have been successful. In particular, a project organized by the Community Nutrition Institute continues to bring trade and environmental advocates together to discuss the most difficult policy differences of opinion between them. World Wide Fund for Nature—WWF's international sister organization—recently began a project involving experts from trade, environment, and development fields designed to produce a similar product. But the concern expressed by participants in both these projects and other activities is that the political opportunity to continue pressing for trade policy reform has passed. These issues will be taken up as part of the discussion in the next chapter.

ENDNOTES

1. *North American Free Trade Agreement, Texts of Agreement, Implementing Bill, Statement of Administrative Action, and Required Supporting Statements.* 1993. 103rd Congress, 1st session. House Document no. 103–59 vol. 1–3 (referred to as NAFTA).

2. Author's personal notes taken during meetings with officials from the British Columbian government, British Columbia, Canada, during consultations over the summer, 1994.

3. Trade constraints found in two bilateral environmental agreements— the *Agreement Between the Government of Canada and the Government of the United States of America Concerning the Transboundary Movement of Hazardous Waste,* and the *Agreement Between the United States of America and the United Mexican States on Cooperation for the Protection and Improvement in the Border Area* (the la Paz Accord)—are also recognized as legitimate environmental agreements. See NAFTA, Articles 104, 105, and Annex 104.1.

4. According to negotiators from the United States and Canada, the term is founded in the GATT terminology "least trade restrictive," one that has been interpreted to strike down environmental regulations in favor of trade liberalization. Author's personal notes, 1994.

5. Article 712(1)(2), NAFTA. Sanitary and phytosanitary measures generally deal with protecting human, animal, and plant life and health from risks of plant- and animal-borne pests and diseases, and with additives and contaminants in foods and feedstuffs. Article 904(1), NAFTA. A technical regulation means any document that specifies goods' characteristics or related processes and production methods. It also includes information and labeling requirements. See Article 915, NAFTA.

6. The "tuna-dolphin" cases brought under GATT will be discussed at greater length later in this chapter.

7. United States House of Representatives, 1993. International Dolphin Conservation Act, H.R. 2823.

8. Message from the president of the United States, 1993.

9. They are *Status of Pollution Prevention in North America; Dispute Avoidance: Weighing the Values of Trade and the Environment Under the NAFTA and the NAAEC; Assessing Latin American Markets for North American Environmental Goods and Services; Status of PCB Management in North America; Putting the Pieces Together: The Status of Pollutant Release and Transfer Registers in North America; NAFTA Effects: Potential NAFTA Effects Claims and Arguments, 1991–1994; CEC Secretariat Report on the Death of Migratory Birds at Selva Reservoir;* and *NAFTA Effects: A Survey of Recent Attempts to Model the Environmental Effects of Trade.* Each report is available from the CEC via its internet website at http://www. cec.org.10.

10. Observations based upon author's interviews with stakeholders attending a CEC workshop held in San Diego, California, May 1996.

11. For specific information regarding the cases filed with the CEC see their website at http://www.cec.org.

12. *North American Free Trade Agreement Supplemental Agreements and Additional Documents.* 103rd Congress, 1st session. House Document no. 103-160 (NAAEC, BECC, or NADBANK).

13. Message from the president of the United States, 1993.

14. For current information regarding the make up of the Board of Directors and other members of the BECC, contact them at the internet website at http://cocef.interjuarez.com.

15. BECC, 1996. Those projects were: Wastewater Treatment Plant, Ensenada, B.C.; Water Treatment Plan, Brawley, Ca.; Wastewater Reuse Project, El Paso, Tex.

16. See NADBANK's website at http://www.quicklink.com/mexico/nadbank.

17. Both the Mexican and U.S. governments agreed to contribute equal payments of $225 million. As of this writing, the bank has $112.50 million in paid capital and $637.50 million in callable capital (NADBANK Website, 19 August 1996).

18. Meeting Minutes of the National and Governmental Advisory committees to the U.S. Representative to the North American Commission for Environmental Cooperation, 26 September 1995 (author's files).

19. The *Mararakesh Proposals for Sustainable Trade,* April 1994, was signed by more than fifty NGOs worldwide in opposition to the passage of the Uruguay Round.

20. See the Report of the WTO Committee on Trade and the Environment, 14 November 1996.

21. These nations are Australia, Brunei, Canada, China, Hong Kong, Indonesia, Japan, South Korea, Malaysia, New Zealand, Philippines, Singapore, Chinese Taipei, Thailand, United States (United States Department of State, 1993).

22. See *APEC Watch,* a series of newsletters published by the International Conveners Committee of the November Manila People's Forum on APEC '96, Quezon City, Philippines. Website http://www.nautilus.org/focusweb/focus.html.

23. This analysis is based upon Audley, n.d. "Negotiating the International Organization for Standardization 14000 Environmental Management System." See also Cascio, 96; Robt Arriaza, 95, Saunders, 95.

24. Repeated attempts by the author to obtain financial information regarding the source of Public Citizen's financial support for the Trade Watch produced only marginal information.

25. This cannot be said of FoE's director, who continues to participate as a spokesperson involved with anti-NAFTA events.

7

Explaining Regime Change in U.S. Trade Policy

One of the many stories of the North American Free Trade Agreement, and the story central to this analysis, is the collision between two fundamentally important but vastly different policy domains. One governs the way market-based societies organize themselves to produce and distribute wealth. The dominant worldview is constant growth; expanding human scale creates the wealth necessary to ensure a higher quality of human life and protect the environment. The other domain seeks a balance between nature and human activity. Here, the world view is characterized by biological limits to human scale. The quality of human life is not measured in terms of human wealth or consumption but by using benchmarks not easily quantified with numbers.

While these two characterizations are overly simple, they make an important point. The collision of these two policy domains was an important component of NAFTA's political life. NAFTA marks the first step toward reconciling trade and environmental policies. Few environmentalists, even NAFTA's strongest supporters, expected major trade policy reform. But even its opponents understood that NAFTA was an important move toward policy integration. Both groups hoped these timid steps held the promise of continued progress toward balancing global economic and environmental policies. But while the environment was politically important to NAFTA's outcome, it was never central to the political debate about trade liberalization. Growth or no growth and trade's impact on jobs and agriculture were the issues that ultimately determined whether NAFTA would pass or fail in Congress. Environmental issues in NAFTA provided some policy makers the leverage they needed to pursue other goals more important to their constituents. Once the leverage was fully exploited, environmental issues receded into the background of the larger debate about growth and jobs and national sovereignty.

Understanding the nature of the changes resulting from the North American Free Trade Agreement is best explained by analyzing the nature of the new norms, rules, and procedures arising from this policy nexus, and by observing how the politics between trade policy elites produced an Agreement capable of gaining congressional support. Negotiated within the framework of growth-oriented trade rules and norms, the environmental components of the NAFTA are best understood as a defensive response to trade policy's most environmentally insensitive aspects than a complete integration of environmental norms and rules into trade. National environmental organizations overcame those most onerous trade rules and procedures by using both adversarial and accommodating political strategies to sustain and use leverage, but ultimately this kind of leverage was insufficient to produce reforms in the U.S. trade policy capable of sustaining efforts toward balancing the interests of trade and of the environment. In the end it appeared that environmental groups traded the preemptive leverage they once enjoyed during trade negotiations for procedural inclusion in trade policy decisions but did not then realize the political leverage enjoyed by older members of the trade policy regime.

NAFTA is just one step in a long-term process responsible for reforging trade policy regimes, but it is an important first step in the trade and environment nexus. As trade continues to link economies worldwide, the structure, rules, and norms now a part of NAFTA impact future trade and environment discussions. NAFTA made an impression on the completion of the Uruguay Round of GATT, the policy discussions at the OECD, and the APEC declarations on economic development and the environment in the Pacific. But whether NAFTA's environmental provision will continue to influence trade negotiation is already uncertain, as efforts to include environmental issues as part of Chile's accession to NAFTA met stiff opposition from Congress.[1] Trade and environment linkages with other Latin American countries such as Brazil and Argentina, plus agreements with existing regional trading blocks, even with Australia or New Zealand, all hinge upon these discussions between political leaders. Understanding the nature of the intersection of trade and environment embodied in NAFTA becomes much more important than a single policy event when one considers the broader implications of its form as a model that others will follow.

TRADE OVER THE ENVIRONMENT

NAFTA as the lodestone for the trade and environment nexus is significant because its structure, rules, and norms characterize the introduction of environmental interests into trade policy. But with the exception of decision-making procedures, the institutional characteristics of the U.S. trade regime were not altered to accommodate the conflicts caused by environmental issues. The complete domination of trade over the environment forged in NAFTA set the stage for future policy dialogue. Trade norms and scope will most likely define the agenda and trade regimes will, at best, consider changing the scope of negotiations only to the point that modification does not hinder trade policy's orientation toward growth. NAFTA codified this constraint when negotiators refused to consider the broader range of issues suggested by NGOs. For example, NAFTA's Energy Chapter encourages governments to ". . . strengthen the important role that trade in energy and basic petrochemical goods plays in the free trade area and to enhance this role through sustained and gradual liberalization" (NAFTA, Chapter 6, Article 601[2]). Nothing is mentioned of the internationally acknowledged importance of reducing human dependence upon fossil fuels. There is no direct discussion of the impact on environmental quality by changing land use patterns caused by integrating agricultural industries in three countries, nor of the effect of the increased use of pesticides and fertilizers normally occurring with corporate farming, nor of the importance of conserving the world's natural resources. Expanding the agenda to include such important environmental issues would obviously have made negotiations that much more difficult. More importantly, it would have legitimated claims made by environmental interest groups regarding trade policy, something just not possible under these conditions. Therefore, many sections of NAFTA that could have better balanced the intersection did not.

Confining the scope of NAFTA's negotiations to exclude fundamental issues of concern to environmentalists produced a situation in which the dialogue surrounding these issues is now dominated by the scope and normative principles of free trade. Yet while these trade organizations question their own competency in environmental affairs, it is their norms and rules that continue to shape the policy dialogue. The policy recommendations made by the OECD and the WTO's CTE, even the more informal dialogues between trade and environmental advocates, are now shaped by the scope of traditional trade regimes. Long-standing discussions surrounding production process, the role of unilateral action and multilateral environmental agreements, and the effects of trade liberalization on the environment now reflect the assumption that trade liberalization will occur or even that it is good for the environment. This is not meant to imply that trade liberalization is necessarily bad for the environment, or that some old policy tools have been ineffective. However, when the domination of trade over the environment is so complete, the future agenda for negotiations between them is so targeted that such a consideration is no longer part of the dialogue.

An intersection defined in terms of existing trade norms and principles also established the tone and use of rhetoric. In a debate character-ized by the language of "free trade," the word "protectionism" can be taken as harmful for the environment. "Protectionism" has always enjoyed an important place in the symbolic language of environmental-ism, just as protecting one's home and family is considered appropriate in U.S. culture and society (Lang and Hines, 93). During trade negotia-tions, protectionism took on a negative, self-interested image that com-pelled environmental organizations to avoid the term, fearing adverse responses from trade advocates. Anti-NAFTA groups also avoided the term to minimize public accusations of economic protectionism, a decision which ultimately led them to employ the much less influential concept of "fair trade" over "free trade." But "fair trade" does not resonate like "free trade," and the symbolic language of growth-oriented trade policy dominated every aspect of the trade policy negoti-ations. The irony of the "free trade" and "protectionism" rhetoric is that neither are truly possible, nor perhaps desirable, even to the most avid trade proponent.

Another implication of the domination of trade over the environ-ment affects the tools used to implement environmental policies. NAFTA and GATT establish guidelines in which national and interna-tional environmental policies will now be evaluated for their impact on efforts to liberalize trade. Conditions such as "least inconsistent with the terms of this Agreement," "equivalence," and "sound science" will play a much greater role in environmental policy making. Policy tools such as trade restrictions and sanctions will increasingly be un-available to policy makers in the international environmental arena, not because they are or are not effective policy tools for environmental protection, but because they clash with trade goals and objectives. The efforts by environmentalists to convince NAFTA negotiators to include "green taxes" as a means of generating revenue for environmental remediation failed, due, in part, to the opposition to taxes as a form of tariff, a policy tool prohibited by trade rules.

These new guidelines for acceptable environmental policies suggest a number of directions for future environmental policies. First, national policy makers will likely be much more conscious of the "trade effects" of environmental regulations. While it is difficult to measure this im-pact, at the very least this can be said of bureaucrats working within regulatory agencies. Second, multilateralism, common in the area of setting and implementing international environmental policies, will have a much greater effect on the direction and scope of national environmental policies. The combination of these two trends will likely direct policy makers toward more voluntarily implemented, less per-formance-oriented, environmental policy. Nowhere is this more evi-dent than in the adoption of ISO 14000; governments and industries worldwide are moving toward this system where it will cost governments less to enforce and businesses less to comply with voluntarily adopted guidelines for business management. Whether or not this new policy direction will result in higher levels of environmental quality is uncertain; what is evident, however, is that the political tools once used by environmental groups to ensure that both businesses and governments followed regulatory guidelines will require rethinking and serious adaptation to a newly defined political regime.

Had the intersection between trade and the environment been characterized by environmental structure, rules, and norms, many of the fundamentally opposed issues would have been discussed. Under the institutional rules of the United Nations, for example, participation by government and nongovernment organizations is fundamental to the decision-making process. Organized input in the agenda-setting process, formalized access to representatives from participating nation-states, and media coverage of NGOs' response to policy statements characterized environmental participation at UNCED (Prudencio, 93). Within the scope of traditional environmental regimes, only the desire expressed by some organizations to maintain the right to take unilateral action to protect the environment would have been so completely rejected.

Perhaps it was inevitable that trade, and not the environment, characterized the formal intersection. Nations can and do discuss setting priorities for environmental protection. But, while important to almost every nation, concern for the environment is not as eminently important an issue as is economic growth. Recent international conventions such as UNCED and the U.N. Conference on Population held in Cairo, Egypt, show that multilateral agreement on priorities, goals, cost allocation, and effective implementation is difficult, if not impossible. But whether or not countries agree with one another on social and environmental issues, they can and do still trade. Trade norms reject any suggestion that exchange is coercive; therefore, if countries voluntarily engage in multilateral exchange, it must be better for everyone. So countries can continue to disagree about the merits of environmental issues yet still trade as long as rules for trade can be negotiated. With the predominance of growth-oriented norms, it is precisely assumptions like "voluntary exchange leads to better outcomes for all" that produce trade policy so insensitive to environmental priorities.

SIGNIFICANT ENVIRONMENTAL GAINS

Given the dominance of trade over the environment, the environmental provisions found in the NAFTA Package are actually quite incredible.

New institutions—the NAAEC, BECC, and NADBANK, even the CTE—were created specifically to monitor the long-term effects of liberalized trade and to correct environmental problems caused by past trade. In one sense it is still too early to judge the success of these new institutions. At the same time objections raised by NGOs raise important points. Can institutions created by trade rules, norms, and procedures balance economic and environmental interests? Of all the new institutions, the CEC and BECC/NADBANK hold the greatest potential for success. During their development both institutions were dedicated to developing procedures that maximized public input in a way that attempted to balance actors' leverage. Both institutions bring financial resources to areas of environmental need. And both increase the political leverage of environmental uses in trade policy. At the same time both institutions remain tenuous. The CEC is constrained by its narrow influence over national political decisions. Opposition by elected officials to its influence over domestic policy reveals how vulnerable both it and the BECC are to the political debates of each member nation. The rules codifying environmental issues in the Agreements themselves are ambiguous at best, or harmful at worst, because they establish a framework for evaluating environmental policies on the basis of trade policy goals. Formal participation by environmental groups in the development of U.S. trade policy has been made permanent. Dialogues between NGOs and business and government officials continue to elaborate these issues. These procedural changes institutionalized the role environmental actors and their issues now play in the development of U.S. trade policy. But these trade institutions now home to a few environmental groups are largely hostile to these goals without affective political leverage. NGOs are generally frustrated by the lack of continued progress toward a balance between trade and environment within these institutional settings; whether these criticisms are merited or not, the fact remains that these new procedures create forums for continued dialogue and opportunity for continued change. Recommendations made by APEC countries to promote "sustainable cities," however flawed, mark new and important policy territory where potential for better balance between trade and environmental interests exists. The environmental provisions found in recent APEC discussions offer evidence that political actors speaking on behalf of the environment can expand trade objectives to include ecological concerns.

There were also a number of rule changes that represent important concessions made by trade advocates. NAFTA shifts the burden of guilt in dispute procedures, recognizes some international environmental laws, and is more sensitive to sanitary and phytosanitary guidelines.

These rule changes represent the first real steps toward internalizing environmental costs in trade. But while each of these changes to trade rules represents unprecedented joining of trade and the environment, the gains must be considered cautiously. Each of these changes in existing trade rules was made consistent to norms and rules for trade. None of the changes can be declared unqualified environmental success stories as each role change is conditioned by other trade rules that narrow its scope.

Other trade and Fast Track rules underscore the difficulties environmental groups face when they rely on formal trade rules to engage in negotiations. In both Congress and the executive branch, Fast Track codifies the political power over trade in the hands of actors whose interests are served by trade liberalization. Efforts to formalize NGO involvement as advisors in future trade agreements, or to formally link trade negotiations with environmental concerns, failed to pass Congress. If future administrations choose not to include environmentalists in negotiations, NGOs may find themselves forced to threaten to preempt reauthorization again. What is interesting to note in the aftermath of the passage of both NAFTA and the Uruguay Round is that Fast Track itself may no longer be as necessary for multilateral negotiations. NAFTA was designed to allow other nations to accede to its provisions without major negotiations. Reducing the need for step-by-step negotiation of the various commodities and trade items eliminates the political need to restrict Congress from intervening in the final outcome. Modification to multilateral trade agreements was made easier with the creation of the WTO. Unlike the GATT, the WTO is a dynamic organization capable of policy modification without the onerous task of negotiating rounds. But even with its reduced influence as the formal vehicle for negotiations, Fast Track authorization will remain a focal point for U.S. politics because it creates an opportunity for actors to negotiate compromises among themselves.

NEW RELATIONSHIPS FAVOR TRADE ADVOCATES

As environmentalists' dissatisfaction with the fruits of their participation in post-NAFTA trade regimes indicates, procedural institutionalization did not produce the level of effectiveness in trade policy negotiations they sought. One of the reasons for this outcome is that procedural change does not seem adequate to change normative behavior of the principal actors involved in regime performance. The procedural changes responsible for institutionalizing environmental interests occurred within the existing framework of trade regimes. What this means is that environmentalists must now effectively operate in a new policy environment, one whose normative principles, rules for interaction, and relationship ties are based on principles they do not share.

Long-term participation by individual environmental organizations is an important indicator of the effect of this reality. With very few exceptions, organizations that were supportive of NAFTA, or at the very least not hostile to its goals, have better access to trade policy elites. Perhaps this point is obvious; it is only natural for presidents to reward interest groups with political appointments or for other interest group communities to forge ties with environmental groups whose philosophies are not in direct conflict with their own. This fact explains why President Bush sought the support from a smaller portion of the environmental community than did President Clinton, who in the end was compelled to stop short of supporting of some of his strongest supporters during his 1992 presidential campaign. It also helps explain why organizations such as Greenpeace and Public Citizen do not enjoy formal access to trade negotiations today. Had the dialogue taken place under the direction of environmental regimes, their strong positions against trade would not have resulted in their formal exclusion. Operating outside traditional environmental regimes also helps to explain why environmental groups struggle to remain actively involved in all of the new trade and environment forums. With no support from the internal budgets of these organizations and so few staff persons dedicated to the issue, maintenance over such diverse dialogues is virtually impossible. Had environmental organizations been better able to coordinate their activities in the period immediately following NAFTA, they may have been able to pool their resources to collectively cover these issues. But the combination of competition for funding after NAFTA and the divisive relationship that developed between groups during the voting stage made this scenario virtually impossible until enough time transpired to reduce the tension between the groups. As environmental groups now respond to efforts by the Clinton administration to extend NAFTA to include Chile, they find themselves struggling to maintain their place in negotiations, facing a hostile Congress, a weakly interested administration, and a trade regime still resistant to their efforts.

THE SOURCE AND USE OF POLITICAL LEVERAGE

When the intersection of trade and the environment is so dominated by the structure, rules, and normative principles responsible for trade liberalization, how can the dramatic procedural changes produced by NAFTA be explained? The answer to this question lies in an examination of the source and use of the political leverage enjoyed (or fought over) by environmental groups. In a phrase, that leverage is best described as *situational preemptive leverage*. It was situational because of the sequence of events responsible for positioning environmental groups in such a strategic position during the Fast Track period. It was preemptive because both the good cop and bad cop roles played by environmental groups relied upon the creation and maintenance of a credible threat to defeat NAFTA. And since their support was sought by both pro- and anti-NAFTA policy elites, until their issues were neutralized, they found themselves in the strategic position to preempt passage depending on which coalition they chose to side with.

History and Events Create Opportunities to Preempt NAFTA

One of the most important lessons taught by the intersection of environmental interests in trade policy is that political history and significant events create opportunities for actors to change a policy's agenda. Through these windows interest groups, normally outside a policy subgroup's cast of political actors, can and do affect the nature of the policy dialogue.

The windows for agenda change that occurred during NAFTA can be categorized in two groups. One group of events was caused by formal rules or norms of behavior. Fast Track, the congressional cycle, and the 1992 presidential election created significant opportunities for environmental groups to pressure Congress and the administration to consider their demands for trade policy. Of these, congressional Fast Track reauthorization was perhaps the most important political event in the early stages of NAFTA. President Bush's request to extend GATT negotiations and include a request to begin NAFTA negotiations under Fast Track gave environmental groups the political event they needed to capitalize on environmental problems along the Mexico-U.S. border and to link trade and environmental issues. Had environmentalists been unsuccessful in their efforts to link environmental issues to Fast Track, they would not have made their concerns part of the agenda for negotiations. It was the linkage that gave environmental groups the political leverage in Congress to press for their demands.

What is interesting to note is that the preemptive leverage generated during the Fast Track period was the product of activities by environmental organizations across the philosophical spectrum regarding trade. During no other period surrounding NAFTA was there so much coordination between what eventually became the pro- and anti-NAFTA environmental organizations. Perhaps this occurred because until the president formally responded to congressional concerns regarding trade and the environment, none of the environmental groups had any guarantee that any of them would take part in negotiations.

Another interesting thing to note about the preemptive leverage enjoyed by environmental groups was that it was as much a product of their association with other more traditionally influential trade actors opposed to NAFTA as it was their own importance as a political issue for members of Congress. Alliances with organized labor prove to be an essential element of their circumstantial leverage for two reasons. First, together both labor and environmental issues carry a good deal of weight in Congress, but it was the strength of anti-NAFTA labor forces that really challenged NAFTA's success. Second, labor's opposition to NAFTA negotiations during the Bush administration created the political incentive for the USTR to engage an interest group they otherwise felt no obligation or political pressure to engage. Labor's opposition to NAFTA and the potential for a environment-labor coalition was an important historical circumstance that enhanced environmental leverage during negotiations. The inability to re-create such circumstances during GATT negotiations, and the current inability of environmental groups to unanimously realign themselves with labor groups who may be opposed to Chilean accession to NAFTA in 1997, may prove to be important weaknesses in environmental groups' strategy to sustain linkages between environmental issues and U.S. trade policy negotiations.

The 1992 presidential elections and the completion of the first phase of the NAFTA negotiations also created a political window to influence the agenda for negotiations. The combination of the two events, plus the long history of support for environmental issues within the Democratic party, empowered environmental groups to pressure President Bush to agree to negotiate a Supplemental Agreement. It also gave them the power to push the Democratic candidate, Bill Clinton, to pursue further linkages in his October NAFTA speech. Each of these events was cast in the blacklight of historical events: a Democratic Congress and a Republican president, worsening environmental conditions along the Mexico-U.S. border, and strong support for environmental issues in the United States. The combination of history and significant events enabled environmental groups to target their resources and press for more concessions.

The other category of preemptive windows were "manufactured" by environmental groups; that is to say, they occurred as the result of specific actions taken by actors with specific goals in mind. H.C.R. 246 is a good example of this. Public Citizen, the Fair Trade Campaign, and Citizen's Trade Campaign orchestrated H.C.R. 246 to pressure congressional members into rejecting NAFTA if certain conditions weren't met in the terms of the Agreement. H.C.R. 246 was a very useful tool for mobilizing grassroots activity and as a vehicle to lobby Congress. But as a political tool to influence the final vote, H.C.R. 246 was a poor device. Resolutions provide a "sense of Congress," and as such are not firm commitments to act. Over one-third of those members endorsing H.C.R. 246 did not return to Congress following the 1992 elections, further weakening the commitment of the new Congress to its language. The divisions within the environmental community over the utility of H.C.R. 246 may also have weakened it as a political tool. Of the accommodating environmental organizations, only NRDC supported its passage. And when the Bush administration endorsed H.C.R. 246 in its eleventh hour by actually supporting it, H.C.R. 246 was effectively emasculated by a vote of 316 to 0 in its favor. The vote in support of H.C.R. 246 by House Republicans implied President Bush had met the conditions of the resolution.

Legal efforts to block NAFTA also provide a good example of a "manufactured" political event. The legal suit brought against the USTR for failure to comply with portions of NEPA ultimately failed on appeal, but it did serve a number of other useful purposes for anti-NAFTA environmental groups. The NEPA case attracted a great deal of media attention, resulted in congressional hearings to vet the issue, and gave anti-NAFTA environmental groups a political platform from which to voice their concerns over trade policy. The GATT Tuna/Dolphin case shares these characteristics with the NEPA case, but it was initially "manufactured" by trade advocates opposed to what they considered unfair U.S. environmental laws. Regardless of its origin, Tuna/Dolphin shocked everyone involved in trade policy negotiations and provided environmental groups with the political "smoking gun" to support their allegations that trade rules actually harmed domestic environmental efforts.

The sequence of events involving Fast Track reauthorization, the GATT Tuna/Dolphin Decision, completion of the first stage of NAFTA negotiations, the 1992 presidential elections, and the NEPA decision, combined with the historical circumstances linking trade and environment in North America, gave environmental groups ample opportunities to preempt successful trade policy negotiations. Alliances with more traditional antitrade interest groups heightened environmental groups' political leverage, but they had a politically "legitimate" concern about restricting trade.

The High Cost of Maintaining Preemptive Leverage

Preemptive leverage was the ticket environmentalists used to gain access to NAFTA negotiations, but it was leverage they enjoyed only because of the unique circumstances that brought trade and environment together in 1991: three neighboring countries gave the U.S. government greater leverage to set the agenda during negotiations; despite the shifting winds within the environmental movement, environmental interest groups enjoyed access to political decision makers within this tripartite negotiating scenario to present their political demands; and a history of environmental degradation along their common borders caused, in part, by economic expansion gave environmentalists their "poster child" to sell their message to the media. But as this analysis suggests, it wasn't just a regional proximity and border environmental degradation that produced preemptive power. Presidential politics and political leverage generated by intrainterest coalitions also played an important role in positioning environmental groups to negotiate unprecedented environmental provisions in NAFTA.

The circumstances responsible for generating preemptive leverage during NAFTA negotiations did not also characterize the completion of the Uruguay Round. Many politically influential countries negotiated a multiparty trade agreement, each responding to domestic political pressures. More negotiating countries dispersed the ability of the United States to dictate the agenda for negotiations. Neither was there a transboundary environmental problem similar to the Mexico-U.S. border to influence politics in each negotiating country. Not all GATT countries share a history of interest group pressure which characterizes U.S. politics. Absent internal domestic pressure, even in countries where environmental concern for trade existed, political leaders might not have incentive to respond to public pressure to expand the trade policy agenda to include the environment (Lang and Hines, 93).

Within the United States political circumstances involving interest group pressure also changed. Organized labor was not actively opposed to passage of the Uruguay Round. The Democratic presidential victory in 1992 meant that political opposition from environmental groups directed at an unpopular president was no longer a unifying theme among organizations. And perhaps most importantly, in the course of one national election, the mood of Congress shifted dramatically away from support for linkages between trade and environmental policies. Now, environmentalists not only face challenges to the linkages forged between trade and the environment in NAFTA, but they are confronted with efforts to rewrite the conventional norms and rules of U.S. environmental institutions. So while preemptive leverage was enough to gain access to a trade policy regime where environmentalists were previously unwelcome, the circumstances responsible for generating this kind of political leverage are difficult to re-create or sustain.

Preemptive leverage is also expensive to maintain. Sustaining a constant threat to NAFTA's success would have required a greater

number of national environmental organizations employing an adversarial strategy. But as a number of negotiators for President Bush indicated, a more aggressive challenge to President Bush's parallel track
jeopardized the willingness of the Bush administration to keep environmental issues part of the negotiating agenda. Had all environmental
organizations set their demands as high as the adversarial coalition,
they may have compelled the administration to actually challenge the
legitimacy of their preemptive threat by removing their concerns from
NAFTA's agenda. Given the dominance of a growth-oriented trade
philosophy, it is doubtful that NAFTA negotiations would somehow
have failed had environmentalists not gotten the demands they asked
for during Fast Track or during initial negotiations. In all likelihood,
environmentalists would have faced early defeat.

Good Cops and Bad Cops

Adversarial and cooperative powers enjoyed by U.S. environmental
organizations were instrumental in the efforts to reform trade policy.
Many organizational factors set each environmental group on its own
course toward support or opposition to NAFTA, but no one group
orchestrated the good cop/bad cop scenario responsible for NAFTA's
environmental provisions.

The willingness and ability of some environmental organizations
to cooperate with protrade policy elites are the key to understanding
how environmentalists gained policy concessions during trade negotiations. Cooperative environmental organizations accepted the limits to
the negotiating agenda outlined in President Bush's parallel approach
in order to keep President Bush from rejecting environmental issues
from negotiations. NWF's formal endorsement of the original NAFTA
gave the Bush administration a marginal political victory, even though
it fell short of the goals set by most environmental organizations. When
it became apparent that the Clinton administration was unable to respond to the more aggressive demands made by environmental groups
in the March 1993 letter, accommodating groups forged a new set of
more moderate demands to avoid a public impasse on environmental
issues. In short, accommodating groups actively worked to set an
agenda for the Supplemental Agreement that did not challenge the
weaknesses of the original NAFTA and ensured that the Clinton administration would be able to negotiate a NAFTA Package acceptable to
their organizations. They were able to accomplish their objectives because their demands were not a direct challenge to growth-oriented
trade policy and because they could control the tone of the environmental agenda using their ties to protrade policy elites.

But cooperation by the accommodating coalition was not possible unless responding to their demands offered some benefit to protrade policy elites. Responding to their moderated demands was necessary because the adversarial environmental coalition sustained the threat to defeat NAFTA. Credible opposition to NAFTA in the summer of 1992 compelled the Bush administration to reconsider its resistance to negotiating an additional agreement for the environment and to revisit controversial language regarding food safety and environmental standards. Opposition to the September 1992 NAFTA advocated by adversarial environmental groups enabled accommodating groups to help the Clinton campaign develop his "NAFTA, with conditions" policy position. Other events such as the NEPA suit against the USTR helped to sustain the threat to NAFTA established during Fast Track, as did H.C.R. 246, the Trade in the 21st Century Conference, and the media attention anti-NAFTA groups drew to their opposition. Therefore, sustaining the threat to preempt NAFTA beyond the significant events was an essential part of negotiating environmental provisions in NAFTA. Cooperation with trade policy elites by some environmental groups appears to be the reason environmental organizations enjoyed such attention from protrade elites, but it was the combination of good cops and bad cops that produced institutional reform of U.S. trade policy.

EXPLAINING DIFFERENTIATED BEHAVIOR

One of the goals of this research was to explain why environmental groups adopted both cooperative and adversarial roles. Upon reflection, this was an impossible task because it required reaching into the minds of the people and organizations involved in negotiations to explain the motivations behind their actions. Organizations represent a complex bundle of personal history, motivations, and people, making explanation of their behavior difficult without employing simplifying assumptions of self-interest (Brewer and deLeon, 83). The set of organizations examined and the number of discrete interactions amenable to statistical analysis was too small to allow for more than direct observation of behavioral differences. Therefore, I will avoid the temptation to offer detailed explanations as to why each group acted as it did and instead offer some observations based on behavior patterns detected during my research.

First, a clear distinction between grassroots environmental organizations and top-down groups delineates NAFTA supporters from its opponents. Grassroots environmental organizations opposed the Agreement, while nongrassroots supported it. The only exception to this rule is the National Audubon Society. With six hundred

independent chapters, it is certainly classified as a grassroots organization. Endorsement was not an easy subject for NAS staff; approximately
twelve of their chapters joined in opposing the Agreement, and strong
differences of opinion between staff members and the board of directors
marked their decision-making process (Rogers, 94). But the fact that
NAS supported NAFTA, and other grassroots organizations did not,
compels me to look for characteristics that distinguish these organizations.

One difference can be found in terms of relationship ties with trade
policy elites. Organizations whose staff had relationship ties with both
Republican and Democratic party elites and whose board members
personally or professionally benefited from trade liberalization tended
to support the Agreement; organizations with fewer ties to political
and economic elites did not. This observation helps to differentiate the
behavior of NAS from other grassroots environmental organizations.
While NAS is noted for grassroots activism, the organization's board
consists largely of people from the business and finance communities
whose economic interests directly benefit from trade liberalization.
Based upon the final position taken by the organization, their interests
apparently held sway. NAS supported the final agreement, but minimized its lobbying role because of the internal tension created by
internal differences of opinion.

The most active supporting environmental organizations—NWF,
EDF, and WWF—are closely tied to economic elites who benefit from
trade liberalization. These organizations had the most number of relationship ties with Bush administration officials, many of which were
relationships between high-ranking political appointees like the EPA
administrator, William Reilly, or with active USA*NAFTA corporations. While only a small portion of their overall budget, corporate
donations are accepted by each organization to fund projects. But because of these linkages, these were also the environmental organizations best positioned to use informal leverage to influence key trade
policy actors. Few environmental organizations could match the access
to USTR and EPA officials or to political elites in Mexico and in Canada.
As Reilly said to the NWF president, Jay Hair, just prior to his departure
from EPA, "Jay, you were the one organization that made the difference" (Reilly, 93).

Perhaps stronger relationship ties with protrade policy elites
through staff and board membership explains why the accommodating
coalition was able to dominate the set of policy alternatives presented
by environmental organizations and explains their less aggressive attitude toward trade liberalization. Access to administration negotiations,
protrade policy elites, and protrade members of the business commu-

nity enabled them to better determine which policy alternatives could be considered without rejecting environmental demands completely. But in addition to better access to protrade policy elites, the accommodating coalition's public message that the absence of an Agreement would mean a return to the status quo of environmental degradation along the Mexico-U.S. border was nonthreatening to the efforts to expand economic growth. The anti-NAFTA groups' message, however, that the Agreement would endanger both environmental protection and democratic institutions threatened not only protrade economic elites but many members of Congress who believe they play a vital role in maintaining democracy in America.

From the perspective of informal relationships and formal appointment to NAFTA institutions, members of the accommodating environmental coalition are easy prey for political pundits critical of NAFTA's passage. However, NAFTA, like most policy outcomes, is much too complicated to draw such simple conclusions. Had accommodating environmental groups not enjoyed privileged access *and* been unwilling to moderate their demands for trade policy, it is possible that the gains earned in NAFTA would not be so substantial. Although I argue that these gains are far from certain, perhaps the only fair thing to conclude is that different environmental organizations believed their positions on NAFTA were in the best interest of the environment. Given the vagueness of the principles of sustainable development, it would be wrong to challenge WWF's belief, on the grounds that others do not share their view, that alleviating poverty in developing countries will help improve environmental quality. At the same time it would also be wrong to dismiss Public Citizen's fear that external influence over domestic environmental policies spells the end of environmental protection. What this dilemma suggests is that more attention must be given to developing a set of widely held principles of sustainable development in order to provide organizations with better guidelines on how to achieve their goals.

Members of the accommodating coalition also used their private resources to dominate the message from the environmental community. Access to trade advocates gave them better insight into what was under consideration during negotiation and, to some degree, the limits for inclusion of environmental demands. Their energy over the content of environmental demands became more assertive during the Clinton administration, when other organizations had other avenues to influence the agenda for negotiating NAFTA's Supplemental Agreement. More than any other event, the May 1993 letter authored by WWF revealed the degree to which accommodating members were willing to dominate the message of the environmental community.

While the accommodating coalition received most of the criticisms for their compromise, in the end it may have been their ability to establish a set of conditions within reach of the U.S. negotiators, and neutralize the opposition voice from within the environmental community, that gained environmental organizations the concessions now embodied in NAFTA. In the end the procedural inclusions won by environmental groups in 1993 may have been all they could have hoped for.

Political leverage for environmentalists did not come from their ability to define the agenda but from the need to be neutralized as a reason to oppose NAFTA. Organizations responsible for establishing and maintaining that threat were incapable of using the leverage to change the agenda but were essential in creating the space for cooperative environmental organizations to translate preemptive power into concessions. Institutional reform of U.S. trade policy can, therefore, be explained in terms of the existence of a preemptive threat to an existing policy regime and the willingness of some environmental groups to exchange "threat leverage" for a formalized role in trade policy. However, it is doubtful that the combination of preemption and cooperation produced a new form for U.S. trade policy that promotes greater balances between the interests of trade and that of the environment.

THE FUTURE FOR TRADE AND THE ENVIRONMENT

Now that a new policy atmosphere has so dramatically altered the political agenda in Washington, D.C., progress in efforts to reconcile trade and environment goals is now in jeopardy. Business leaders no longer feel the need to maintain the dialogue with environmental organizations because they now have members of Congress who are actively hostile to any restrictions to economic growth placed on business activity. National environmental organizations have cut back on their work on trade and the environment, even those who secured the most favorable political appointments or received foundation support to continue the work. The economic crisis in Mexico has threatened the full implementation of both the NAAEC and the BECC, as Mexican officials now doubt whether they can meet the financial obligations required of participation. And as negotiations on the Chilean accession to NAFTA begin, it is doubtful that the Clinton administration will risk stalling efforts to "grow the economy" through trade by attaching environmental and labor conditions to the Agreement that Republican leaders have already pledged to oppose.

U.S. politics and political actors are no longer at center stage in the international efforts to balance trade with the environment. Instead, the locus has shifted to other institutions such as the United Nations and the World Trade Organization. Within these institutions, the debate over growth and development has sparked tremendous interest on the part of officials from developing countries as they struggle for a balance between the need to exploit their natural resources to provide wealth for their citizens with the importance of preserving their ecosystems to create long-term economic viability. However, the hostility toward environmental goals at the WTO make it an unlikely institution to balance issues. Environmentalists will likely shift their attention to other international forces to counteract the influence of the WTO on environmental policy. Alternative forces such as the U.N. are not promising, as they lack the political power to challenge the WTO.

It is unrealistic to expect that environmental interests in trade could produce a new institutional form which balances trade and the environment when popular and elite faith in the growth model is so strong. Whether the belief is justified or not, the fact remains that most people in the United States have not reconciled these two issues themselves, finding refuge in the argument that the problem does not really exist or that technology will ultimately provide a costless solution to human encroachment on biological realities. Until some change in this belief system occurs, interest in the market will continue to dominate interest in the environment, and policies will reflect this reality. But what we can hope for are new institutional structures, rules, and norms which encourage policy elites to take steps toward reconciling the conflict between economic growth and ecological sustainability. To that end, U.S. NGOs will likely spend more time and energy helping build public awareness among their constituents. The CEC and BECC offer their members access to trade related institutions which were designed to balance trade and environment interests. If NGOs begin to more actively pursue these two institutions, perhaps they can bring the relevance of trade and environment home to U.S. citizens.

The nature of the environmental provisions in NAFTA suggests that efforts to streamline environmental regulations to facilitate global trade will continue. Environmental organizations whose own philosophies are most adaptable to this worldview are the most likely participants in future negotiations. The policy areas around which discussions will focus will most likely be related to privatizing regulatory enforcement, not the continuation of the debate surrounding production processes or multilateral versus unilateral action. Therefore, private initiatives such as ISO 14000 and ecolabelling will likely play a larger role in the trade and environment debate. It also suggests more attention will be paid to the shift toward private lending by multilateral lending institutions such as the World Bank. More and more often environmental groups must directly confront trade institutions. The world has embraced the growth paradigm and will continue to pursue it during periods of massive government reordering of priorities. Environmental organizations will either move with this trend or work to generate the necessary political leverage to threaten its continued progression. Given the broad appeal of a message that suggests "more growth" solves social and environmental problems, the likelihood of environmental groups using the second strategy is remote; at present the third strategy remains just a vision. But it is in visions like this that concrete ideas are born.

NOTE

1. See the letter from the Sierra Club, NWF, FoE, Defenders, WWF, and CNI to Vice President Al Gore, 14 February 1997. See also "Enviro Provisions Left out of Fast Track Offer," *Greenwill*, 13 February 1997.

Appendix A:
Environmental Organizations and NAFTA*

Organization	Human/ Financial Resources	NAFTA Resources	Access	Strategy
World Wildlife Fund (WWF)	1.2 million members $60 million Sources: indiv, fdn, corp, federal	Staff: 1 executive, 1 staff (1 link**) Trade resources: internal; pro bono work Active since: 9/92 Congressional hearings	Trade advisor, Republican and Democratic party elites, EPA administrator, informal agency access, business associations, Mexican political elites	"Trade as instrument for environmental benefits" Informal, cooperative efforts to ensure environmental support for NAFTA
Environmental Defense Fund (EDF)	200,000 members $22 million, Sources: corp, indiv, fdtn, litigation	Staff: 1 executive 2 staff (plus share link with WWF) Financial resources: internal; pro bono Active since: 5/9/91 "Consensus Document"	Presidential advisor, Republican and Democratic party elite, informal agency access, business associations	"Market-driven solutions to environmental problems" Utilize informal access to both Bush and Clinton administrations to push for change

Continued on next page

Organization	Human/ Financial Resources	NAFTA Resources	Access	Strategy
National Wildlife Federation (NWF)	5.8 million members $71 million Sources: indiv, corp, sales, fdtn	Staff: 2 executives, 2 staff (share link with WWF) Financial resources: internal; foundation; pro bono Active since: 11/27/90 trade and environment document	Trade advisor, Republic and Democratic party elites, EPA administrator, informal agency access, business association, Mexican political elites	"Important opportunity to link trade and environment" Used pivotal role as Bush administration target to influence environmental agenda in manner consistent with trade policy objectives; generated grassroots support when needed
The Nature Conservancy (TNC)	724,000 members $100 million Sources: indiv, fdtn, corp, federal	Staff: 1 executive 25 staff Financial resources: internal Active since: 5/93 "Group of 7" letter	Trade advisor, Republican and Democratic party elite, business association	"Nonconfrontational" Cooperate; maintenance; played small role in policy process; withdrew from public debate in summer 1993
Natural Resources Defense Council (NRDC)	170,000 members $16 million Sources: indiv, fdtn, corp, litigation	Staff: 1 executive, 2 staff Financial resources: internal; foundation Active since: 5/9/91 "Consensus Document"	Trade advisor, Democratic and Republican party elite, informal agency access, business and labor associations	"Influence trade policy by incorporating environmental reforms" Focused on technical advice and resolving environmental problems.
The National Audubon Society (NAS)	600,000 members $44 million Sources: indiv, corp, fdtn	Staff: 1 executive, .5 staff Financial resources: internal Active since: 1/93	Trade advisor, Democratic and Republican party elite, informal agency access, business association	"Inside pressure, outside silence" Focused attention on lobbying Clinton administration to include greater assurance for wildlife protection mixed

Organization	Human/ Financial Resources	NAFTA Resources	Access	Strategy
Defenders of Wildlife (Defenders)	85,000 members $5 million Sources: indiv, sales, corp, fdtn	Staff: 1 staff Financial resources: internal Active since: 3/12/93 Kantor letter	Not active on NAFTA during Bush administration, Democratic party elite, informal informal agency access, business association	"Wildlife preservation laws" Consensus builder looking for adequate guarantees of environmental protection
Sierra Club	600,000 members $34 million Sources: indiv, sales, corp, fdtn	Staff: 1 executive 1 staff Financial resources: internal; foundation Active since: 5/91 Fast Track Opposition	Democratic Party elite, informal agency access	"Opposition unless strong environmental protection" Adversarial role, focused on grassroots education and congressional lobbying
Friends of the Earth (FoE)	50,000 members $3.4 million Sources: indiv, fdtn	Staff: 1 executive 1.5 staff Financial resources: internal; foundation Active since: 1990 Canada Coalitions	No formal or informal party elite access No formal or informal agency labor association	"Global trade threatens the environment" Focused on Congress constituency, education, broad-based coalition building
Public Citizen	Not available	Staff: 1 executive 4 staff Financial resources: internal; foundation Active since: 3/91	Anti-NAFTA elites	"Trade agreements undermine national sovereignty" Adversarial, focus on Congress constituency, education, broad-based coalition building

Continued on next page

Organization	Human/ Financial Resources	NAFTA Resources	Access	Strategy
Greenpeace	1.6 million members $34 million Sources: indiv, sales	Staff: .5 executive, .5 staff Financial re- sources: internal Active since: 1/93	None	"Global commerce threatens the envi- ronment and com- munity" Slow to engage in public debate be- cause of differ- ences of opinion between U.S. and Mexican affili- ates; adversarial, increase public awareness

*See Appendix A: Explanatory Information for details regarding categorizations.
**Refers to the use of Ken Berlin, partner at Winthrop, Stimson, Putnam and Roberts, who worked pro bono on behalf of WWF, NWF, and EDF during 1993.

EXPLANATORY INFORMATION

The data contained in this chart combines interview information and published organizational literature. Some explanatory information follows.

HUMAN/FINANCIAL RESOURCES

Membership information obtained from "Inside the Environmental Groups, 1994." *Outside Magazine* XIX (no. 3, March 1994): 65–73. *Outside Magazine* annu- ally publishes their scorecard of environmental organization performance. Fi- nancial resources and their sources are taken from the 1993 Annual Reports of the various environmental organizations. Information regarding the source of funds differs from group to group, direct inquiries with each organization did not result in greater detail; therefore, revenue sources are listed with no specific determination as to the percentage of total revenue from each source.

NAFTA RESOURCES

Resources on NAFTA were obtained during interviews with representatives from each organization and from Wathen, Thomas A. *A Guide to Trade and the Environment.* New York: Environmental Grantmakers Association, 1992. Percentages of each staff person's time dedicated to trade is based upon inter- views with each staff person. The following people represent the staff focused on NAFTA:

Defenders of Wildlife: John Fitzgerald, counsel for wildlife policy (until March 1993); William Snape, associate counsel (after March 1993).

Environmental Defense Fund: Scott Hajost, international counsel; Peter Emerson, senior economist; Jim Marston, senior attorney; Marsha Aranof, vice-president, worked on trade during the final stages of NAFTA, in large part due to her relationship with Mickey Kantor and other staff members at the USTR. EDF also employed Alan Neff, attorney for specific research projects and used Ken Berlin of Winthrop, Stimson, Putnam and Roberts, pro bono on NAFTA.

Friends of the Earth: Alex Hittle, international coordinator; Andrea Durbin, policy associate; Brent Blackwelder, vice-president.

Greenpeace: Cameron Duncan, economist; Barbara Dudley, executive director.

National Audubon Society: Kathleen Rogers, attorney (July 1992 to present); Peter A.A. Berle, president.

National Wildlife Federation: Stewart Hudson, legislative representative; Lynn A. Greenwalt, vice-president of international affairs; Jay Hair, president. The following people worked as NWF's trade and environment specialists throughout the NAFTA policy event: Paul Speck (November 1990 through May 1991); Ted Stimson (May 1991 through May 1992); Kelly Wojohowitz (May 1992 through September 1992); and Rodrigo Prudencio (September 1992 to present).

Natural Resources Defense Council: Justin Ward, senior resource specialist; Jacob Scherr, international program director; Lynn Fischer, international program associate; Glenn Prickett, senior international program associate; John Adams, executive director.

The Nature Conservancy: Tia Nelson, attorney; Katherine Scott, attorney; John Sawhill, executive director.

Public Citizen's Congress Watch: Lori Wallach, staff attorney; and the following people throughout the NAFTA process: Tom Hilliard, (July 1991 through December 1991); Atlanta McIlwraith (December 1991 through May 1993); Chris McGinn (throughout NAFTA); plus Gabriela Boyer and Angela Ledford. In addition to these people, Patti Goldman, attorney, Public Citizen Litigation Group; Joan Claybrook, president, Public Citizen; and Ralph Nader, founder, all spent some of their energies on NAFTA.

Sierra Club: John Audley, program director, trade and the environment (May 1991 through July 1993); J. Michael McCloskey, chairman; Larry Williams,

director, international program; Carl Pope, executive director; Dan Seligman, trade specialist (May 1993 to December 1993).

World Wildlife Fund: Russell Train, chairman (August 1991 through January
1993); Kathryn Fuller, president (January 1993 to present); Doug Siglin,
assistant to chairman of the board (May 1992 to present). In addition,
WWF was assisted by Ken Berlin, partner of Winthrop, Stimson, Putnam
and Roberts, to coordinate environmental goals for NAFTA from February
1993 until September 1993. Mr. Berlin remained involved, working on
behalf of EDF, NWF, and WWF until November 1993.

Trade Resources were determined during interviews with representatives
from each organization. *Internal* denotes that work was done on NAFTA
using financial resources of the organizations; *foundation* indicates that
involvement was assisted by nonprofit foundation support.

Active Participation is based upon interviews with individual representatives
of each organization.

ACCESS

Access to political elites was determined using biographical information on staff
and board members of each environmental organization involved in NAFTA.
Information on staff was obtained during interviews with each staff member.
Information regarding board members was obtained either directly from each
organization (as in the case of the Sierra Club, World Wildlife Fund, Friends
of the Earth, and Public Citizen) or by searching each board member's name
in the NEXIS data base. Only those board members who could be clearly
identified are included as informal links for political access. The following
links to political elites were established for each organization.

Informal agency access to the Clinton administration indicates those organizations whose leaders had working or personal relationships with Bruce
Babbitt, secretary of the interior, and Tim Wirth, associate secretary, Department of State.

National Audubon Society

Bush: Peter Berle, advisor, USTR; Scott Reed, board member, NAS, and execu-
tive director of Republic National Committee (board member); John Carroll
Whitaker, cofounder of the Richard Nixon Library Foundation (board
member).
Clinton: Peter Berle, advisor, USTR; Madeline Kunin (board member) and
Clinton cabinet member; informal access.
Other elites: None.

Business: (Through board members): Peter W. Stroh (Stroh Brewery); John J. Phelan, Jr., New York Stock Exchange chairman; Phillip B. Rooney, president, Waste Management, Inc.

Environmental Defense Fund

Bush: Fred Krupp, advisor, Presidents Council on Environmental Quality; Scott Hajost, political appointee, Department of State; President Reagan.
Clinton: Marsha Aranof, personal acquaintance of Mickey Kantor; Wren Wirth (board member), wife of assistant secretary of state, Tim Wirth.
Business elites: (Through board members or advisory councils): James Miscoll, Bank of America; Roger Sant, chairman, AES Corporation; R. E. Turner, Turner Broadcasting.

National Wildlife Federation

Bush: Jay Hair, advisor to USTR, personal friends with William Reilly, EPA administrator.
Clinton: Jay Hair, advisor to USTR.
Business: Corporate Conservation Council members: Asea Brown Boceri, AT&T, Bank of America, Browning-Ferris Industries, Ciba-Geigy Corporation, Dow Chemical, Duke Power Company, DuPont Company, Johnson and Johnson, 3M, Merck and Company, Monsanto, Pacific Gas and Electric, Proctor and Gamble, Shell Oil, USX, WMX. Board members: Gene Stout, Coachman Industries.
Other trade elites: Jay Hair developed a personal relationship with President Carlos Salinas de Gortari during NAFTA negotiations.

Friends of the Earth

Bush: None.
Clinton: Informal access to the Departments of State and the Interior.
Business: None.
Other trade elites: None.

The Nature Conservancy

Bush: John Sawhill, USTR advisor.
Clinton: John Sawhill, USTR advisor.
Business: Board members: Joseph Williams, Williams Oil Company; Ian Cummings, Cummings International; James Harvey, Transamerica Corporation; Richard Heckert, E.I. Du Pont.
Other elites: John C. Whitehead (board member), former chairman of Goldman Sachs and friends with Mexican President Salinas.

Natural Resources Defense Council

Bush: John Adams, USTR advisor.

Clinton: John Adams, USTR advisor; political appointees to Clinton administration but none directly involved in trade policy.

Business: None identified directly with trade liberalization.

World Wildlife Fund

Bush: Russell Train, chairman, USTR advisor, and personal friend of George Bush; William Reilly, EPA administrator; Gordon Binder, ex-chief of staff to EPA administrator, Reilly.

Clinton: Kathryn Fuller, USTR advisor; Ken Berlin, personal friend of USTR staff.

Business: Joseph Cullman, Philip Morris Companies; Russell Train, Union Carbide; Rodney Wagner, Saudi Arabian Oil Company; G. A. Buder III, Texas oil exploration; H. Eugene Mcbrayer, Exxon Chemical Company; Nelson Mead, The Mead Corporation; William Ruckelshaus, Browning Ferris Industries and former EPA director, Weyerhauser.

Other trade elites: WWF has overseen projects in Mexico since 1980. They work on sea turtle conservation and monarch butterfly projects, plus are involved in the Lacadonia Rainforest preservation project. Kathryn Fuller and Russell Train are personal friends of President Carlos Salinas.

Sierra Club

Bush: None.

Clinton: Political appointees but none involved in trade policy; informal access to the Department of State and the Interior.

Business: None through board members.

Other trade elites: Mike McCloskey, chairman, Sierra Club, and Tom Donahue, secretary, AFL-CIO, developed a professional relationship during NAFTA debate.

Public Citizen

Bush: None.

Clinton: Political appointees but none involved in trade policy; Ralph Nader and USTR ambassador, Mickey Kantor, have been acquainted for years through Kantor's advocacy work in California.

Business: Associated with Rupert Murdoch and H. Ross Perot during NAFTA debate.

Other trade elites: Professional relationship with AFL-CIO.

Defenders of Wildlife

Bush: None.

Clinton: Informal access to the Departments of State and the Interior.

Business: None through board members specifically identified with trade policy.

Greenpeace

Bush: None.
Clinton: None.
Business: None through board members specifically identified with trade policy.

Appendix B:
Acronyms and Abbreviations

ACTPN	Advisory Committee on Trade Policy Negotiations
ACTWU	Amalgamated Clothing and Textile Workers Union
AFSC	American Friends Service Committee
APEC	Asia-Pacific Economic Cooperation
ATI	Arizona Toxics Information
BECC	Border Environmental Cooperation Commission
BEP	Border Ecology Project
BTA	Border Trade Alliance
CEC	Commission for Environmental Cooperation
CFTA	Canada-U.S. Free Trade Agreement
CI	Conservation International
CIEL	Center for International Environmental Law
CNI	Community Nutrition Institute
CTC/CTWC	Citizen's Trade (Watch) Campaign
CTE	Commission for Trade and Environment (World Trade Organization)
Defenders or DoW	Defenders of Wildlife
EDF	Environmental Defense Fund
ENR	(Office of) Environment and Natural Resources
FAO	Food and Agriculture Organization
FoE	Friends of the Earth
GATT	General Agreements on Tariffs and Trade
IATP	Institute for Agriculture and Trade Policy
IBEP	Integrated Border Environmental Plan
IBWC	International Boundary and Water Commission
IEA	International Environmental Agreement
ITC	International Trade Commission
IUCN	International Union for the Conservation of Nature
JPAC	Joint Public Advisory Committee
MMPA	Marine Mammal Protection Act
MODTLE	Mobilization on Development, Trade, Labor, and the Environment
NAAEC	North American Agreement on Environmental Cooperation
NAC	National Advisory Committee

NADBANK	North American Development Bank
NAFTA	North American Free Trade Agreement
NAS	National Audubon Society
NEPA	National Environmental Policy Act
NGO	Non-Governmental Organization
NRDC	Natural Resources Defense Council
NWF	National Wildlife Federation
OECD	Organization for Economic Cooperation and Development
TCPS	Texas Center for Policy Studies
TEPAC	Trade and Environment Policy Advisory Committee
TNC	The Nature Conservancy
UNCED	United Nations Conference on the Environment and Development
UNCTAD	United Nations Conference on Trade and Development
UNEP	United Nations Environmental Program
Uruguay Round	Uruguay Round of GATT
USTR	Office of United States Trade Representative
WTO	World Trade Organization
WWF	World Wildlife Fund-U.S.

Appendix C: NAFTA Timeline and Environmental Participation in Significant Events

Date	Description	Participants
6/90	Consultation begins between Mexico and the United States on the possibility of negotiating a free trade agreement.	Trade ministers plus private ACTPN advisors participate.
8/90–9/90	Mexican President Carlos Salinas de Gortari writes President George Bush to formally propose the negotiation of a free trade agreement (8/21/90). President Bush informs Congress of his intention to negotiate an agreement with Mexico (9/25/90).	
11/90	Bush and Salinas meet in Monterrey, Mexico, to discuss a bilateral trade agreement; agree to negotiate a bilateral border environmental agreement.	Business leaders attend meeting. EPA administrator, William Reilly, also attends.
1/15/91	Capitol Hill Briefing: "U.S.-Mexico Free Trade: Setting the Agenda." First time environmental issues formally raised in context of trade negotiations.	Organized by NWF, MODTLE, BEP, with attendance by TCPS, and FoE.
1/23/91	Canada formally announces its desire to take part in negotiations.	

Date	Description	Participants
2/6/91	Press conference in opposition to Fast Track for NAFTA, "The Environmental Agenda."	Organized by NWF, AFL-CIO, MODTLE; included NRDC, FoE, BEP.
3/1/91	Bush formally requests Fast Track extension for UR-GATT and Fast Track for NAFTA.	
3/7/91	Letter from Senate Finance Committee chairman, Lloyd Bentsen, and House Ways and Means Committee chairman, Dan Rostenkowski, requesting President Bush to respond to labor and environmental concerns prior to the Fast Track vote scheduled for mid-May. Bush agrees to respond by 1 May.	
3/4/91	USTR ambassador, Carla Hills, meets with leaders of national environmental organizations in meetings arranged by EPA administrator, William Reilly.	WWF, EDF, NWF, Sierra Club, NAS, NRDC.
5/1/91	President Bush: "Response to Congressional Concerns Arising from the North American Free Trade Agreement"; NRDC and NAS endorse response, Public Citizen announces its opposition	Written by USTR with assistance from EPA and the Department of Labor.
5/7/91	Letter from Senator Timothy Wirth to EPA administrator, Reilly, suggesting compromises on Fast Track; CTW initiates campaign to defeat Fast Track in Congress.	NWF and EDF assist Wirth's staff. Public Citizen, Sierra Club, and FoE active in CTW campaign.
5/10/91	"A Response to the Bush Administration's Environmental Action Plan."	Organized by NWF, endorsed by NRDC, NAS, EDF, CNI.

Continued on next page

Date	Description	Participants
5/17/91	EPA administrator Reilly's response to Wirth.	
5/19/91	NWF endorses Fast Track in *NY Times* article.	
5/23–4/91	Fast Track approved for NAFTA.	

NAFTA NEGOTIATIONS

Date	Description	Participants
7/91	Negotiations begin.	EPA officials included in negotiations for first time in history of U.S. trade policy.
8/16/91	Environmental advisors selected.	WWF, NWF, NRDC, TNC, NAS.
8/16/91	GATT Tuna/Dolphin Decision; 9/13/91 environmental community response.	Sierra Club, Public Citizen, FoE, Defenders, Greenpeace, CNI; NRDC responds in separate release.
10/17/91	USTR Environmental Review released.	Written by USTR, with EPA assistance.
10/23/91	Draft border environmental plan released.	EPA authored.
10/26/91	Zacatecas, Mexico, ministerial meeting where parallel track to negotiations accepted by Canada and Mexico.	
12/10/91	"Dunkel Draft" of GATT released. Criticized by environmental groups in December press release.	Public Citizen, Sierra Club, FoE, Greenpeace, Defenders. NRDC criticized Draft in separate release (2/21/91).
1/3/92	NWF correspondence with Ambassador Hills regarding investment conditions of Agreement. 2/27/92 letter from Hills to NWF rejecting proposals; 3/9/92 NWF letter to Hills, backing away from position.	
5/92	Meetings between Ambassador Hills and environmental groups, organized by Senator Max Baucus.	WWF, NWF, NRDC, NAS, EDF, Defenders.

Date	Description	Participants
5/28/92	"Minimal Environmental Safeguards" position paper released.	Organized by NWF. NRDC, Sierra Club, and border groups participated in development, but did not endorse it. Endorsed by EDF.
6/92	"Environmental Safeguards" position paper.	Organized by NRDC. Endorsed by Sierra Club, EDF, NAS, Defenders, Public Citizen, CNI, border groups.
7/24/92	NRDC letter to Ambassador Hills indicating they cannot support NAFTA as negotiated.	
7/26/92	Environmental Community letter to negotiators in all three countries.	Organized by NWF, endorsed by Sierra Club, NRDC, Defenders, EDF, NAS, Public Citizen, FoE.
8/17/92	Negotiators "shake hands" on completed Agreement.	
8/25/93	Environmental opposition to Agreement.	NRDC, Public Citizen, Sierra Club, FoE, Greenpeace in separate statements.
9/9/92	"Trade in 21st Century Conference" where Richard Gephardt calls for renegotiation of text.	Organized by AFL-CIO, Public Citizen, FoE, Sierra Club, NFFC; attended by NRDC.
9/17/92	Meeting between environmental ministers of Mexico, Canada, and United States, Agreement to negotiated North American Commission on Environment announced. WWF informally endorses Agreement in testimony before Senate Finance Committee.	
9/30/92	NWF officially endorses "environmental" language in NAFTA text.	
10/92	Meetings to discuss NACE begin, but called off by Mexico until after presidential election.	

Continued on next page

Date	Description	Participants
10/92	Presidential candidate, Bill Clinton, developed NAFTA position: supports Agreement "with strong supplemental agreement for environment, labor, and import surges" during speech at Raleigh-Durham, NC, 10/24/92.	Sierra Club, NRDC, NWF, WWF contribute information to campaign; NWF and WWF asked to help draft final position.
11/92	Election of Bill Clinton as president of the United States.	

Supplemental Agreement Negotiations

Date	Description	Participants
2/1/93	Congressmen Ron Wyden and Robert Matsui send letter to Clinton supporting his position on NAFTA.	
2/17/93	Environmental community meets with new USTR ambassador, Mickey Kantor, to discuss environment and trade. Marks beginning of more open dialogue between USTR and environmental community regarding NAFTA.	Attendance by entire environmental community; however, Kantor did not revise the private advisors.
2/25/93	NAFTA introduced to Canadian parliament.	
3/93	Border recommendations paper.	NRDC, EDF, border groups.
3/12/93	Letter from environmental community to Ambassador Kantor regarding supplemental agreement.	Organized by Defenders and CIEL; endorsed by Sierra Club, Public Citizen, FoE, Greenpeace, NAS.
3/5/93	Senate Environment and Public Works staff tries to mediate compromise between USTR and environmental groups.	NWF, NRDC, Defenders, Sierra Club, FoE, EDF, WWF.
3/5/93	Environmental community meetings with staff from all executive agencies to press environmental agenda for Supplemental Agreement.	Meetings attended by most organizations working on trade policy.

Date	Description	Participants
4/29/93	Robert Matsui (D-CA) selected to head NAFTA effort in House by Dan Rostenkowski.	
5/8/93	Letter to Ambassador Kantor restating environmental objectives.	Organized by Ken Berlin for WWF. Organizers included WWF, NWF, EDF; endorsing organizations included NRDC, Defenders, NAS, TNC.
5/26/93	Canadian MP endorses NAFTA.	
6/4/93	Business opposition to Supplemental Agreements formally expressed in letters from USA*NAFTA.	
6/30/93	*Public Citizen v. United States Trade Representative* decided against USTR; eventually overturned by superior court on 8/24/93.	Litigants include Public Citizen, Sierra Club, FoE. Defenders, NRDC, NAS filed amicus brief in support of decision; WWF critical of decision in 7/16/94 Senate Environment and Public Works Hearing.
8/13/93	Supplemental Agreement negotiations concluded.	
8/19/93	Richard Daly selected to head White House NAFTA team. Team includes Howard Paster, White House director for legislative affairs, and Bill Frenzel, former Minnesota Republican congressman.	
9/13/93	Letter from Ambassador Kantor to NRDC addressing their outstanding concerns with document.	
9/13/93	Opposition press conference organized by David Bonior (D-MI).	Sierra Club, Public Citizen (among others).
9/14/93	NAFTA Supplemental Agreement signing at White House.	NWF, WWF, NRDC, EDF, NAS.

Continued on next page

Date	Description	Participants
9/15/93	Pro-NAFTA press conference sponsored by Senator Max Baucus.	WWF, NWF, NAS, EDF, NRDC.
10/11/93	Period of competition between environmental groups divided over NAFTA. Decreased public attention on environment.	Leading groups opposed, Sierra Club, Public Citizen, FoE; Supportive, WWF, NWF, EDF.
11/22/93	NAFTA passed by House.	

Appendix D: Congressional Testimony and Hearings

RECORD OF CONGRESSIONAL HEARINGS, SIGNIFICANT DOCUMENTS, AND ENVIRONMENTAL PANELISTS ON ISSUES PERTAINING TO THE NORTH AMERICAN FREE TRADE AGREEMENT

Fast Track

6/14/90 and 6/28/90, House Committee on Ways and Means, Subcommittee on Trade, "Mexico-US Free Trade Agreement, prospects and implications," Y4.W36:101–108

6/28/90, House Committee on Foreign Affairs, "Enterprise for the Americas Initiative," Y4.F76/1:En8/4
> Geoffrey Barnard, Nature Conservancy
> Barbara Bramble, NWF (representing EDF)

2/6/91 and 2/20/91, Senate Committee on Finance, "United States-Mexico Free Trade Agreement," S102-75
> Mary Kelly, TCPS

2/20/91a, House Committee on Ways and Means, Subcommittee on Trade, "Proposed Negotiation of a Free Trade Agreement with Mexico," Y4.W36:102-19
> David Ortman, FoE

2/28/91a, House Committee on Agriculture, "Review of the Uruguay Round of Multilateral Trade Negotiations Under the General Agreements on Tariffs and Trade," Y4.Ag8/1:102-4

3/6/91, House Committee on Foreign Relations, Subcommittees on International Economic Policy and on Western Hemispheric Affairs, "The North American Free Trade Agreement," Y4.F76/1:N 81/16
> Stewart Hudson, NWF

3/12/91 and 4/11/91b House Committee on Ways and Means, Subcommittee on Trade, "President's Request for Extension of Fast Track Trade Agreement Implementing Authority"

3/13/91b, House Committee on Agriculture, "Review of Fast Track Extension Request Submitted by the Administration, House Committee on Agriculture," Y4.Ag8/1:102-17

3/14/91b, Senate Committee on Finance, "Extension of Fast Track Legislative Procedures," Y4.F49:S.hrg.102-81

3/14/91, House Committee on Banking, Finance and Urban Affairs, "The US-Mexican Free Trade Agreement," Y4.B22/1:102-20

3/14/91, Senate Committee on Judiciary, "Hearings on Fast Track: Intellectual Property," Y4.J89/2:S.hrg.214

3/14/91, Senate Committee on Foreign Relations, "Issues Relating to a Bilateral Free Trade Agreement with Mexico," Y4.F76/2:S.hrg.102-95

    Michael McCloskey, SC

3/20/91, 5/8/91, and 5/15/91, House Committee on Energy and Commerce, Subcommittee on Consumer Protection and Competitiveness, "North American Free Trade Agreement," Y4.EN2/3:102-88, Y4.En2/3:102-15

    Peter Emerson, EDF

    Alex Hittle, FoE

    Richard Kamp, BEP

    Craig Merrilees, FTC, NTC

    Lori Wallach, Public Citizen

    Mary Kelly, TCPS

4/16/91, House Committee on Banking, Finance and Urban Affairs, Subcommittee on International Development, Finance, Trade and Monetary Policy, "The U.S.-Mexican Free Trade Agreement," Y4.B22/1:102-20

    Stewart Hudson, NWF

4/17/91c, Senate Committee on Finance, "Review of the Uruguay Round: Commitments To Open Foreign Markets," Y4.F49:S.hrg.102-105

4/23/91 and 5/8/91, Senate Committee on Environment and Public Works, Subcommittee on Labor and Human Resources, "Economic and Environmental Implications of the Proposed U.S. Trade Agreement With Mexico," Y4.P96/10:S.hrg.102-116

    Homero Aridjis, Grupo de Cien

    Michael Gregory, ATI

    Craig Merrilees, FTC

4/24/91c, House Committee on Agriculture, "Proposed U.S.-Mexico Free Trade Agreement and Fast Track Authority," Y4.Ag8/1:102-9

4/24/91d, Senate Committee on Finance, "Enterprise of the Americas Initiative Related to Fast Track," Y4.F49.S.hrg.102-232

4/24/91, Committee on Small Business, "U.S.-Mexico Free Trade Agreement: The Small Business Perspective," Y4.Sm1:102-71

4/30/91, House Committee on Education and Labor, Subcommittee on Labor Management Relations and Subcommittee on Employment Opportunities, "Hearing on Implication for Workers of the Fast Track Process and the Mexican Free Trade Agreement," Y4.Ed8/1:102-12

5/1/91c, House Committee on Ways and Means, "Exchange of Letters on Issues Concerning the Negotiation of a North American Free Trade Agreement," Y4.W36:WMCP 102-10

5/7/91c, Senate Committee on Finance, "The President's United States-Mexico Free Trade Letter," Sr. 102-202

    EPA administrator, William Reilly

5/8/91, Senate Committee on Agriculture, Nutrition and Forestry, "Fast Track Procedures for Agricultural Trade Negotiations, Y4.Ag8/3:S.hrg.102-397

5/8/91, House Committee on Public Works and Transportation, Subcommittee on Economic Development, "Fast Track Authority and North America Free Trade Agreement," Y4.P 96/11:102-12
    Craig Merrilees, NTC and FTC
    Lori Wallach, Public Citizen

5/14/91, House Committee on the Budget, "Economic Impact of the Mexico Free Trade Agreement," Y4.B85/3:102-6-1

5/14/91, Senate Committee on the Judiciary, "Hearings on Fast Track: Intellectual Property," Y4.J89/2:S.hrg.102-214

5/15/91, House Subcommittee on Intellectual Property and Judicial Administration, "Intellectual Property and International Issues," Y4.J89/1:102/74

5/16/91, House Committee on Banking, Finance, and Urban Affairs, "U.S. Mexican Free Trade Agreement," Y4.B22/1:102-20

NAFTA

8/2/91, Senate Committee on Finance, "Review of Ongoing Trade Negotiations and Completed Trade Agreements," S.hrg.102-423

9/27/91b, House Committee on Energy and Commerce,
    Ralph Nader, Public Citizen
    David Phillips, Earth Island
    Steven Shrybman, Canadian Environmental Law Association
    Statement of Charles Arden-Clarke, policy analyst, WWF

9/30/91, House Committee on Small Business, Subcommittee on Regulation, Business Opportunities and Energy, "Protecting the Environment in North American Free Trade Agreement Negotiations," Y4.Sm1:102-44
    Pet Emerson, EDF
    Lynn Greenwalt, NWF
    Mary Kelly, TCPS
    Michael McCloskey, Sierra Club
    Enrique Medina, Industrial Ecology International

10/16/91, House Committee on Foreign Affairs, "Update on Recent Developments in Mexico," Y4.F76/1:M57/15
    Stewart Hudson, NWF
    Brent Blackwelder, FoE
    Larry Williams, Sierra Club
    Letter from Justin Ward, NRDC

10/25/91, Senate Committee on Finance, Subcommittee on International Trade, "Trade and the Environment," S.hrg.102-566
    Lynn Greenwalt, NWF
    Justin Ward, NRDC
    Roy Manik, EDF

12/9/91, House Committee on Foreign Affairs, Subcommittee on International Economic Policy, and Subcommittee on Western Hemispheric Affairs, "American Jobs and Environmental Protection," Y4.F76/1:F87/2

2/21/92, House Committee on Small Business, Subcommittee on Regulation, Business Opportunities and Energy, "North American Free Trade Agreement," Field Hearing in Nogales, Arizona, Y4.Sm1:102-65
>   Richard Kamp, BEP
>   Fernando Medina-Robles, Comité Civico de Divulgacion Ecologica

5/5/92, House Committee on Foreign Affairs, Subcommittees on International Economic Policy and Western Hemispheric Affairs, "North American Free Trade Agreement: Mexico's Petroleum Sector," Y4.F76/1:F87/4/pt.1/2

4/24/92, House Committee on Education and Labor, "Joint Field Hearing To Address Proposed North American Free Trade Agreement With Mexico and Canada, and Hr 3878, the American Jobs Protection Act," Y4.ED 8/1:102-129
>   Craig Merrilees, FTC
>   Carl Pope, Sierra Club
>   Al Meyerhoff, NRDC

4/24/92, Senate Committee on Labor and Human Resources, "Save American Jobs Act," Y4.L11/4:S.hrg.102-550

4/8/92, 7/9/92, 9/16–9/23/92, and 9/30/92, House Committee on Agriculture, "Review of Issues Related to the North American Free Trade Agreement," Y4.AG8/1:102-70
>   Timothy Atkeson, EPA
>   John Audley, Sierra Club
>   William Barclay, Greenpeace

5/7/92, House Committee on Energy and Commerce, "Impact of Textile Fraud on Commerce," Y4.En2/3:102-144

5/12/92 and 7/1/92, House Committee on Foreign Affairs, Subcommittees on International Economic Policy and Western Hemispheric Affairs, "Beyond the North American Free Trade Agreement: Chile, the Caribbean, and Administration Views," Y4.F76/1:F87/5/PT.1/2 part 1

7/22/92, Senate Committee on Finance, "Trade Policy Legislation," S 102-1065

9/8/92, Senate Committee on Finance, Subcommittee on International Trade, "North American Free Trade Agreement," Y4.F49:S.hrg.102-1032
>   Katheryn Fuller, WWF
>   Stewart Hudson, NWF
>   Peter Emerson, EDF
>   Justin Ward, NRDC

9/9/92, House Committee on Ways and Means, Subcommittee on Trade, "North American Free Trade Agreement," Y4.W36:102-135
>   John Audley, Sierra Club
>   Rodney Leonard, CNI
>   Pete Emerson, EDF
>   Kathryn Fuller, WWF

3/9/92, Senate Committee on Finance, "US Trade Policy and NAFTA," Y4.F49:S.hrg.103-66

9/18/92, House Committee on Small Business, "The North American Free Trade Agreement," Y4.SM1:102-90

9/30/92, House Committee on Science, Space and Technology, "The Role of Science in Adjudicating Trade Disputes under the North American Free Trade Agreement," Y4.SCI2:102/159
> Robert Housman, CIEL

12/15/92, House Committee on Small Business, "North American Free Trade Agreement," Y4.SM1:102-93

2/18/93, House Committee on Energy and Commerce, Subcommittee on Commerce, Consumer Protection and Competitiveness, "North American Free Trade Agreement," Y4.En2/3:103-10
> Lori Wallach, Public Citizen

2/24/93, House Committee on Foreign Affairs, Joint Hearing Before Subcommittees on Economic Policy, Trade and Environment and Western Hemisphere, "The North American Free Trade Agreement: Environment and Labor Agreements," Y4/F76/F87/6
> Stewart Hudson, NWF

2/25/93, House Committee on Small Business, "North American Free Trade Agreement: Mexico's Political and Legal Environment for Doing Business," Y4.SM1:103–4

3/9/93, Senate Committee on Finance, "U.S. Trade Policy and NAFTA," Y4.f49:S.hrg.103-66

3/10/93, House Committee on Merchant Marine and Fisheries Subcommittee on Environment and Natural Resources, "Impacts of Trade Agreements on US Environmental Protection and Natural Resource Conservation Efforts," Y4.M53:103–5
> Robert Housman and Paul Orbuch, CIEL
> Bill Snape, Defenders
> Ralph Nader and Lori Wallach, Public Citizen
> Barbara Dudley, Greenpeace
> John Audley, Sierra Club

3/11/93a, House Committee on Ways and Means Subcommittee on Trade, "Supplemental Agreements to the North American Free Trade Agreement," Y4.W36:103-8
> John Audley, Sierra Club
> Pete Emerson, EDF
> Lori Wallach, Public Citizen
> Stewart Hudson, NWF

3/16/93a, Senate Committee on Environment and Public Works, "Environmental Aspects of the North American Free Trade Agreement," Y4.P96/10:S.hrg.103-75
> Jay Hair, NWF
> Justin Ward, NRDC
> Larry Williams on behalf of J. Michael McCloskey, Sierra Club

3/16/93, House Subcommittee on Technology, Environment, and Aviation, "Technology Policy: Trade and Technology Issues, Vol. II," Y4.SCI2:103/11

3/17/93a, House Committee on Agriculture, "Review of the President's Supplemental Agreements to the North American Free Trade Agreement and

an Update on the Uruguay Round of the GATT Negotiations,"
Y4.AG8/1:103–10

3/30–31/93, 4/20/93, 5/3–4/93, and 5/6/93, House Committee on Appropriations, "Departments of Commerce, Justice, and State, the Judiciary, and
Related Agencies Appropriations for 1994," Y4.AP6/1:C73/2/994/PT.6

3/3/93–3/5/93, House Committee on Government Operations, Subcommittee
on Commerce, Consumer and Monetary Affairs, "The North American
Free Trade Agreement and Its Impact on the Textile/Apparel/Fiber and
Auto Parts Industries," Y4.G74/7:AM

4/2/92, Joint Committee on Economics, "U.S.-Latin American Economic Relations," Y4.EC7:L34/6/993

4/22/93, Senate Committee on Banking, Housing, and Urban Affairs, "The
Impact of the North American Free Trade Agreement on U.S. Jobs and
Wages," Y4.B22/3: S.hrg. 103-20

4/27/93b, House Committee on Ways and Means, "President's Request for
Extension of Fast Track Procedures for Uruguay Round Implementation
and Possible Administration Requests for Extensions of Expiring Trade
Programs," Y4.W36.103-11

4/28/93, House Subcommittee on Oversight of Government Management,
"Federal Job Movement Data and the Implications for NAFTA," Y4.G74/
9:S.hrg.103-106

4/29/93, House Committee on Public Works and Transportation, "Transportation Infrastructure and Safety Impacts of the North American Free Trade
Agreement," Y4.P96/11:103-21

5/4/93, "Surface Transportation Implications of NAFTA," Y4.C73/7:S.hrg.
103-157

5/4/93, House Committee on Government Operations, "North American Free
Trade Agreement (NAFTA) and Its Impact on the Textile/Apparel/Fiber
and Auto Parts Industries," YA.G74/7:AM3/3

5/6/93, Senate Committee on Commerce, Science and Transportation, "Effects
of the North American Free Trade Agreement," Y4.C73/7:S.hrg.103-917

5/18/93, Senate Committee on Commerce, Science, and Transportation, "U.S.
Competitiveness in the Global Marketplace," Y4.C73/7:S.hrg.103-390

5/20/93, Senate Committee on Finance, "Renewal of Fast Track Authority and
the Generalized System of Preferences Program," Y4.F49: S.hrg. 103-285

5/20, 27/93, House Committee on Government Operations, Subcommittee
on Employment, Housing, and Aviation, "North American Free Trade
Agreement: Are There Jobs for American Workers?" Y4.F74/7:AM3/4

5/20/93, House Committee on Small Business, "NAFTA and Peso Devaluation:
A Problem for US Exporters?" Y4.SM1:103-18

6/11/93, Field Hearing by Committee on Agriculture, Subcommittee on General Farm Commodities, "Impact of Canadian Grain Imports," Y4.AG8/
1:103-22

6/24/93c, House Committee on Ways and Means, "Caribbean Basin Free Trade
Agreements Act," Y4.W36:103-28

7/22/93, Senate Committee on Commerce, Science, and Transportation, "Agricultural Trade With Mexico," Y4.C73/7/:S.hrg.103-473

7/22/93, Committee on Banking, Finance, and Urban Affairs, Subcommittee on International Development, Finance, and Trade and Monetary Policy, "North American Development Bank," Y4.B22/1:103-57
> Mary Kelly, TCPS

7/22/93, Senate Committee on Environment and Public Works, "National Environmental Policy Act and the North American Free Trade Agreement," Y4.P96/10:S.hrg.103-219
> Rodger Schlickeisen, Defenders
> Kathryn Fuller, WWF

7/31/93, 9/29-30/93, 10/14/93, and 10/19/93, House Committee on Agriculture, "North American Free Trade Agreement," Y4.AG8/1:103-45

8/3/93, House Committee on Education and Labor, "Telecommunications Trade," Y4.EN2/3:103-60

8/5/93, House Committee on Government Operations, "High Skills, Low Wages, Productivity and the False Promise of NAFTA," Y4G74/7:SK3

9/8/93, House Committee on Banking, Finance and Urban Affairs, "North American Free Trade Agreement," Hearing to Examine Implications of U.S. Financial Services Industry of NAFTA, Y4.B22/1:103-64 CIS/MF/5

9/9/93, 10/7/93, House Committee on Government Operations, "Can the Labor Side Agreement Save NAFTA?" Y4.G74/7:L11/11

9/14/93d, 9/15/93, 9/21/93, and 9/23/93, House Committee on Ways and Means, Subcommittee on Trade, "North American Free Trade Agreement (NAFTA) and Supplemental Agreements to the NAFTA," Y4.W36:103-48
> Andrea Durbin, FoE
> Pete Emerson, EDF
> Stewart Hudson, NWF
> Carl Pope, Sierra Club
> Lori Wallach, Public Citizen

9/15/93, 9/21/93, and 9/28/93, Senate Finance Committee, "NAFTA and Related Side Agreements," Y4.F49:S.hrg. 103-439
> Fred Krupp, EDF
> Lori Wallach, Public Citizen

Voting Stage

9/21/93, Senate Committee on Agriculture, Nutrition and Forestry, "How NAFTA Will Affect U.S. Agriculture," Y4.AG8/3:S.hrg.103-465

9/22/93, House Committee on Energy and Commerce, "NAFTA: Energy Provisions and Environmental Implications," Y4.EN2/3:103-70
> Brent Blackwelder, FoE
> Cameron Duncan, Greenpeace

9/23/93, and 11/4/93, House Committee on Energy and Commerce, "North American Free Trade Agreement," Y4.EN2/3:103-81
> Alan Hecht, EPA
> Irving Fuller, EPA
> Michael Shapiro, EPA
> David van Hoogstraten, EPA

9/28/93, House Committee on Banking, Finance, and Urban Affairs, "Financial Services Chapter of NAFTA," Y4.B22/1:103-71

9/29/93, House Committee on Government Operations, "Maquiladora Detention: Mexican Trade of Trade Unionists," Y4.G74/7:M32/2

10/5/93, House Committee on Government Operations, "Oversight of U.S. Customs Service and Textile Transshipment," Y4.G74/7:C96/3

10/13/93, Senate Committee on Labor and Human Resources, "North American Free Trade Agreement: Affects on Workers," Y4.L11/4:S.hrg.103-226

10/19/93, Senate Committee on Environment and Public Works, "North American Free Trade Agreement and Its Environmental Side Agreements," Y4.P96/10:S.hrg.103-329

> Jay Hair, NWF
> Fred Krupp, EDF
> Lori Wallach, Public Citizen

10/19/93, House Committee on Government Operations, "Trade Adjustment Assistance: A Failure for Displaced Workers," Y4.G74/7:T67/10

10/21/93, House Committee on Foreign Affairs, "NAFTA and American Jobs," Y4.F76/1:F87/7

10/27/93, Senate Committee on Foreign Relations, "Foreign Policy Implications of the North American Free Trade Agreement and Legislative Requirements for the Side Agreements," Y4.F76/2:S.hrg.103-360

11/9/93, Senate Committee on Energy and Natural Resources, "Use of Risk Analysis and Cost-Benefit Analysis in Setting Environmental Priorities," Y4.EN2.S.hrg.103-336

> Robert Housman, CIEL

11/10/93, Senate Committee on Governmental Affairs, "NAFTA Job Claims: Truth in Statistics?" Y4.G74/9:S.hrg.103-386

11/10/93, House Committee on Merchant Marine and Fisheries, "Environmental Implications of NAFTA," Y4.M53:103-80

> Barbara Dudley, Greenpeace
> Jay Hair, NWF
> Carl Pope, Sierra Club
> Roger Schlickeisen, Defenders

10/28/93, House Committee on Government Operations, "Mexican Agricultural Policies: An Immigration Generator?" Y4.G74/7:M57

10/28/93, 11/5, House Committee on Foreign Affairs, "North American Free Trade Agreement (NAFTA)," Y4.F76/1:F87/6

11/3/93, House Committee on the Judiciary, "Immigration-Related Issues in the North American Free Trade Agreement," Y4.J89/1:103/18

11/8/93, House Committee on Banking, Finance and Urban Affairs, "Abuses Within the Mexican Politican Regulatory and Judicial Systems and Implications for the North American Free Trade Agreement," 103-93

11/10/93, House Committee on Government Operations, "NAFTA: A Negative Impact on Blue Collar, Minority and Female Employment?" Y4.G74/7:AM/5

11/15/93, House Committee on Energy and Commerce, "North American Free Trade Agreement Implementation Act"

No recommendation reported; some aspects related to environment, especially pertaining to Corporate Average Fuel Economy (Clean Air Act) CAFE and to NADBANK, and the ambiguity between U.S. laws and NAFTA.

11/15/93, House Committee on Banking, Finance and Urban Affairs, "North American Free Trade Agreement Implementation Act"
·   Recommends against passage.

11/15/93, House Committee on Ways and Means, "North American Free Trade Agreement Implementation Act"
Reported favorably on passage of NAFTA.

11/18/93, Senate Committees on Finance; Agriculture, Nutrition and Forestry; Commerce, Science and Transportation; Government Affairs; Judiciary; and Foreign Relations, "North American Free Trade Agreement Implementation Act"
Reported favorably on passage of NAFTA (S 1627).

Bibliography

Adams, John. 1993. "Statement of John H. Adams, executive director, Natural Resources Defense Council on Environmental Issues Surrounding the North American Free Trade Agreement." 14 September 1993. Mimeographed.

Adams, John. 1992. Letter to USTR ambassador, Carla Hills, 24 July 1992. Mimeographed.

Advisory Committee for Trade Policy. 1992. "Report on the North American Free Trade Agreement." September 1992.

AFL-CIO. *How They Voted, 1992.* Washington, D.C.: AFL-CIO.

Agusto de Castro, Jeao. 1995. "Environment and Development; The Case of the Developing Countries," In *Green Planet Blues,* edited by Ken Conca, Michael Alberty, and Geoffrey Dabelko. Boulder, Colo.: Westview Press.

Alexander, Carol, and Ken Stump. 1992. *The North American Free Trade Agreement and Energy Trade.* Washington, D.C.: Greenpeace U.S.A.

Alliance for Responsible Trade. 1993. "A Just and Sustainable Trade and Development Initiative for North America." 28 September 1993. Mimeographed.

Almon, Clopper, Alberto Ruiz-Moncayo, and Luis Sangines. 1991. "Simulation of a Mexico-U.S. Free Trade Agreement." *Economic Systems Research* 3, no. 1.

Altschiller, Donald, ed. 1988. *Free Trade Versus Protectionism.* New York: H.W. Wilson.

Anderson, Mark. 1994. Interview with author given by AFL-CIO international economist.

Anderson, Terry L., and Donald R. Leal. 1991. *Free Market Environmentalism.* Boulder, Colo.: Westview Press.

Arden-Clarke, Charles. 1992. *South-North Terms of Trade, Environmental Protection and Sustainable Development.* Gland, Switzerland: World Wide Fund for Nature.

———. 1991a. *Green Protectionism.* Gland, Switzerland: World Wide Fund for Nature.

———. 1991b. *The General Agreement on Tariffs and Trade, Environmental Protection and Sustainable Development.* Gland, Switzerland: World Wide Fund for Nature.

Aridjis, Homero. 1993. "Mexico's Environmental Movement and Its Influence on the NAFTA Negotiations." Grupo de Cien. 19 February 1993. Mimeographed.

Arizona Toxics Information. 1995. Letter to Victor Miramontes, deputy manager, and Alfredo Phillips Olmedo, general manager, North American Development Bank, 18 December 1995. Mimeographed.

Arizona Toxics Information. 1992. Memorandum to Stewart Hudson, NWF, Regarding the 21 May 1992 Draft Trinational Declaration. Mimeographed.

Arnold, R. Douglas. 1990. *The Logic of Congressional Action*. New Haven: Yale University Press.

Asia-Pacific Economic Community Cooperation. 1996a. *Overview of APEC Initiatives on Sustainable Development*. Manila, Philippines, 19 July 1996. APEC Document 96/SD-SOM.

———. 1996b. *APEC Ministerial Meeting on Sustainable Development*, Manila, Philippines, 11/12 July 1996.

Atkeson, Timothy. 1994. Interview with author given by the former assistant director for international affairs, Environmental Protection Agency.

Audley, John. 1996. "Privatizing Public Regulation: The International Organization for Standardization, 14000 Environmental Management Series." unpublished paper.

———. 1993a. "The Greening of Trade Agreements: Environmental Window Dressing and NAFTA." In *North American Free Trade Agreement: Opportunities and Challenges*, edited by Khosrow Fatemi. New York: Macmillan Company.

———. 1993b. "Why Environmentalists Are Angry About NAFTA." In *Trade and the Environment*, edited by Durwood Zaelke, Robert Housman, and Paul Orbuch. Washington, D.C.: Island Press.

———. 1993c. "Issues Regarding Group of Six Document." Sierra Club. 30 April 1993.

———. 1992a. *A Critique of the February 21, 1992 Draft of the North American Free Trade Agreement*. Washington, D.C.: Sierra Club Center for Environmental Innovation.

———. 1992b. Letter to EPA, Department of International Affairs counsel, David van Hoogstraten, 15 April 1992. Original.

———. 1992c. Memorandum to the environmental community regarding the Trinational Declaration. 18 May 1992. Original.

———. 1992d. Memorandum to Bob Baum and Ali Webb, Clinton/Gore for President, regarding trade and the environment. 12 August 1992. Original.

———. 1992e. Memorandum to USTR deputy assistant, Sandord Gaines, regarding the Tri-National Commission on Trade and the Environment. 16 October 1992. Mimeographed.

———. 1992f. Memorandum to Rod Leonard, Community Nutrition Institute; Justin Ward, Natural Resources Defense Council; and Stewart Hudson, National Wildlife Federation regarding proposed NAFTA language. 30 April 1992. Original.

———. n.d. "Policy Proposal for NAFTA in Response to NRDC Environmental Language Proposal." Original.

Audley, John, and Eric Uslaner. 1997. "NAFTA, the Environment, and American Domestic Politics." In *Through a Glass Darkly: Building the New Workplace for the 21st Century*, edited by James Auerbach. New York: Cambridge University Press.

————. 1994. "NAFTA, the Environment, and American Domestic Politics." *North American Outlook* 4, no. 3.

Avery, Natalie, Martine Drake, and Tim Lang. 1993. *Cracking the Codex: An Analysis of Who Sets World Food Standards*. London: National Food Alliance.

Bacharach, Peter and Morton Boratz. 1970. *Power and Poverty; Theory and Practice.* New York: Oxford University Press.

Bailey, Ronald, ed. 1995. *The True State of the Planet.* New York: The Free Press.

————. 1994. *Ecoscam: The False Prophets of Ecological Apocalypse.* New York: St. Martins Press.

Baker Fox, Annette. 1995. "Environment and Trade: The NAFTA Case." *Political Science Quarterly* 10, no. 1.

Barclay, William. 1991. Letter to EPA coordinator regarding U.S.-Mexico environmental review. 30 November 1991. Mimeographed.

Baucus, Max. 1993a. "NAFTA's Environmental Benefits." United States Committee on the Environment and Public Works. 15 September 1993. Mimeographed.

————. 1993b. Press conference in support of NAFTA's environmental provisions. 15 September 1993. Mimeographed.

————. 1992. Letter to USTR ambassador, Carla Hills. 6 July 1992. Mimeographed.

Bauer, Raymond A., Ithiel de Sola Poole, and Lewis Anthony Dexter. 1972. *American Business and Public Policy: The Politics of Foreign Trade.* Chicago: Aldine-Atherton.

Baum, Robert. 1992. Memorandum to John Audley regarding the Clinton campaign and environmental issues teams. 20 July 1992. Mimeographed.

Baumgartner, Frank and Bryan Jones. 1993. Agendas and Instability in American Politics. Chicago: University of Chicago Press.

Becker, Gary. 1979. "Economic Analysis and Human Behavior." In *Sociological Economics,* edited by Louis Levy-Garboua. London: SAGE Publications.

Beil, Eric. 1994. Interview with author given by the counsel to the Senate Finance Committee.

————. 1993. Speech given by the counsel to the Senate Finance Committee during a Capitol Hill briefing meeting. 22 January 1993. Author's notes.

Bentsen, Lloyd. 1996. Letter to USTR ambassador, Carla Hills. *Inside U.S. Trade.* Washington, DC. 30 November 1990.

Bentsen, Lloyd, and Dan Rostenkowski. 1991. Letter to President George Bush, 7 March 1991. House Document no. 102-51.

Bergsten, C. Fred. 1986. *America in the World Economy: A Strategy for the 1990's.* Washington, D.C.: International Institute for Economics.

Berle, Peter. 1993. Letter to chapter leaders from the president of the National Audubon Society explaining their position on NAFTA. 17 September 1993. Mimeographed.

Berlin, Kenneth. 1994. Interview with author.

————. 1993a. "Side by Side Comparison." 24 September 1993. Mimeographed.

———. 1993b. Memorandum to national environmental groups regarding the NAFTA Environmental Side Agreement. 13 September 1993. Mimeographed.

———. n.d. "The NAFTA Environmental Agreements." Mimeographed.

Bhagwati, Jagdish. 1993. "The Case For Free Trade." *Scientific American*. (November): 42–49.

———. 1988. *Protectionism*. Cambridge: MIT Press.

Bhagwati, Jagdish, and Hugh T. Patrick, eds. 1990. *Aggressive Unilateralism: America's 301 Trade Policy and the World Trading System*. Ann Arbor: University of Michigan Press.

Binder, Gordon. 1993. "NAFTA and the Environment." Washington, D.C.: World Wildlife Fund White Paper. Mimeographed.

Blackwelder, Brent. 1994. Interview with author by the president of Friends of the Earth.

Border Trade Alliance. 1991. "The North American Free Trade Agreement: Business and Employment Benefits." 26 April 1991. Mimeographed.

Border Environmental Cooperation Commission. 1996a. *Year End Summary Report for the BECC*. San Antonio, Texas. 16 January 1996.

BECC. Guidelines for Project Submission and Criteria for Project Evaluation. El Paso, Texas. 1995–1996.

———. cocef.interjuarez.com.

———. Monthly newsletter, *BECC News*, available online: http:cocef.interjuarez.com.

Brinza, Daniel. 1994. Author interview with the counsel, Office of United States Trade Representative.

Broad, Robin, et al. 1991. "Development: The Market Is Not Enough." *Foreign Policy* 81 (Winter 1990–91): 144–160.

Brock, William, and Robert Hormats, eds. 1990. *The Global Economy: America's Role in the Decade Ahead*. New York: W.W. Norton.

Brookhart, Larry, and Robert Wallace. 1993. "Potential Impact on the U.S. Economy and Selected Industries of the North American Free Trade Agreement." Washington, D.C.: United States International Trade Commission. January 1993. Mimeographed.

Bullard, Robert, ed. 1994. *Unequal Protection: Environmental Justice and Communities of Color*. San Francisco: Sierra Club Books.

———. 1993. *Confronting Environmental Racism: Voices From the Grassroots*. Boston: South End Press.

(The) Business Roundtable. 1993. "Protecting the Global Environment and Promoting International Trade: Principles and Action Plan." March 1993. Mimeographed.

Caldwell, Lynton Keith. 1990. *International Environmental Policy: Emergence and Dimensions*. 2d. ed. Durham, N.C.: Duke University Press.

Cameron, James, et al. 1994. *Sustainable Development and Integrated Dispute Settlement in GATT*. Switzerland: World Wide Fund for Nature.

Canadian Government. 1993. Memorandum to USTR and State Department officials regarding Canadian environmental group comments on objects for a NACE. March 1992. Mimeographed.

Cascio, Joseph. 1996. *The ISO 14000 Handbook*. Fairfax, VA: CEEM Information Systems.

The Case Against Free Trade: GATT, NAFTA, and the Globalization of Corporate Power. 1993. New York: Earth Island Press.

Center for International Environmental Law. 1992a. "NAFTA Is Just One More Addition to the Bush Administration's Long List of Broken Environmental Promises." 6 October 1992. Mimeographed.

———. 1992b. Letter to the Honorable Curtis Bohlen, assistant secretary for Oceans, International Environment and Scientific Affairs, Department of State. 18 November 1992. Mimeographed.

Center for International Environmental Law and Defenders of Wildlife. 1992. Memorandum to Gus Speth, Garry Carter, Katie McGinty, and Mollie Olson, Clinton/Gore Transition Team, regarding immediate trade/environment concerns. 29 December 1992. Mimeographed.

Charnovitz, Steve. 1996. "The TWO Panel Decision on U.S. Clean Air Act Regulations." *International Environmental Reporter*. 6 March 1996.

———. 1994a. "Dolphins and Tuna: An Analysis of the Second GATT Panel Report." *ELR News and Analysis* 24, October 1994.

———. 1994b. "The GATT Panel Decision on Automobile Taxes." *International Environmental Reporter*. 2 November 1994.

———. 1992. "The Regulation of Environmental Standards by International Trade Agreements." *International Environmental Reporter*. August 1992.

Christensen, Eric. 1991. "GATT Nets an Environmental Disaster." Washington, D.C.: Community Nutrition Institute Internal Paper. October 1991.

Christensen, Eric, and Samantha Geffin. 1991–2. "GATT Sets Its Net on Environmental Regulation: The GATT Panel Ruling on Mexican Yellowfin Tuna Imports and the Need for Reform of the International Trading System." *The University of Miami Inter-American Law Review* 23, no 2 (Winter 1991–92).

Chubb, John E., and Paul E. Peterson, eds. 1989. *Can the Government Govern?* Washington, D.C.: Brookings Institution.

Citizen's Trade Campaign. 1993a. "Lobbying Target List." 20 October 1993. Mimeographed.

———. 1993b. "Swing Members With Enviro Concerns." Mimeographed.

———. 1993c. "Citizen's Trade Campaign Policy Statement on NAFTA." 15 April 1993. Mimeographed.

———. 1991. Open letter to Congress urging endorsement of Waxman-Gephardt Resolution. 20 November 1991. Mimeographed.

———. n.d. "Democratic Members of Congress—Target List Conflicts." Mimeographed.

Clark, Michael. 1991a. Open letter to members of the U.S. House of Representatives in opposition to Fast Track. 10 May 1991. Mimeographed.

———. 1991b. Memorandum to national conservation leaders regarding the White House attempt to divide and conquer on free trade. 7 May 1991. Mimeographed.

Clegg, Stewart. 1989. *Frameworks of Power*. London: SAGE Publications.

Clinton, William. 1992. "Expanding Trade and Creating American Jobs." Remarks by Governor Bill Clinton, North Carolina State University. 4 October 1992. Mimeographed.

———. n.d. "Bill Clinton on Protecting Our Environment." Clinton/Gore Campaign Committee position paper. Mimeographed.

———. n.d. "Bill Clinton on Trade." Clinton/Gore Campaign Committee position paper. Mimeographed.

Coalition for Justice in the Maquiladoras. n.d. *Maquiladoras: A Broken Promise.* New York: Interfaith Center of Corporate Responsibility.

Coleman, James. 1990. *Foundations of Social Theory.* Cambridge: Harvard University Press.

Commission for Environmental Cooperation. 1996a. "CEC Announces Winners of First Grants Under North American Environment Fund." 1 August 1996.

———. 1996b. *Bridling a Framework for Assessing NAFTA Effects.* Montreal, Canada.

———. 1995. Guidelines for Submissions on Enforcement Matters under Articles 14 and 15 of the North American Agreement on Environmental Cooperation. Montreal, Canada.

Committee for Economic Development. 1945. *International Trade, Foreign Investment, and Domestic Employment.* New York: Research Committee, Committee for Economic Development.

Conca, Ken, et al. 1995. *Green Planet Blues.* Boulder, Colo.: Westview Press.

Congressional Record. Washington, D.C. 22 November 1993.

———. Washington, D.C. 23 May 1991.

Conservation International. 1993. "Conservation International Declares Support for NAFTA." 14 September 1993. Mimeographed.

Costanza, Robert, et al. 1995. "Sustainable Trade: A New Paradigm for World Welfare." *Environment* 37, no. 5.

Council on Scientific Affairs. 1990. "A Permanent U.S.-Mexico Border Environmental Health Commission." *Journal of the American Medical Association* 262, no. 3319.

Cronon, William. 1983. *Changes in the Land.* New York: Hill and Wang.

Culbertson, John. 1992. "The Folly of Free Trade." *Focus.* (Spring).

Dahl, Robert. 1961. *Who Governs?* New Haven: Yale University Press.

Daly, Herman. 1993. "The Perils of Free Trade." *Scientific American.* (November): 49–53.

———. 1992. "From Adjustment to Sustainable Development: The Obstacle of Free Trade." *Loyola Latin American Law Journal* 15, no. 33.

———. 1991. "Elements of Environmental Macroeconomics." In *Ecological Economics,* edited by Robert Costanza. New York: Columbia University Press.

Daly, Herman, ed. 1973. *Toward a Steady-State Economy.* San Francisco: W.H. Freeman and Company.

Daly, Herman, and John Cobb. 1989. *For the Common Good.* Boston: Beacon Press.

Dam, Kenneth. 1970. *GATT Law and International Economic Organization.* Chicago: University of Chicago Press.

Danforth, John. 1994. Letter to USTR ambassador, Mickey Kantor. *Inside U.S. Trade.* Washington, D.C. 13 May 1994.

———. 1993. Letter to President Bill Clinton 7 May 1993. Mimeographed.

Davis, Charles and James Lester. 1989. "Federalism and Environmental Policy." In *Environmental Politics and Policy,* edited by James Lester. Durham: Duke University Press.

Defenders of Wildlife. 1993a. Letter to USTR ambassador, Mickey Kantor. 4 March 1993. Mimeographed.

———. 1993b. "Conservation Group Withholding Support on NAFTA." 14 September 1993. Mimeographed.

———. Annual Reports. 1992–1993.

Destler, I.M. 1992. *American Trade Politics.* 2d ed. Washington, D.C.: Institute for International Economics with the Twentieth Century Fund.

———. 1980. *Making Foreign Economic Policy.* Washington, D.C.: Brookings Institution.

Dudley, Barbara. 1993a. Memorandum to "Green Group" regarding letter on NAFTA and resources to congressional leaders. 22 April 1993. Mimeographed.

———. 1993b. Letter to USTR ambassador, Mickey Kantor. 12 March 1993. Mimeographed.

Duncan, Cameron. 1993. Interview with author given by international economist for Greenpeace.

Durbin, Andrea. 1995. "Trade and the Environment: The North-South Divide." *Environment* 37, no. 7.

———. 1994. Conversation with author and Friends of the Earth international program staff.

———. n.d. "Additional Comments to the Draft Letter to Ambassador Kantor." Mimeographed.

Durning, Alan B., and Holly B. Brough. 1991. "Taking Stock: Animal Farming and the Environment." World Watch Institute Paper no. 103. (July).

Eckersley, Robyn. 1992. *Environmentalism and Political Theory: Toward an Ecocentric Approach.* Albany: State University of New York Press.

Edelman, Murray. 1973. Political Language: Words that Succeed and Policies that Fail. New York: Academic Press.

Edwards, David, and R. Harrison Wagner. 1969. *Political Power: A Reader in Theory and Research.* New York: The Free Press.

Elkin, Stephen. 1987. *City and Regime in the American Republic.* Chicago: University of Chicago Press.

Environmental Defense Fund. 1993. "Environmental Defense Fund Joins Groups in Support of NAFTA." 14 September 1993. Mimeographed.

———. Annual Reports 1991–1993.

Environmental Protection Agency. 1992a. Internal memo circulated with copy of NWF testimony before House Banking, Finance, and Urban Affairs Committee. April 1992. Mimeographed.

———. 1992b. "First Joint Meeting of North American Environment Ministers." *EPA Activities Update.* Washington, D.C.: EPA Communications, Education and Public Affairs. (28 September).

———. 1991. Draft Review of U.S.-Mexico Environmental Issues. October.

Esty, Daniel. 1994a. *Greening the GATT: Trade, Environment, and the Future.* Washington, D.C.: Institute for International Economics.

———. 1994b. Interview with author given by the former EPA deputy administrator for policy, planning, and evaluation.

(The) European Commission. 1994. *Report on United States Barriers to Trade*

Investment. Brussels: Services of the European Commission, Document no. I/194/94.

Fair Trade Campaign. n.d. "Tools for Grassroots Leaders to Educate Congress About the GATT and NAFTA Agreements." Mimeographed.

Federal Register. Document nos. 91-32456; 91-21672; 92-5593.

Ferguson, Dieneke, et al. 1995. *Curves, Tunnels and Trade: Does the Environment Improve With Economic Growth?* London: The New Economics Foundation for the World Wide Fund for Nature International.

Ferretti, Janine. 1992a. Memorandum to Stewart Hudson, National Wildlife Federation, regarding "Green" NAFTA language. 21 May 1992. Mimeographed.

———. 1992b. "Proposed Amendments to the Draft North American Free Trade Agreement." 1 May 1992. Mimeographed.

Fisher, Linda. 1994. Interview with author given by the former EPA assistant deputy for pesticides under President Bush.

Freeman, A. Myrick. 1994. "Economics, Incentives, and Environmental Regulations." In *Environmental Policy in the 1990's* by Norman Vig and Michael Kraft. Washington, D.C.: CQ Press.

French, Hillary. 1993. "Costly Tradeoffs." World Watch Institute Paper no. 113.

Friends of the Earth. 1993a. "The North American Free Trade Agreement and the Environment: Provisions To Include in the Environmental Supplemental Agreement." 4 March 1993. Mimeographed.

———. 1993b. "Friends of the Earth Evaluates NAFTA and the Side Agreements: Environmental Side Agreements Fall Short of Fixing NAFTA's Flaws." 13 September 1993. Mimeographed.

———. Annual Reports. 1991–1993.

———. n.d. (a). "International Environmental Agreements With Trade Provisions Omitted from Article 104 in the NAFTA." Mimeographed.

———. n.d. (b). "Does the NAFTA Measure Up?" Mimeographed.

Gamson, William A. 1968. *Power and Discontent.* Homewood, Ill.: The Dorsey Press.

Gaventa, John. 1980. *Power and Powerlessness.* Urbana, Ill.: University of Illinois Press.

General Agreements on Tariffs and Trade. n.d. "Trade and the Environment— News and Views from the GATT." Information and Media Relations Division of GATT. Centre William Rappard, 154 rue de Lausanne, CH-1211 Geneva 21.

General Accounting Office. *Environmental Infrastructure Needs in the U.S.-Mexican Border Region Remain Unmet.* Washington, D.C.: GAO/RCED-96-179.

Gephardt, Richard. 1992. *Remarks of Congressman Richard A. Gephardt Address on the Status of the North American Free Trade Agreement Before the Institute for International Economics.* 27 July 1992. Mimeographed.

Gephardt, Richard. 1991. Letter to President George Bush. 27 March 1991. Mimeographed.

Gephardt, Richard, et al. 1991. Letter from Richard Gephardt, Ed Markey, Donald Pease, Jim Moody, Ron Wyden, Henry Waxman, Sander Levin, and Charles Schumer to USTR ambassador, Carla Hills. 29 July 1991.

Mimeographed. Also published in *Inside U.S. Trade*. Washington, D.C. 2
August 1991.

Gingrich, Newt, Richard Armey, and David Drier. 1994a. Letter to President
Bill Clinton. *Inside U.S. Trade*. Washington, D.C. 29 July 1994.

Gingrich, Newt, et al. 1994b. Letter to USTR ambassador, Mickey Kantor. *Inside
U.S. Trade*. Washington, D.C. 12 December 1994.

Goebel, Martin. 1993. Memorandum to WWF staff regarding press strategy on
Mexico Conservation Fund. 6 October 1993. Mimeographed.

Goldman, Patti, and Alan Morrison. 1991. Letter on behalf of Public Citizen,
Friends of the Earth, and the Sierra Club to USTR ambassador, Carla Hills.
2 July 1991. Mimeographed.

Gottlieb, Robert. 1993. *Forcing the Spring: The Transformation of the American
Environmental Movement*. Washington, D.C.: Island Press.

Goulet, Denis. 1992. "Development: Creator and Destroyer of Values." *World
Development* 20, no. 3: 467–475.

Gray, H. Peter. 1985. *Free Trade or Protection? A Pragmatic Analysis*. New York:
St. Martins Press.

Greenpeace U.S.A. 1993a. "NAFTA Threatens the Environment: Proposals for
a New Agreement." February 1993. Mimeographed.

———. 1993b. Letter to members of the United States Congress. 29 April 1993.
Mimeographed.

———. 1993c. "NAFTA Undermines Natural Resource Conservation." 30
April 1993. Mimeographed.

———. n.d. "NAFTA & the North American Agreement on Environmental
Cooperation (NAAEC): Side-Stepping the Environment." Mimeographed.

———. n.d. "Eleven Environmental Myths NAFTA's Supporters Hope You'll
Believe." Mimeographed.

Greenwalt, Lynn. 1992. Letter to Curtis Bohlen, assistant secretary of state. 6
November 1992. Mimeographed.

Gregory, Michael. 1992. "Environment, Sustainable Development, Public Participation, and the NAFTA: A Retrospective." *Journal of Environmental Law
and Litigation* 7.

———. 1992b. "Memorandum to Stewart Hudson, National Wildlife Federation, regarding the Trinational Declaration." 21 May 1992. Mimeographed.

Gregory, Michael, and Dick Kamp. 1993. Letter to Bill Pistor, United States
Environmental Protection Agency. 31 August 1993. Mimeographed.

———. 1991. "Structuring a Free Trade Agreement: A Draft for Discussion."
24 March 1991. Mimeographed.

Grilli, Enzo, and Enrico Sassoon, eds. 1990. *The New Protectionist Wave*. New
York: New York University Press.

Hass, Peter, Robert Keohane, and Marc Levy. 1993. *Institutions for the Earth*.
Cambridge: MIT Press.

Hair, Jay. 1993. Letter to Sierra Club chairman, Michael McCloskey. 17 September 1993. Mimeographed.

———. 1992a. Letter to EPA administrator, William K. Reilly. 16 October 1992.
Mimeographed.

———. 1992b. Letter to Sierra Club chairman, Michael McCloskey. 27 July 1992. Mimeographed.

———. 1992c. Letter to USTR ambassador, Carla Hills. 22 July 1992. Mimeographed.

———. 1992d. Letter to USTR ambassador, Carla Hills. 9 March 1992. Mimeographed.

———. 1992e. Letter to USTR ambassador, Carla Hills. 8 January 1992. Mimeographed.

———. 1991a. Memorandum to USTR ambassador, Carla Hills, regarding environmental impact of NAFTA investment provisions. 20 November 1991. Mimeographed.

———. 1991b. Memorandum to John Adams, NRDC; Peter Berle, NAS; Fred Krup, EDF; and Michael McCloskey, Sierra Club regarding North American Free Trade Agreement and White House meeting. 8 May 1991. Mimeographed.

Hansen-Kuhn, Karan. 1991. Memorandum to members of MODTLE and the Citizen's Trade Watch regarding briefing materials on NAFTA. 5 September 1991. Mimeographed.

Haq, Mahbub ul-, et al., eds. 1995. *The UN and the Bretton Woods Institutions: New Challenges for the Twenty-First Century.* New York: St. Martins Press.

Hardin, Garrett. 1991. "Paramount Positions in Ecological Economics." In *Ecological Economics: The Science of Management of Sustainability,* edited by Robert Costanza. New York: Columbia University Press.

Hechtor, Michael. 1987. *Principles of Group Solidarity.* Berkeley, Ca.: University of California Press.

Held, David. 1987. *Models of Democracy.* Stanford, Ca.: Stanford University Press.

Hill, Cam. 1991. Memorandum to Tim Atkeson regarding National Wildlife Federation testimony on the U.S.-Mexico FTA. 18 April 1991. Mimeographed.

Hills, Carla. 1992. Letter to NWF president, Jay Hair. 27 February 1992. Mimeographed.

Hittle, Alex. 1994. Interview with author.

———. 1991. Letter to USTR deputy assistant trade representative, Charles Ries. 20 August 1991. Mimeographed.

Hittle, Alex, et al. 1992a. Memorandum to President-elect William Clinton regarding implementing the ideas of the North American Free Trade Agreement (NAFTA) presented in his Raleigh speech. 21 December 1992. Mimeographed.

———. 1992b. Letter from environmental organizations to USTR ambassador to GATT, Warren Lavorel. 8 February 1992. Mimeographed.

Housman, Robert. 1996. *Reconciling Trade and the Environment: Lessons from the North American Free Trade Agreement.* New York: United Nations Environmental Program.

Hudec, Robert. 1986. *Developing Countries in the GATT Legal System.* Brookfield, Vt.: Gower Publishing.

Hudson, Stewart. 1994. Interview with author given by the former legislative liaison, National Wildlife Federation.

———. 1992a. Letter to environmental colleagues regarding upcoming "green language" discussions pertaining to NAFTA text. 21 May 1992. Mimeographed.

———. 1992b. Memorandum to colleagues in Mexico, Canada, and the United States regarding the trinational statement on NAFTA's "green language." 15 May 1992. Mimeographed.

———. 1991. Letter to USTR deputy assistant trade representative, Charles Ries. 10 July 1991. Mimeographed.

Hudson, Stewart, and Rodrigo Prudencio. 1993. *The North American Commission on Environment and Other Supplemental Environmental Agreements: Part Two of the NAFTA Package.* Washington, D.C.: National Wildlife Federation.

Hufbauer, Gary Clyde, and Jeffrey J. Schott. 1993. *NAFTA: An Assessment.* Washington, D.C.: Institute for International Economics.

———. 1992. *North American Free Trade: Issues and Recommendations.* Washington, D.C.: Institute for International Economics.

Hunter, David, Julia Sommer, and Scott Vaughan. 1996. *Concepts and Principles of International Law: An Introduction.* New York United Nations Environmental Program.

Industrial Effects of a Free Trade Agreement Between Mexico and the U.S.A. An INFORUM report prepared for the U.S. Department of Labor, Bureau of International Labor Affairs. Clopper Almon, principal investigator. Washington, D.C. September 1990.

Institute for Agriculture and Trade Policy. 1994. "The Marrakesh Proposals for Sustainable Trade." Minneapolis, Minn.: Institute for Agriculture and Trade Policy. 12 April 1994. Mimeographed.

Inter-American Tropical Tuna Commission. 1992. "Resolution: La Jolla, California. April 1992." Mimeographed.

Jackson, John E., ed. 1991. *Institutions in American Society.* Ann Arbor, Mi.: University of Michigan Press.

Johnson, Pierre Marc, and Andre Beaulieu. 1995. *The Environment and NAFTA: Understanding and Implementing the New Continental Law.* Washington, D.C.: Island Press.

Journal of the American Medical Association. 1990. "A Permanent U.S. Mexican Border Environmental Health Commission." Chicago: 27 June 1990.

Kamp, Dick. 1993. Memorandum to Carol Browner, EPA administrator, regarding the establishment of a North American Commission on Environment and Health. 2 February 1993. Mimeographed.

Kantor, Mickey. 1994. Speech given at the Georgetown Law Center. 18 January 1994.

———. 1993a. Letter to Carl Pope, executive director, Sierra Club. 28 September 1993. Mimeographed.

———. 1993b. Letter to NRDC executive director, John Adams. 13 September 1993. Mimeographed.

―――. 1993c. Letter to the Honorable Henry Waxman, chairman, Subcommittee on Health and the Environment. 7 September 1993. Mimeographed.

Kaptur, March, and Byron Dorgan. 1991. Letter regarding the Fair Trade Caucus. 30 September 1991. Mimeographed.

Katz, Jules. 1994. Interview with author given by the former assistant United States trade representative.

Kindleberger, Charles. 1984. Multinational Exclusions. Cambridge: MIT Press.

Kingdon, John W. 1984. *Agendas, Alternatives, and Public Policies*. Glenview, Ill.: Scott, Foresman and Company.

Sale, Kirkpatrick. 1993. *The Green Revolution: The American Environmental Movement, 1962–1992*. New York: Hill and Wang.

Keohane, Robert. 1996. *Institutions for Environmental Aid: Pitfalls and Promises*. Cambridge: MIT Press.

Knight, Jack. 1992. *Institutions and Social Conflict*. Cambridge: University Press.

Kochan, Leslie. 1990. *The Maquiladoras and Toxics: The Hidden Costs of Production South of the Border*. Available as part of the formal submission to the Subcommittee on Trade of the House Committee on Ways and Means, *United States-Mexico Economic Relations*. 14 June 1990.

Kock, Karen. 1969. *International Trade Policy and the GATT 1947–1967*. Stockholm: Almqvist and Wiksell.

KPMG Peat Marwick. 1991. *Analysis of Economic Effects of a Free Trade Area Between the United States and Mexico*. Prepared for the U.S. Council of the Mexico-U.S. Business Committee. Washington, D.C.

Krasner, Stephen. 1983. *International Regimes*. Ithaca, N.Y.: Cornell University Press.

Krauss, Melvyn B. 1978. *The New Protectionism: The Welfare State and International Trade*. New York: New York University Press.

Kriz, Margaret. 1992. "The New Economics." *National Journal* (30 May): 1280–1285.

Krugman, Paul, ed. 1988. *Strategic Trade Policy and the New International Economics*. Cambridge: MIT Press.

Krugman, Paul. 1987. "Is Free Trade Passe?" *Economic Perspectives* 1, no. 1.

Land, Geoffrey. 1993. "North American Free Trade and the Environment: Border Environmental Groups and the NAFTA." *Frontera Norte* 5, no. 10.

Lang, Tim, and Colin Hines. 1993. *The New Protectionism*. New York: The New Press.

La Red Fronteriza de Salud. 1993. "NACE Must Strengthen Mexico's Environmental Management If Sanctions Are To Be Applied." 2 July 1993. Mimeographed.

Lawrence, Robert. 1990. *An American Trade Strategy: Options for the 1990's*. Washington, D.C.: Brookings Institution.

Lawrence, Robert, and Robert Litan. 1986. *Saving Free Trade: A Pragmatic Approach*. Washington, D.C.: Brookings Institution.

Leonard, Rodney. 1994–96. Interviews with author given by the Executive Director of the Community Nutrition Institute.

Leonard, Rodney. 1991. Letter to USTR deputy assistant trade representative, Charles Ries. 16 July 1991. Mimeographed.

Levin, Sander, et al. 1991. Letter from Sander Levin, Donald Pease, Jim Moody, Richard Gephardt, and Ron Wyden to USTR ambassador, Carla Hills. 23 October 1991.

Lindblom, Charles E. 1977. *Politics and Markets: The World's Political-Economic Systems.* New York: Basic Books.

List, Peter C. 1993. *Radical Environmentalism: Philosophy and Tactics.* Belmont, Ca.: Wadsworth Publishing Co.

Low, Patrick. 1993. *Trading Free: The GATT and U.S. Trade Policy.* Washington, D.C.: Twentieth Century Fund.

Lowi, Theodore J. 1969. *The End of Liberalism: Ideology, Policy, and the Crisis of Public Authority.* New York: W.W. Norton.

Magraw, Daniel. 1995. *NAFTA and the Environment: Substance and Process.* Washington, D.C.: American Bar Association.

———. 1994. "NAFTA's Repercussions: Is Green Trade Possible?" *Environment* 36, no. 2.

Mann, Thomas E., ed. 1990. *A Question of Balance: The President, the Congress, and Foreign Policy.* Washington, D.C.: Brookings Institution.

March, James G., and Johan P. Olsen. 1989. *Rediscovering Institutions: The Organizational Basis of Politics.* New York: The Free Press.

Marcich, Christopher. 1995. Interview with author given by the assistant deputy USTR.

Mathews, Ami. "The Impact of NEPA on the North American Free Trade Agreement." 12 August 1992. The American University, Washington, D.C.

Mazur, Laurie Ann. 1994. *Beyond the Numbers: A Reader on Population, Consumption, and the Environment.* Washington, D.C.: Island Press.

McAlpine, Jan, and Patricia Le Donne eds. *The Greening of World Trade.* Library of Congress. Document no. 93-83602. Washington, D.C.: U.S. Government Printing Office.

McCloskey, Michael. 1991–1996. Interviews and conversations with author given by the chairman of the Sierra Club.

———. 1993. Letter to the Honorable Alice Rivlin, deputy director, Office of Management and Budget. 16 August 1993. Mimeographed.

———. 1992. Personal notes taken during conversation with Senator Al Gore regarding the North American Free Trade Agreement. 2 November 1992. Mimeographed.

———. 1991a. Memorandum to John Audley regarding discussions with USTR assistant trade representative, Chip Roh. 12 April 1991. Mimeographed.

———. 1991b. Memorandum regarding meeting with Carla Hills on Mexican Free Trade Agreement. 28 March 1991. Mimeographed.

———. 1991c. Open letter to members of the U.S. House of Representatives. 13 May 1991. Mimeographed.

McCloskey, Michael and Durwood Zaelke. 1992. Letter to Barry Carter, Clinton administration transition team. 16 December 1992. Mimeographed.

McCord, Norman. 1970. *Free Trade: Theory and Practice from Adam Smith to Keynes.* New York: Barnes & Noble.

Meade, Walter Russell. 1992. "Bushism Found." *Harpers*, September.

Meadows, Donella, Dennis L. Meadows, and Jorgen Randers. 1992. *Beyond the Limits: Confronting Global Collapse, Envisioning A Sustainable Future*. Post Mills, Vt.: Chelsea Green Publishing.

Merchant, Carolyn. 1987. *Radical Ecology: The Search for a Livable World*. New York: Routledge Press.

Mikesell, Raymond, and C. Ford Runge. n.d. "Statement on NAFTA and the Environment." Mimeographed.

Mikesell, Raymond, and Michael McCloskey. 1991. *A Critique of the USTR's Review of U.S./Mexico Environmental Issues*. Washington, D.C.: Sierra Club Center for Environmental Innovation.

Mills, C. Wright. 1956. *The Power Elite*. New York: Oxford University Press.

Miller, A.L. 1995. *The Third World in Global Environmental Politics*. Boulder, Colo.: Lynne Reinner.

Mobilization on Development, Trade, Labor, and the Environment. 1992. "Leaked NAFTA Text a Disaster for Labor, the Environment, and Family Farms." 26 March 1992. Mimeographed.

———. 1992. "U.S. Citizen Groups Call for Renegotiation of North American Agreement in Broader, More Democratic Talks." 16 September 1992. Mimeographed.

———. "Public Opinion and the Free Trade Negotiations—Citizen's Alternatives Final Declaration." Zacatecas, Mexico. 25 October 1991. Mimeographed.

Morici, Peter. 1990. "The Environment for Free Trade." In *Making Free Trade Work: The Canada-U.S. Agreement*, edited by Peter Marici. New York: Council on Foreign Relations Press.

Nader, Ralph. 1992. Letter to Sierra Club chairman, Michael McCloskey. 4 June 1992. Mimeographed.

———. 1991. Letter to House Majority Leader, Richard Gephardt. 3 May 1991. Mimeographed.

Naess, Arne. 1972. "The Shallow and the Deep, Long Range Ecology Movement: A Summary." *Inquiry*, no. 16: 95–100.

Nash, Roderick. 1989. *The Rights of Nature*. Madison: University of Wisconsin Press.

National Audubon Society. Annual Reports. 1990–1993.

National and Governmental Advisory Committee. "Minutes of the Meeting of the NAG and NAC to the U.S. Representative to the North American Commission for Environmental Cooperation." 26 September 1996. Mimeographed.

National Wildlife Federation. 1993a. "Rapid Response #1 to Sierra Club Analysis of NAFTA and the North American Agreement on Environmental Cooperation." 6 October 1993. Mimeographed.

———. 1993b. "North American Free Trade Agreement: Jobs and the Environment; Setting the Record Straight on Environmental Concerns About NAFTA." 14 September 1993. Mimeographed.

———. 1993c. *America's Largest Environmental Group Supports NAFTA*. Washington, D.C.: National Wildlife Federation Public Affairs Department.

————. 1993d. "Greening World Trade: Environmental Conditions for the 1993 United States Fast Track Reauthorization." 14 May 1993. Mimeographed.

————. 1993e. *Trade and the Environment Information Packet.* Washington, D.C.: National Wildlife Federation International Programs.

————. 1992a. "Environmental Provisions of Free Trade Agreement Win Support of National Wildlife Federation." 30 September 1992. Mimeographed.

————. 1992b. Letter to USTR ambassador, Carla Hills. 20 July 1992.

————. 1991a. "Initial Response to the Draft Environmental Review." 23 October 1991. Mimeographed.

————. 1991b. "Comments on the Draft Review of U.S.-Mexico Environmental Issues." 23 October 1991. Mimeographed.

————. 1991c. Meeting agenda for discussions with the Honorable Richard Gephardt. 16 September 1991. Mimeographed.

————. 1991d. "Key Environmental Commitments Made by the Bush Administration Regarding NAFTA." 9 July 1991. Mimeographed.

————. 1991e. "Consensus Position by National Audubon Society, Environmental Defense Fund, National Wildlife Federation, Natural Resources Defense Council Regarding President Bush's Action Plan for Addressing Environmental Issues Related to the North American Free Trade Agreement." 9 May 1991. Mimeographed.

————. 1991f. "Environmental Concerns Related to the U.S.-Mexico-Canada Free Trade Agreement." 6 February 1991. Mimeographed.

————. 1991g. "U.S.-Mexico Free Trade: Opening up the Debate." 15 January 1991. Mimeographed.

————. Annual Reports. 1990–1993.

————. 1990. "Environmental Concerns Related to a United States-Mexico-Canada Free Trade Agreement." 17 November 1990. Mimeographed.

————. n.d. (a). "The North American Free Trade Agreement: Creating U.S. Jobs in Environmental Industries." Mimeographed.

————. n.d. (b). "Eight Reasons Why NAFTA Is Good for the Environment." Mimeographed.

————. n.d. (c). Comments on draft border Environmental Plan. Mimeographed.

————. n.d. (d). "North American Free Trade Agreement: Jobs and Environment." Mimeographed.

————. n.d. (e). "Environmental Principals Related to Trade Agreements." Mimeographed.

————. n.d. (f). *Corporate Conservation Council.* Washington, D.C.

National Wildlife Federation and Pollution Probe-Canada. 1992. "Binational Statement on Environmental Safeguards That Should Be Included in the North American Free Trade Agreement." 28 May 1992. Mimeographed.

Natural Resources Defense Council. 1992a. Internal memorandum regarding the status of NAFTA environmental issues. November 1992. Mimeographed.

————. 1992b. Statement of NRDC on administration announcement of the North American Free Trade Agreement. 12 August 1992. Mimeographed.

————. 1992c. Open letter to members of the United States Congress urging rejection of the Uruguay Round on General Agreements on Tariffs and Trade. Mimeographed.

———. 1992d. "Environmental Safeguards for the North American Free Trade Agreement." June 1992. Mimeographed.

———. 1992e. "Draft Position on Environmental Safeguards for the North American Free Trade Agreement." 3 June 1992. Mimeographed.

———. 1991. "NRDC Urges Environmental Protection Within North American Free Trade Agreement: Administration Proposal Called Positive Step in Need of Additional Environmental Enforcement and Review Measure." 1 May 1991. Mimeographed.

———. Annual Reports. 1990–1993.

Natural Resources Defense Council and the Environmental Defense Fund. 1993. "Recommendations for a North American Commission on the Environment." March 1993. Mimeographed.

Natural Resources Defense Council and Grupo de Cien. 1991. "Comments on the Draft Review of U.S.-Mexico Environmental Issues." December 1991. Mimeographed.

Nessman, Alan. 1993. *The NAFTA Package: Funding Needs and Options.* National Wildlife Federation and the Environmental Defense Fund. 16 July 1993. Mimeographed.

NGO Forum. "Statement from 1995 NGO Forum on APEC." 14 November 1995. Mimeographed.

Nicholson, Max. 1987. *The New Environmental Age.* New York: Cambridge University Press.

North American Development Bank. 1996. http://www.quicklink.com/mexico/nadbank.

———. 1995. "Loan and Guaranty Policies, Section II, Project Evaluation Criteria." San Antonio, Texas: Border Environment Cooperation Commission and the North American Development Bank. (20 December 1995.)

Occhipiniti, Jon. Unpublished. "New Institutionalism." College Park: University of Maryland, Department of Government and Politics. 1994.

Odell, Rice. 1980. *Environmental Awakening: The New Revolution to Protect the Earth.* Cambridge, Mass.: Ballinger Publishing. The Conservation Foundation. QH 75. O33.

Office of the President, 1994. Trade and Environment Policy Advisory Committee. Executive Order 12905. 25 March 1994.

———. 1992. List of members to the Advisory Committee for Trade Policy and Negotiations. 10 September 1992. Mimeographed.

———. 1991. Response of the administration to issues raised in connection with the negotiation of a North American Free Trade Agreement. 1 May 1991.

Office of the United States Trade Representative. 1992. *Agreement Between the Government of the United States of America and the Government of the United Mexican States Regarding the Strengthening of Bilateral Cooperation Through the Establishment of a Joint Committee for the Protection and Improvement of the Environment.* 28 September 1992. Mimeographed.

Office of the United States Trade Representative. 1991. *Review of Environmental*

Concerns Relating to the Proposed North American Free Trade Agreement. Washington, D.C.: U.S. Government Printing Office.

Organization for Economic Cooperation and Development. 1993. *Trade and the Environment.* Paris: OECD Publications. Mimeographed.

———. 1992. *Environment and Economics: A Survey of OECD Work.* Paris: OECD Publications.

———. 1990. *Costs and Benefits of Protection.* Paris: OECD Publications.

Ostrom, Elinor. 1990. *Governing the Commons: The Evolution of Institutions for Collective Action.* New York: Cambridge University Press.

Outside 18 (March 1993).

Oxley, Alan. 1990. *The Challenges to Free Trade.* New York: Harvester Wheatsheaf.

Paehlke, Robert. 1989. *Environmentalism and the Future of Progressive Politics.* New Haven: Yale University Press.

Pastor, Robert. 1980. *Congress and the Politics of U.S. Foreign Economic Policy, 1929–1976.* Berkeley: University of California Press.

Pastor, Robert, and Jorge Castaneda. 1989. *Limits to Friendship: The United States and Mexico.* New York: Vintage Books.

Pearce, David, and R. Kerry Turner. 1990. *Economics of Natural Resources and the Environment.* Baltimore: Johns Hopkins Press.

Pearson, Charles S. 1993. "The Trade and Environment Nexus: What Is New Since '72?" In *Trade and the Environment: Law, Economics, and Policy,* edited by Durwood Zaelke, et al. Washington, D.C.: Island Press.

Perkins, Jane. 1993. Letter to USTR ambassador, Mickey Kantor. 4 May 1993. Mimeographed.

Petricioli, Gustavo. 1992. Letter to the Honorable Richard Gephardt from the Mexican ambassador to the United States. 15 June 1992. Mimeographed.

Piven, Francis. 1977. *Poor Peoples Movement: Why They Succeed, How They Fail.* New York: Pantheon.

Porter, Gareth, and Janet W. Brown. 1991. *Global Environmental Politics.* Boulder, Colo.: Westview Press.

Postel, Sandra, and Lori Heise. 1988. "Reforesting the Earth." World Watch Institute Paper no. 83. (April).

Powell, Walter, and Paul DiMaggio. 1989. "Iron Cage Revisited." *American Sociological Review* 48. (April 1983): 147–60.

Public Citizen. 1996. *NAFTA's Broken Promises: The Border Betrayed.* Washington, D.C.: Public Citizen's Global Trade Watch.

———. 1993a. "Announcement Confirms: Most of Clinton's NAFTA Problems Never Made It Onto the Table." 13 August 1993. Mimeographed.

———. 1993b. Letter to USTR ambassador, Mickey Kantor. 13 September 1993. Mimeographed.

———. 1993c. "NAFTA Vote 'Buying' to Cost Taxpayers Billions." 12 November 1993. Mimeographed.

———. 1992a. "Why Voters Are Concerned: Environmental and Consumer Problems in GATT and NAFTA." November 1992. Mimeographed.

———. 1992b. Memorandum to Citizen's Campaign on International Trade regarding passage of H.C.R. 246. 14 August 1992. Mimeographed.

———. 1992c. *GATT and NAFTA: Consumer and Environmental Briefing Packet.* Washington, D.C.: Public Citizen.

———. Annual Reports. 1991–1993.

———. 1991. "Joint Statement by Over 300 Groups Nationwide in Opposition to Fast Track." 9 May 1991. Mimeographed.

———. n.d. "The NAFTA Does Not Measure Up on the Environment and Consumer Health and Safety." Mimeographed.

———. n.d. "The NAFTA-Breast Cancer Link." Mimeographed.

Public Citizen, Friends of the Earth, and the Sierra Club. 1992. "NEPA Lawsuit Refiled by Consumer; Environmental Groups Would Require Environmental Impact Statement for NAFTA; NAFTA Completion Makes Case Ripe." 15 September 1992. Mimeographed.

Putnam, Robert. 1993. *Making Democracy Work: Civic Traditions in Modern Italy.* New Jersey: Princeton University Press.

Red de Salud y Ambiente, et al. 1992. Open letter to negotiators of the North American Free Trade Agreement. 24 July 1992. Mimeographed.

Reifman, Alfred. 1991. *A North American Free Trade Area?* Washington, D.C.: Congressional Research Report for Congress. Document no. IB90140.

Reilly, William. 1993. Letter to NWF president, Jay Hair. 20 January 1993. Mimeographed.

———. 1992. "Statement on the North American Free Trade Agreement." 13 August 1992.

———. 1991. Letter to Senator Timothy Wirth in response to 7 May letter. 17 May 1991. Mimeographed.

Renner, Michael. 1988. *Rethinking the Role of the Automobile.* World Watch Institute Paper no. 84. (June).

Repetto, Robert. 1996. *Trade and Sustainable Development.* New York: United Nations Environmental Program.

Richie, Mark, and Hariett Barlow. 1992. Information pertaining to meeting at Blue Mountain Center. 14–16 May 1992. Original.

Ripley, Randall. 1985. *Policy Analysis in Political Science.* Chicago: Nelson Hall Publishers.

Robertson, David. 1993. "Return to History and the New Institutionalism in American Political Science." *Social Science History* 17, no. 1.

Rogers, Kathleen. 1994. Interview with author given by the attorney, National Audubon Society.

———. 1993. Letter to USTR ambassador, Mickey Kantor. 1 June 1993. Mimeographed.

Roh, Charles Jr. 1994. Interview with author given by the USTR deputy administrator for Latin America.

———. 1991. Letter to Patti Goldman from the assistant USTR for North American Affairs. 16 July 1991. Mimeographed.

Rosenbaum, Walter. 1991. *Environmental Politics and Policy,* 2d ed. Washington, D.C.: CQ Press.

Sale, Kirkpatrick. 1993. *The Green Revolution: The American Environmental Movement, 1962–1992.* New York: Hill and Wang.

Salisbury, Robert, ed. 1970. *Interest Group Politics in America.* New York: Harper and Row.

Samuel, Bryan. 1994. Interview with author at Department of State.

Samuelson, Robert. 1987. *Problems of the American Economy.* London: Athlone.

Schattschneider, E.E. 1935. *Politics, Pressures and the Tariff.* New York: Prentice Hall.

Schelling, Thomas. 1978. *Micromotives and Macrobehavior.* New York: W.W. Norton.

Scherr, Jacob, and Justin Ward. 1993. Letter to USTR ambassador, Mickey Kantor. 18 July 1993. Mimeographed.

Schott, Jeffrey. 1990. *Completing the Uruguay Round.* Washington, D.C.: Institute for International Economics.

Scott, Catherine, and Tia Nelson. 1996. Memorandum concerning the 28 April 1996 draft Kantor letter. Mimeographed.

Seligman, Dan. 1994. Interview with author.

———. 1993. Memorandum to International Committee members regarding Sierra Club decision on NAFTA. 3 September 1993. Mimeographed.

Sessions, George. 1991. "Ecocentrism and the Anthropocentric Detour." *Revision* 13, no. 3 (Winter): 109–115.

Shabecoff, Philip. 1993. *A Fierce Green Fire.* New York: Hill and Wang.

Shrybman, Steven. 1993. Memorandum regarding World Wildlife Fund critique of anti-NAFTA groups analysis. 30 September 1993. Mimeographed.

Shepsle, Kenneth. 1979. "Institutional Arrangements and Equilibrium in Multidimensional Voting Models." *American Journal of Political Science* 32: 27–59.

Shepsle, Kenneth, and Barry Weingast. 1987. "The Institutional Foundations of Committee Power." *American Political Science Review* 81: 85–104.

Sierra Club. 1994. "Environmentalists Oppose NAFTA." November. Mimeographed.

———. 1993. "Not This NAFTA." 13 September 1993. Mimeographed.

———. 1992a. "Environmentalists Call NAFTA Flawed: Criticize Bush for Planned Photo-Op." 6 October 1992. Mimeographed.

———. 1992b. "Response of Environmental and Consumer Organizations to the September 6, 1992 Text, North American Free Trade Agreement." 6 October 1992. Original.

———. 1991. "Administration Mexican Free Trade Proposal—Sierra Club Charges a Lack of Assured Environmental Performance Measures." 2 May 1991. Mimeographed.

———. 1991. "Statement of Sierra Club, Friends of the Earth, Public Citizen, Environmental Action, National Toxics Campaign, Clean Water Action, National Coalition Against the Misuse of Pesticides: National Environmental Groups United in Opposition to Fast Track." 14 May 1991. Mimeographed.

———. Annual Reports. 1990–1993.

———. n.d. (a). "NAFTA: Trade Away the Environment." Mimeographed.

———. n.d. (b). "Most National Environmental Organizations Oppose NAFTA." Mimeographed.

———. n.d. (c). "How To Respond to Questions Regarding the Split Among Environmental Organizations and NAFTA." Mimeographed.

Siglin, Douglas. 1994. Interview with author given by the legislative liaison, World Wildlife Fund.

Smith, Denis. 1992. *Business and the Environment: Implications for the New Environmentalism.* New York: St. Martin's Press.

Smith, Dick. 1993. Letter to J. Michael McCloskey, chairman, Sierra Club from the special negotiator, Department of State. 18 August 1993. Mimeographed.

Snape, William. 1995. "Searching for GATT's Environmental Miranda: Are 'Process Standards' Getting Due Process?" *Cornell International Law Journal,* no. 3.

———. 1994. Interview with author.

Snape, William, Robert Housman, and Paul Orbuch. 1993. Letter to Ken Berlin. 29 April 1993. Mimeographed.

Snow, Donald, ed. 1992. *Voices From the Environmental Movement: Perspectives for a New Era.* Washington, D.C.: Island Press.

Soroos, Marvin. 1994. "From Stockholm to Rio: The Evolution of Global Environmental Governance." In *Environmental Policy in the 1990's,* edited by Norman Vig and Michael Kraft. Washington, D.C.: CQ Press.

Speck, Paul 1994. *Issues in Sustainable Development.* Washington, D.C.: Environmental and Energy Institute. 1 August 1994.

Stokes, Bruce. 1992. "On the Brink." *National Journal.* (29 February): 504–509.

———. Stokes, Bruce. 1990a. "Will Trade Talks Ever Conclude?" *National Journal,* no. 19 (12 May).

———. 1990b. "Little Hope for Stalled GATT Talks." *National Journal,* no. 50. (15 December).

Stone, Clarence. 1989. *Regime Politics: Governing Atlanta, 1946–1988.* Lawrence, Ks.: University of Kansas Press.

———. 1988. "Preemptive Power: Floyd Hunter's Community Power Structure Reconsidered." *American Journal of Political Science* 32 (February).

Stonehouse, John M., and John Mumford. 1996. *Environment and Trade: Science, Risk Analysis and Environmental Policy Decisions.* New York: United Nations Environmental Program.

Sullivan, Thomas F.P. 1992. *The Greening of American Business: Making Bottom-Line Sense of Environmental Responsibility.* Rockville, Md.: Government Institutes.

Summers, Lawrence. 1991. Office memorandum regarding general environmental program. World Bank. 12 December 1991. Mimeographed.

Switzer, Jacqueline. 1994. *Environmental Politics: Domestic and Global Dimensions.* New York: St. Martin's Press.

Texas Center for Policy Studies, Border Ecology Project. 1991. "Mexico-U.S. Free Trade Negotiations and the Environment: Exploring the Issues." Mimeographed.

Third World Network. 1994. "The World Trade Organization, Trade and the Environment." Malaysia: The Third World Network. March 1994. Mimeographed.

Tolba, Mostafa K. "Counting the Costs." Statement by Dr. Mostafa K. Tolba, executive director, United Nations Environment Program, to the 8th Meeting of the Parties of the Convention in Trade on Endangered Species (CITIES). March 1992.

Tucker, William. 1982. *Progress and Privilege: America in the Age of Environmentalism*. New York: Anchor Press.

United States Chamber of Commerce. 1993. *A Guide to the North American Free Trade Agreement*. Washington, D.C.

———. 1991–1993. *How They Voted*. Washington, D.C.: U.S. Chamber of Commerce.

United States Congress. House. 1993a. *North American Free Trade Agreement, Texts of Agreement, Implementing Bill, Statement of Administrative Action, and Required Supporting Statements*. 103rd Congress, 1st session. House Document no. 103–159, vol. 1–3.

———. House. 1993b. *North American Free Trade Agreement, Supplemental Agreements, and Additional Documents*. House Document no. 103–160. U.S. Government Printing Office.

———. 1993c. *A Budgetary and Economic Analysis of the North American Free Trade Agreement*. Washington, D.C.: Congressional Budget Office.

———. 1992a. *Trade and Environment: Conflicts and Opportunities*. Washington, D.C.: Office of Technology Assessment Document no. OTA-BP-ITE-94.

———. 1992b. *Trade and Environment: Conflicts and Opportunities*. Washington, D.C.: U.S. Government Printing Office Document no. OTA-BP-ITE-94.

———. 1987. *The GATT Negotiations and U.S. Trade Policy*. Washington, D.C.: Congressional Budget Office. U.S. Government Printing Office Document no. 74-479-87-1.

United States Department of State. 1993. "Asia Pacific Economic Cooperation." United States Department of State Fact Sheet. 5 November 1993.

United States Environmental Protection Agency. *Fact Sheet: Free Trade and the Environment: Tools for Progress*. Washington, D.C.: EPA Communications, Education, and Public Affairs. September 1992. Document EPA 175-F-92-001. Mimeographed.

———. n.d. "North American Free Trade Agreement: NAFTA and the Environment." Mimeographed.

———. n.d. Issue Briefs on the NAFTA's Environmental Benefits." Mimeographed.

United States General Accounting Office. 1993. *The North American Free Trade Agreement: Assessment of Major Issues*. Washington, D.C.: GAO/GGD-93-137.

United States International Trade Commission. 1991. *The Likely Impact on the United States of a Free Trade Agreement With Mexico*. Investigation no. 332-297, U.S. International Trade Commission Publication 2353.

United States Trade Representative. 1994a. "Press Statement Announcing the Establishment of a Trade and Environment Policy Advisory Committee (TEPAC)." 30 March 1994. Mimeographed.

———. 1994b. "Joint Press Statement by U.S. Trade Representative, Mickey Kantor, and EPA Administrator, Carol Browner, Announcing Selection of TEPAC Advisors." 4 November 1994. Mimeographed.

———. 1992. "Outline of Reactions of Environmental NGOs to the NAFTA,

Supplemental Agreements and a North American Commission on the Environment (NACE)." Memorandum written EPA & USTR staff. 29 January 1992. Mimeographed.

Vaughan, Scott. 1996. *Trade and Environment: Bridling the Revolutionary Framework*. New York United Nations Environmental Program.

Vig, Norman, and Michael Kraft. 1994. *Environmental Policy in the 1990's*. Washington: CQ Press.

Wall, Derek. 1994. *Green History: A Reader in Environmental Literature, Philosophy, and Politics*. London: Routledge.

Wallach, Lori. 1994. Interview with author given by Public Citizen attorney.

———. 1991. Memorandum to Public Citizen president, Joan Claybrook, regarding Fast Track congressional approval. 21 February 1991. Mimeographed.

———. n.d. Memorandum to John Audley, Sierra Club, regarding Public Citizen's position on the 4 May 1993 "Group of 7 Letter" to USTR ambassador, Mickey Kantor. Mimeographed.

Wallach, Lori, John Audley, and Rodney Leonard. 1991. Statement of the Citizen's Trade Watch Campaign before the Office of the United States Trade Representative. 3 September 1991. Mimeographed.

Wallach, Lori, and Tom Hilliard. 1991. "The Consumer and Environmental Case Against Fast Track." Washington, D.C.: Public Citizen. May 1991. Mimeographed.

Ward, Justin. 1996. Personal correspondence. 12 December 1996.

Ward, Justin. 1994. Interview with author given by the senior resource specialist, Natural Resources Defense Council.

———. 1993. Letter to USTR ambassador, Mickey Kantor. 9 June 1993. Mimeographed.

———. 1992a. Memorandum to EPA deputy administrator, Timothy Atkeson, et al., regarding the North American Environmental Commission. 20 October 1992. Mimeographed.

———. 1992b. "Draft NAFTA Safeguards Paper." 4 June 1992. Mimeographed.

———. 1992c. Memorandum to the environmental community regarding revised NAFTA language. 4 May 1992. Mimeographed.

———. 1992d. Memorandum to Stewart Hudson, National Wildlife Federation, regarding NAFTA Safeguards Project. 19 May 1992. Mimeographed.

———. 1992e. Memorandum to environmental community regarding NAFTA environmental language. 18 March 1992. Mimeographed.

———. 1991a. Letter to the Honorable Henry Waxman regarding NRDC support for H.C.R. 246. 11 December 1991. Mimeographed.

———. 1991b. Statement of the Natural Resources Defense Council before the Office of the United States Trade Representative. 3 September 1991. Mimeographed.

———. 1991c. Comments of the Natural Resources Defense Council on the Integrated Environmental Plan for the Mexico-U.S. Border Area. 30 September 1991. Mimeographed.

———. 1991d. Letter to USTR deputy assistant trade representative, Charles Ries. 9 September 1991. Mimeographed.

Ward, Justin, et al. 1992. Letter to the Honorable Max Baucus. 26 June 1992. Mimeographed.

———. 1993. Letter to the Honorable Lloyd Bentsen. 30 September 1993. Mimeographed.

Wathen, Thomas. 1992. *A Guide to Trade and the Environment*. New York: Environmental Grantmakers Association.

Weaver, R. Kent, and Bert A. Rockman, eds. 1993. *Do Institutions Matter? Government Capabilities in the United States and Abroad*. Washington, D.C.: Brookings Institution.

Weintraub, Sidney. 1991. *Ten Considerations Favoring Free Trade With Mexico*. Washington, D.C.: Center for Strategic & International Studies.

———. 1990. *A Marriage of Convenience: Relations Between Mexico and the United States*. Oxford: Oxford University Press.

(The) White House. 1993. "NAFTA Notes." Daily press releases pertaining to the passage of the North American Free Trade Agreement. (September through November 1993). Mimeographed.

———. Office of the Press Secretary. 1992b. "Integrated Environmental Plan for the Mexico-U.S. Border Area." 25 February 1992. Mimeographed.

———. Office of the Press Secretary. 1992c. "The North American Free Trade Agreement Fact Sheet." 12 August 1992. Mimeographed.

———. 1992d. *Report of the Administration on the North American Free Trade Agreement and Actions Taken in Fulfillment of the May 1, 1991 Commitments*. 18 September 1992. Mimeographed.

———. Office of the Press Secretary. 1992a. "Review of Environmental Effects of Free Trade With Mexico." 25 February 1992. Mimeographed.

———. n.d. "The NAFTA: Expanding U.S. Exports, Jobs and Growth: Clinton Administration Statement on the North American Free Trade Agreement." Mimeographed.

White, Lynn. 1967. "The Historical Roots of Our Ecologic Crisis." *Science* 155, no. 3767. (March 1967): 1203–1207.

Williamson, Oliver E. 1975. *Markets and Hierarchies: Analysis and Antitrust Implications*. New York: The Free Press.

Wilson, James Q. 1973. *Political Organizations*. New York: Basic Books.

Winham, Gilvert. 1992. *The Evolution of International Trade Agreements*. Toronto: University of Toronto Press.

Wirth, Timothy. 1991. Letter to EPA administrator, William Reilly. 7 May 1991. Mimeographed.

World Commission on Environment and Development. 1987. *Our Common Future*. Oxford: Oxford University Press.

World Trade Organization. 1996 Report of the WTO Committee on Trade and Environment. Geneva: World Trade Organization.

World Wildlife Fund. 1993a. Letter and memorandum to USTR ambassador, Mickey Kantor (including early draft letters: 26 April 1993, 28 April 1993, and 2 May 1993). 4 May 1993. Mimeographed.

———. 1993b. "WWF Announces Support for NAFTA: Trade Package Would Aid Global Wildlife Conservation." 14 September 1993. Mimeographed.

———. 1993c. "Swing Members With Environmental Concerns." 6 October 1993. Mimeographed.

———. Annual Reports. 1991–1994.

World Bank. 1992. *World Development Report 1992: Development and the Environ-ment*. Washington, D.C.: The World Bank.

World Commission on Environment and Development. 1987. *Our Common Future*. Oxford: Oxford University Press.

World Trade Organization. 1996. *Trade and the Environment*. Geneva: Informa-tion and Media Relations Division of the World Trade Organization.

Wyden, Ron. 1991a. Letter to USTR ambassador, Carla Hills. 20 October 1991. Mimeographed.

———. 1991b. Letter to USTR ambassador, Carla Hills. 20 August 1991.

———. 1991c. Letter to Business Roundtable chairman, Kay Whitmore. 19 August 1991. Mimeographed.

———. 1991d. Letter to President George Bush. *Inside U.S. Trade*. 22 Febru-ary 1991.

Wyden, Ron, and Robert Matsui. 1993. Letter to President-Elect Bill Clinton. 31 January 1993.

Wyden, Ron, and Richard Gephardt. 1991. Letter to USTR ambassador, Carla Hills. 13 September 1991.

Wyden, Ron, et al. 1991. Letter to USTR ambassador, Carla Hills. 23 October 1991. Mimeographed.

Zaelke, Durwood. 1993. Letter to USTR ambassador, Mickey Kantor. 4 May 1993. Mimeographed.

Zarocostas, John. "Rich, Poor Nations Take Trade Rows to Court." *Journal of Commerce*. (30 January) 1996: 2a.

Index